DATA SCIENCE WITH JUPYTER

Master Data Science skills with easy-to-follow Python examples

by

Prateek Gupta

FIRST EDITION 2019

Copyright © BPB Publications, India

ISBN: 978-93-88511-377

Distributors:

BPB PUBLICATIONS
20, Ansari Road, Darya Ganj
New Delhi-110002
Ph: 23254990/23254991

MICRO MEDIA
Shop No. 5, Mahendra Chambers,
150 DN Rd. Next to Capital Cinema,
V.T. (C.S.T.) Station, MUMBAI-400 001
Ph: 22078296/22078297

DECCAN AGENCIES
4-3-329, Bank Street,
Hyderabad-500195
Ph: 24756967/24756400

BPB BOOK CENTRE
376 Old Lajpat Rai Market,
Delhi-110006
Ph: 23861747

Published by Manish Jain for BPB Publications, 20 Ansari Road, Darya Ganj, New Delhi-110002

About the Author

Prateek Gupta is a seasoned Data Science professional with 6+ years of experience in finding patterns, applying advanced statistical methods and algorithms to uncover hidden insights and maximize revenue, profitability and ensure efficient operations management. He has worked with several multinational IT giants like HCL, Zensar and Sapient.

He is a self-starter and committed data enthusiast with expertise in e-commerce domain. He has also helped clients like NTUC Singapore and Times Group India with his machine learning expertise in automatic product categorization, sentiment analysis, customer segmentation and recommendation engine. He is a staunch believer of the premise "Hard work triumphs talent when talent doesn't work hard".

His keen area of interest is in the areas of cutting-edge research papers on machine learning and applications of natural language processing in various industry sectors. In his leisure time, he enjoys sharing knowledge through his blog and motivates young minds to enter the exciting world of Data Science.

His Blog: **http://dsbyprateekg.blogspot.com/**

His LinkedIn Profile: **www.linkedin.com/in/prateek-gupta-64203354**

Preface

Today, Data Science has become an indispensable part of every organization for which employers are willing to pay top dollars to hire skilled professionals. Due to the rapidly changing needs of the industry data continues to grow and evolve and thereby increasing the demand for data scientists. However, the questions that continuously haunt every company – are there enough highly-skilled individuals who can analyse, how much data will be available, where will it come from, and what the advancement in analysis techniques to serve them greater insights? If you have picked up this book, you must have already come across the above through talks or blogs from several experts and leaders in the industry.

To become an expert in any field, everyone must start from a point to learn. This book is designed keeping such perspective in mind in order to serve as your starting point in the field of data science. When I started my career in this field, I had little luck finding a compact guide which I could use to learn concepts of data science, practise examples and revise them when faced with similar problems at hand. I soon realized Data Science is a very vast domain and having all the knowledge in a small version of a book is highly impossible. Therefore, I decided to accumulate my experience in the form of this book where you'll gain essential knowledge and skill set required to become a data scientist without wasting valuable time finding material scattered across the internet.

I planned the chapters of this book in a chained form. In the first chapter you will be familiarized with the data and the modern data science skill set. The second chapter is all about setting up tools for the trade with the help of which you can practise the examples discussed in the book. From chapter three to six you will learn all types of data structures in Python which you will use in your day-to-day data science jobs. The eighth chapter of this book will teach you most often used statistical concepts in data analysis. By ninth chapter, you will be all set to start your journey of becoming a data scientist by learning how to read, load and understand different types of data in Jupyter notebook for analysis. The tenth and eleventh chapter will guide you through different data cleaning and visualizing techniques.

From twelfth chapter onwards, you will have to combine knowledge acquired from previous chapters to do data pre-processing of real-world use-cases. In the chapters thirteen and fourteen you will learn supervised and unsupervised machine learning problems and how to solve them. Chapters fifteen and sixteen will cover time series data and will teach you how you can handle them. After covering the key concepts I have included four different case studies where you will apply all the knowledge acquired and practise solving real-world problems.

This book is my humble effort to cover fundamentals of Data Science using Python and save the readers' time focussing on practical examples rather than just theory. These practical examples include real-world datasets and real problems which will make you confident to tackle similar or related data problems. I hope you will find this book valuable and it will enable you to extend your data science knowledge as a practitioner in a quick time.

Acknowledgements

I would like to thank some of the brilliant knowledge sharing minds - Jason Brownlee PhD, Hugo Bowne-Anderson and Filip Schouwenaars with whom I have learnt and am still learning many concepts. I would also like to thank open data science community Kaggle and various data science blogs authors in Medium for making data science and machine learning knowledge available to everyone.

I would also like to express my gratitude to the almighty God, my parents, my wife Pragya and my brother Anubhav for being extremely supportive throughout my life and the writing of this book.

Many thanks to the BPB Publications who made this book possible: Manish Jain, Nrip Jain, Varun Jain and many thanks to others who worked behind the scenes.

Finally, I would also like to thank Vinay Argekar, who served as the book's acquisition editor, content reviewer and technical editor for improving the content day by day.

Downloading the code bundle and colored images:

Please follow the link to download the
Code Bundle and the *Colored Images* of the book:

https://rebrand.ly/ab68d

Errata

We take immense pride in our work at BPB Publications and follow best practices to ensure the accuracy of our content to provide with an indulging reading experience to our subscribers. Our readers are our mirrors, and we use their inputs to reflect and improve upon human errors if any, occurred during the publishing processes involved. To let us maintain the quality and help us reach out to any readers who might be having difficulties due to any unforeseen errors, please write to us at :

errata@bpbonline.com

Your support, suggestions and feedbacks are highly appreciated by the BPB Publications' Family.

Table of Contents

## CHAPTER 1

Data Science Fundamentals

"Learning from data is virtually universally useful. Master it and you will be welcomed anywhere." – John Elder, founder of the Elder Research- America's largest and most experienced analytics consultancy. With his vision about data, John has started his company in 1995 yet the importance of the finding information from the data is a niche and the most demanding skill of the 21st century. Today Data Science is everywhere.

The explosive growth of the digital world requires professionals with not just strong skills, but also adaptability and a passion for staying on the forefront of technology. A recent study shows that demand for data scientists and analysts is projected to grow by 28 percent by 2020. This is on top of the current market need. According to LinkedIn, there are more than 11,000 data scientist job openings in the US as of late August. Unless something changes, this skills gap will continue to widen. In this first chapter you will be familiar with data, your role as an aspiring data scientist and importance of Python programming language in Data Science.

Structure

- What is Data?
- What is Data Science?
- What a Data Scientist actually do?
- Real world use cases of Data Science
- Why Python for Data Science?

Objective

After studying this chapter, you should be able to understand the data types, amount of the data generated daily and need of data scientist with currently available real-world use cases.

What is Data?

The best way to describe the data is to understand the types of the data. Data is divided into following three categories.

1. Structured Data

A well-organized data in the form of tables that can be easily operated is known as structured data. Searching and accessing information from such type of data is very easy. For example, data stored in the relational database i.e. sql in the form of tables having multiple rows and columns. Spreadsheet is another good example of structured data. Structured data represent only 5 to 10% of all data present in world. Following image is an example of sql data where a sql table is holding the merchant related data.

merchant_id	merchant_name	subtitle	status	publish_date
83	Texas Chicken		1	2018-03-22 00:00:00
84	ZALORA		1	2018-03-29 00:00:00
85	Caltex		1	2018-04-02 00:00:00
86	COURTS		1	2018-04-09 00:00:00
87	Agoda		1	2018-04-07 00:00:00
88	Lerk Thai		1	2018-03-02 00:00:00
89	Peach Garden @ Gardens Bv the Bav		1	2018-02-16 00:00:00

Fig 1.1

2. Unstructured Data

Unstructured data requires advance tools and software's to access information. For Example, images and graphics, pdf files, word document, audio, video, emails, PowerPoint presentations, webpages and web contents, wikis, streaming data, location coordinates etc fall under the unstructured data category. Unstructured data represent around 80% of the data. Following image shows various unstructured data types.

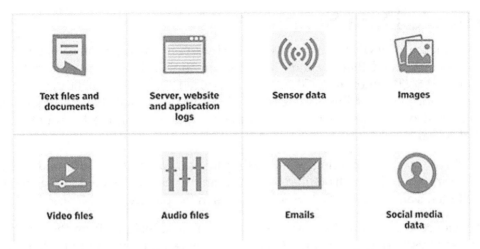

Fig 1.2

3. Semi-Structured Data

Semi-structured data is basically a structured data that is unorganised. Web data such JSON(JavaScript Object Notation) files, BibTex files, .csv files, tab-delimited text files, XML and other markup languages are the examples of Semi-structured data found on the web. Semi-structured data represent only 5 to 10% of all data present in world. Following image shows an example of JSON data.

```
{
    "custkey": "450002",
    "useragent": {
        "devicetype": "pc",
        "experience": "browser",
        "platform": "windows"
    },
    "pagetype": "home",
    "productline": "television",
    "customerprofile": {
        "age": 20,
        "gender": "male",
        "customerinterests": [
            "movies",
            "fashion",
            "music"
        ]
    }
}
```

Fig 1.3

What is Data Science?

It's become a universal truth that modern businesses are awash with data. Last year, McKinsey estimated that big data initiatives in the US healthcare system "could account for $300 billion to $450 billion in reduced healthcare spending, or 12 to 17 percent of the $2.6 trillion baseline in US healthcare costs". On the other hand, though, bad or unstructured data is estimated to be costing the US roughly $3.1 trillion a year.

Data driven decision making is increasing in popularity. Accessing and finding information from the unstructured data is complex and cannot be done easily with some BI tools and here the Data Science comes in the picture.

Data Science is a field that extract the knowledge and insights from the raw data. To do so it uses Maths, Statistics, Computer Science and Programming Language knowledge. A person who has all these skills is known as a Data Scientist. Data scientist is all about being curious, self-driven, and passionate about finding answers. The following picture shows the skills a modern data scientist should have!

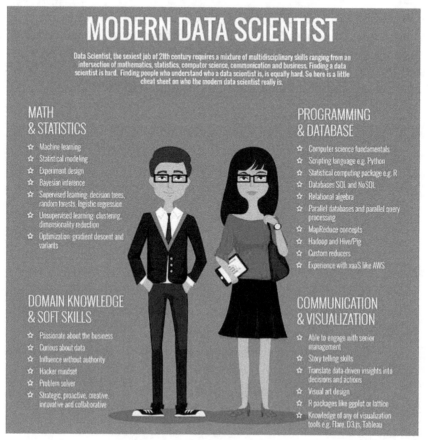

Fig 1.4

What a Data Scientist actually do?

Most data scientists in the industry have advanced and training in statistics, math, and computer science. Their experience is a vast horizon that also extends to data visualization, data mining, and information management. The primary job of a Data Scientist is to ask the right question- It's about surfacing hidden insight that can help enable companies to make smarter business decisions.

The job of a Data Scientist is not bonded to a particular domain. Apart from the scientific research they are working in various domain including shipping , healthcare, e-commerce, aviation, finance, education etc. They start their work by understanding the business problem and then they proceed with data collection, reading the data, transforming the data in required format, visualizing, modelling, evaluating the model and then deployment. You can imagine their work cycle as mentioned in below image

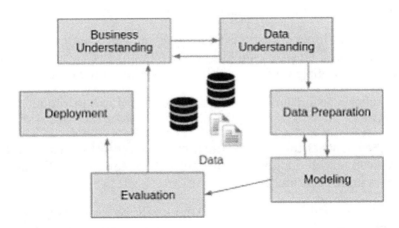

Fig 1.5

80 percent of a data scientist's time is spent in simply finding, cleansing, and organizing data, leaving only 20 percent to actually perform analysis. These processes can be time-consuming and tedious. But it's crucial to get them right since a model is only as good as the data used to build it. And because models generally improve as they are exposed to increasing amounts of data, it's in data scientists' interests to include as much data as they can in their analysis.

In the later chapter of this book you will learn all above required skills to be a data scientist.

Real world use cases of Data Science

Information is the oil of the 21st century, and analytics is the combustion engine. Whether you are uploading a picture on Facebook, posting a tweet, emailing anybody or shopping in e-commerce site, the role of Data Science is everywhere. In modern workplace Data Science is applied to many problems to predict and calculate outcomes that would have taken several times more human hours to process. Following are some list of real-world examples where Data Scientists are playing a key role.

- Google's AI research arm is taking help of Data Scientists to build the best performing algorithm for automatically detecting objects.

- Amazon has built a product recommendation system to personalize their product.

- Santander Group of Bank has built a model with the help of Data Scientists to identify the value of transactions for each potential customer.

- Airbus in maritime industry is taking help of Data Scientists to build a model that detects all ships in satellite images as quickly as possible to increase knowledge, anticipate threats, trigger alerts, and improve efficiency at sea.

- You tube is using an automated video classification model in a limited memory.

- Data Scientists at the Chinese internet giant Baidu Inc. released details of a new deep learning algorithm that they claim can help pathologist identify tumors more accurately.

- The Radiological Society of North America (RSNA®) is using an algorithm to detect a visual signal for pneumonia in medical images which automatically locate lung opacities on chest radiographs.

- The Inter-American Development Bank is using an algorithm that considers a family's observable household attributes like the material of their walls and ceiling, or the assets found in the home to classify them and predict their level of need.

- Netflix data using data science skill on the movie viewing patterns to understand what drives user interest and uses that to make decisions on which Netflix original series to produce.

Why Python for Data Science?

Python is very beginner-friendly. The syntax (words and structure) is extremely simple to read and follow, most of which can be understood even if you do not know any programming. Python is a multi-paradigm programming language: a sort of Swiss Army knife for the coding world. It supports object-oriented programming, structured programming, and functional programming patterns, among others. There's a joke in the Python community that "Python is generally the second-best language for everything."

Python is free, open-source software, and consequently anyone can write a library package to extend its functionality. Data science has been an early beneficiary of these extensions, particularly Pandas, the big daddy of them all.

Python's inherent readability and simplicity make it relatively easy to pick up and the number of dedicated analytical libraries available today mean that data scientists in almost every sector will find packages already tailored to their needs freely available for download.

The following survey done by KDnuggets- a leading site on Business Analytics, Big Data, Data Mining, Data Science, and Machine Learning, clearly shows that Python is a preferable choice for Data Science/Machine Learning.

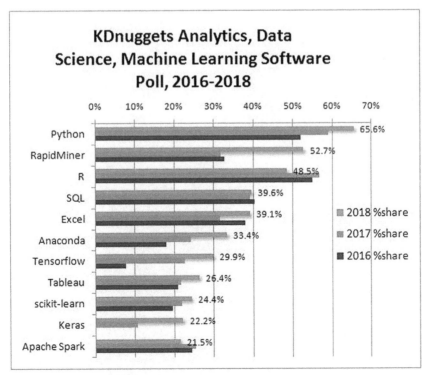

Fig 1.6

Conclusion

Most of the people think that it is very difficult to become a Data scientist. But, let me clear it is not tough!

If you love making discoveries about the world, if you are fascinated by machine learning then you can break into the data science industry no matter what your situation is. This book will push you to learn, improve and master of the data science skill by your own. There is only one thing you need to keep on is LEARN-APPLY-REPEAT. In the next chapter we will setup our machine ready for our data science journey.

CHAPTER 2

Installing Software and Setting up

In the last chapter we covered the Data Science fundamentals and now we are ready to move ahead and prepare \ our system ready for the Data Science. In this chapter we are going to learn about the most popular Python Data Science platform-Anaconda. With this platform you don't need to install Python explicitly- just one installation in your system (Windows, macOS or Linux) and you are ready to use the industry standard platform for developing, testing and training.

Structure

- System Requirements
- Downloading the Anaconda
- Installing the Anaconda in Windows
- Installing the Anaconda in Linux
- How to install a new Python library in Anaconda
- Open your notebook- Jupyter
- Know your notebook

Objective

After studying this chapter, you should be able to install Anaconda in your system successfully and use Jupyter notebook. You will also run your first Python program in your notebook.

System Requirements

- System architecture: 64-bit x86, 32-bit x86 with Windows or Linux, Power8 or Power9

- Operating system: Windows Vista or newer, 64-bit macOS 10.10+, or Linux, including Ubuntu, RedHat, CentOS 6+

- Minimum 3 GB disk space to download and install

Downloading Anaconda

You can download the Anaconda Distribution from the below link:

https://www.anaconda.com/download/

Once you click on the above link you will see the following screen.

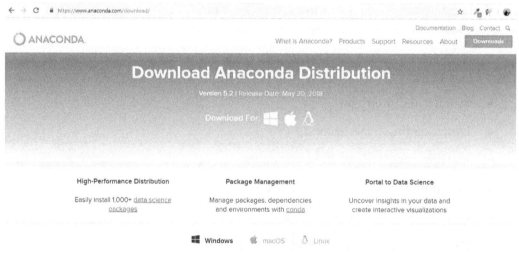

Fig 2.1

The Anaconda Distribution shows different OS options- Windows, macOS and Linux. According to your OS, select the appropriate option and then it will display the two most stable Python versions for download - 3.6 and 2.7. For this example, I have selected the Windows OS as shown in above screenshot. Now it is showing me both two options as below screen.

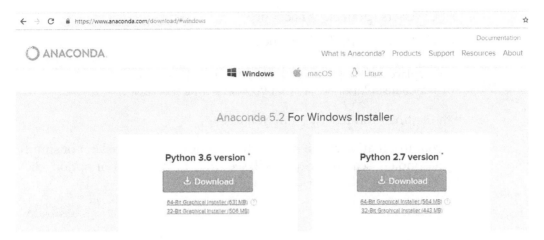

Fig 2.2

We are going to use Python 3.6 version throughout in this book so I will recommend downloading this version only. For downloading the distribution see the two links just below the Download button, there are showing the Graphical Installer for each system architecture type- 64-bit or 32-bit; click on the appropriate link and downloading will be started. This downloading process is same for macOS and Linux also.

Installing the Anaconda in Windows

- Once the downloading is complete, double click on the installer to launch (recommended way is to run the installer with admin privileges)

- Click Next, accept the terms, select the users- Just Me or All Users and click Next

- Select the default destination folder or add a custom location to install the Anaconda, copy this path for later use and click Next

Note	Install Anaconda to a directory path that does not contain spaces or Unicode characters.

- Deselect (uncheck) the first following option (if checked already)- Add Anaconda to my PATH environment variable then click Install, wait till installation is completed

- Click Next, click Skip and then click Finish

- Now open the Advanced system settings in your machine and add the following two values in your PATH environment variable-o   C:\Users\prateek\Anaconda3

o   C:\Users\prateek\Anaconda3\Scripts

Note Here replace the C:\Users\prateek\Anaconda3 with the actual path of your Anaconda installation folder that you have copied earlier

- Save the settings and restart your system

- Verify your installation by clicking on the Windows icon in taskbar or simply type Anaconda in search bar- you will see Anaconda Navigator option, click on this option and following screen will appear.

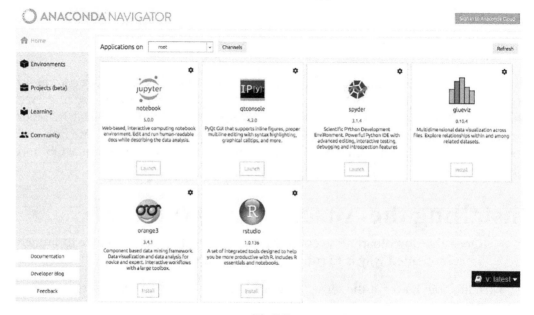

Fig 2.3

Note Installing the Anaconda with Graphical Installer in macOS is same as we did above for Windows.

Installing the Anaconda in Linux

After downloading the 64bit(x86) Installer run the following two commands to check the data integrity.

1. Md5sum /path/filename

2. Sha256sum /path/filename

Note	Replace /path/filename with the actual path and filename of the file you downloaded.

Enter the following to install Anaconda for Python 3.6, just replace ~/Downloads/ with the path to the file you downloaded:

```
bash ~/Downloads/Anaconda3-5.2.0-Linux-x86_64.sh
```

Fig 2.4

- Choose "Install Anaconda as a user" unless root privileges are required.

- The installer prompts "In order to continue the installation process, please review the license agreement." Click Enter to view license terms.

- Scroll to the bottom of the license terms and enter "**Yes**" to agree.

- The installer prompts you to click Enter to accept the default install location, **CTRL-C** to cancel the installation, or specify an alternate installation directory. If you accept the default install location, the installer displays "**PREFIX=/ home/<user>/anaconda<3>**" and continues the installation. It may take a few minutes to complete.

- The installer prompts "**Do you wish the installer to prepend the Anaconda<3> install location to PATH in your /home/<user>/.bashrc ?**" Enter **Yes**.

- NOTE: If you enter "No", you must manually add the path to Anaconda or conda will not work.

- The installer describes Microsoft VS Code and asks if you would like to install VS Code. Enter yes or no. If you selected yes, follow the instructions on screen to complete the VS Code installation.

- NOTE: Installing VS Code with the Anaconda installer requires an internet connection. Offline users may be able to find an offline VS Code installer from Microsoft.

- The installer finishes and displays "**Thank you for installing Anaconda<3>!**"

- Close and open your terminal window for the installation to take effect, or you can enter the command **source ~/.bashrc**.

- After your install is complete, verify it by opening Anaconda Navigator, a program that is included with Anaconda: Open a Terminal window and type anaconda-navigator. If Navigator opens, you have successfully installed Anaconda.

Note	You can find some known issues while installing Anaconda and their solutions in below link-
	https://conda.io/docs/user-guide/troubleshooting.html

How to install a new Python library in Anaconda

Most of the Python libraries/packages are preinstalled with the Anaconda Distribution which you can verify by typing the following command in an Anaconda Prompt:

conda list

```
▨ Anaconda Prompt

C:\Users\prateek1.gupta>set "KERAS_BACKEND=theano"

(base) C:\Users\prateek1.gupta>conda list
# packages in environment at C:\Users\prateek1.gupta\AppData\Local\Continuum\anaconda3:
#
# Name                    Version              Build  Channel
_ipyw_jlab_nb_ext_conf    0.1.0          py36he6757f0_0
absl-py                   0.1.10                  py_0  conda-forge
agate                     1.6.1                  <pip>
agate-dbf                 0.2.0                  <pip>
agate-excel               0.2.2                  <pip>
agate-sql                 0.5.3                  <pip>
alabaster                 0.7.10         py36hcd07829_0
anaconda                  custom         py36h363777c_0
anaconda-client           1.6.5          py36hd36550c_0
anaconda-project          0.8.0          py36h8b3bf89_0
aniso8601                 3.0.0                  py36_0  conda-forge
argparse                  1.4.0                  <pip>
asn1crypto                0.22.0         py36h8e79faa_1
astroid                   1.6.4                  py36_0  anaconda
astropy                   2.0.2          py36h06391c4_4
```

Fig 2.5

Now if you need to install any Python package which is not in the above list and required for your task then follow the below steps.

In same Anaconda Prompt terminal, type conda install <package-name>.

For example if you want to install 'scipy' package, just type **conda install scipy** then press enter and then enter 'y' to continue.

A second recommended approach to install any new package in Anaconda is to search the same (conda install <package-name>) in Google first and then go to the first search result like below.

1. In Google search a package name for example I am searching imageio package i.e. **'conda install imageio'**

2. Go to the first search result; this will open the Anaconda official site showing the installers of the searched package. In our example it is like: <ins>https://anaconda.org/menpo/imageio</ins>

3. Now copy the text under the 'To install this package with conda run:' and paste in Anaconda Prompt. In our case text is: **conda install -c menpo imageio**

Open your notebook- Jupyter

After installing Anaconda the next step is to open the notebook- an open-source web application that allows you to create and share documents that contain live code, equations, visualizations and narrative text. For the notebook open Anaconda Navigator and click on Launch button under the Jupyter Notebook icon or just type Jupyter Notebook in search bar in Windows and then select it as shown in the next screenshot.

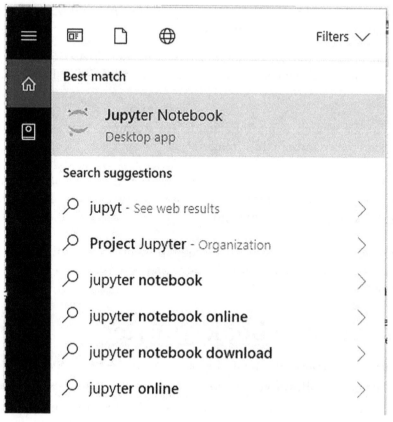

Fig 2.6

Once you select it, a browser window (default is IE) will be opened showing the notebook as showing in below screen shot.

Fig 2.7

Know your notebook

Once your notebook is opened in browser, click on the 'New' dropdown and select the default first option- Python 3 as shown in next screen.

Fig 2.8

After clicking on Python 3 option, a new tab will be opened containing the new untitled notebook-

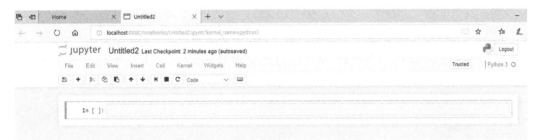

Fig 2.9

Rename your notebook with a proper name by double clicking on the Untitled text and then enter any new name (I have named it MyFirstNotebook) and click Rename.

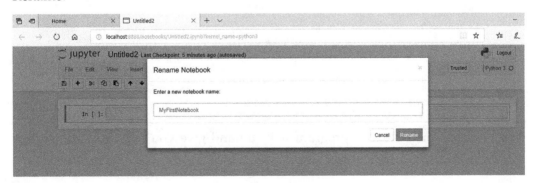

Fig 2.10

Above step will rename your notebook. Now it's time to run your first Python program in your first notebook.

We will print a greeting message in Python for this purpose. In the cell (text bar) just type any welcome message inside the print block as shown in the next screenshot.

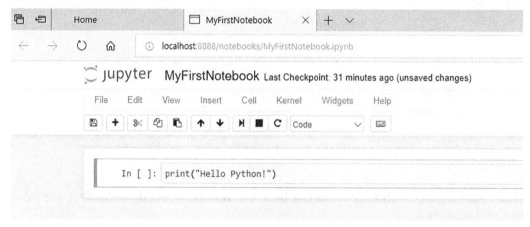

Fig 2.11

In above cell we are printing a string in Python 3.6. Now to run this program you can simply press '**shift**' + '**enter**' keys together or click on the play button just below the Cell column.

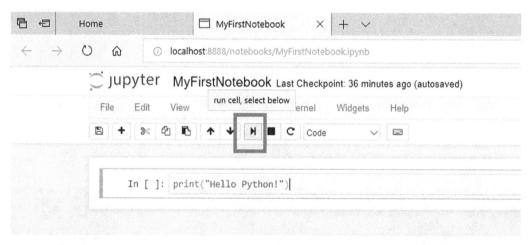

Fig 2.12

Once you run the cell, your program will run and give you output as shown just below the cell-

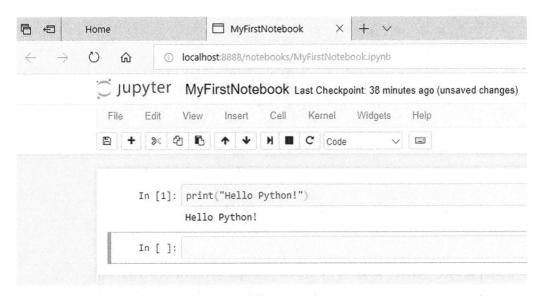

Fig 2.13

Congrats! You have successfully run your first program in Python 3.6. This is it just a one line code using simple plain English text. Let's explore more the simplicity of the Python by doing some mathematics calculations.

Let's add two numbers by entering the FirstNumber + SecondNumber and then run it as below.

```
In [2]:  29+56
Out[2]:  85
```

Fig 2.14

Quite interesting, right! Let's move ahead and ask user to input numbers and let Python do the homework. In below example you need to enter first number, press enter, then enter second number and press enter. The calculation will be done and output displayed within a mili second.

```
a = int(input())
b = int(input())
print("adding of two numbers: ", a+b)
print("difference in numbers: ", a-b)
print("multiplicaton of numbers: ", a*b)
```

```
4
2
adding of two numbers:    6
difference in numbers:    2
multiplicaton of numbers:    8
```

Fig 2.15

Now suppose you have done your given task and want to share the same with your project lead or manager. You can do it easily by going to the File option and hover on **'Download as'** option like below.

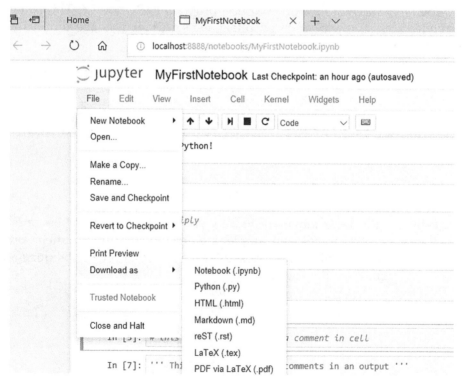

Fig 2.16

Now you can save your current work in different formats- notebook, pdf, python or html. Once you select the required option, it will saved in that format with the same name as you have given while renaming the notebook in default location of your system. By saving in various format you can carry and share your analysis to anyone.

Conclusion

Anaconda Distribution is the fastest and easiest way to do Python and Machine Learning work. You can load the data, pre-process it, visualize it, train your model and evaluate the performance in a single notebook and then share your work to anyone easily. In the next chapter you will learn about the data structures specific to Data Science and will also learn how to use them in your analysis task.

CHAPTER 3
Lists and Dictionaries

Data structures are a way of organizing and storing data in a programming language so that they can be accessed and worked with efficiently. They define the relationship between the data, and the operations that can be performed on the data. As an aspiring Data Scientist, you will use various data structures in your daily job so learning data type is a must have skill. In this chapter we will learn the two most widely used Python data structures specific to Data Science when working with huge data- Lists and Dictionaries. We will also compare the both with the other data structures those looks like same but have fundamental differences.

Structure

- What is list?
- How to create a list?
- Different list Manipulation operations
- Difference between list and tuples
- What is dictionary?
- How to create a dictionary?
- Some operations with dictionary

Objective

After studying this chapter, you will have strong knowledge of using list and dictionary.

What is list?

List is a non-primitive type data structure in Python which means it stores a collection of values in various formats rather than storing only a single value. Lists are mutable- we can change the content of a list. In simple word list is a collection which is ordered, mutable and may contain duplicate values. Here ordered means in which order you entered the elements in a list, the same order will be shown once you print/get that list.

In Python we can store a single value in following primitive data types-

- float represents rational number for examples 1.23 or 3.2

- int represents numeric data like 1,2 or -3

- str represents the string or text

- bool represents True/False

But consider a scenario where your family doctor needs heights and weights of every family member to calculate the body mass index. Now creating a separate variable to store each person height and weight is very inconvenient. Here Python list comes in the picture.

How to create a list?

In Python, a list is an object which is treated like any other data type (e.g. integers, strings, boolean, etc.). This means that you can assign your list to a variable, so you can store and make it easier to access. We can create a list using the square brackets and separating the elements by comma.

In your notebook you can create an empty list, store it in a variable and then can check the type of the variable like below.

```
In [2]: # creating an empty list in Python
        height = []
        type(height)

Out[2]: list
```

Fig 3.1

Let's create a list containing the heights of family members in meters like below.

```
In [3]: # a list containing heights
        height_list = [1.76,1.64,1.79,1,57]
        print(height_list)

        [1.76, 1.64, 1.79, 1, 57]
```

Fig 3.2

One advantage of list is that we can store different types (str, int, float etc) of values in a list and even list of a list itself. Interesting right? For an example we can add names of the family members which is string data type and it's values is in float data type in our above created list like below.

```
In [4]: # a list containing str and float
        name_height_list = ["Tom",1.76,"Harry",1.64,"Lisa",1.79,"Mona",1.57]
        print(name_height_list)

        ['Tom', 1.76, 'Harry', 1.64, 'Lisa', 1.79, 'Mona', 1.57]
```

Fig 3.3

Different list manipulation operations

1. Let's create a list and print it's element by its index one by one. In this example we are storing the values 'python', 'c', and 'java' in a list and then printing each of these values using their position (in other word we are accessing a list by index number) in the list.

   Here the starting point of a list begins with number zero (0) not from one (1). To access the first element of a list you need to use zero index not the first index as shown in below example.

```
In [6]: lang = ['python','c','java']

        print (lang[0] + ' is very easy to learn for Data Science')
        print (lang[1] + ' is the first language I have learnt')
        print (lang[2]+ ' is difficult to learn for Data Science')

        python is very easy to learn for Data Science
        c is the first language I have learnt
        java is difficult to learn for Data Science
```

Fig 3.4

2. Since list is mutable, we can change the existing value of any element , let's do this by changing the java language with *cobol* language as shown in the next example.

```
In [1]:  lang = ['python','c','java']
         print("old list:", lang)
         lang[2] = 'cobol'
         print("new list:", lang)

         old list: ['python', 'c', 'java']
         new list: ['python', 'c', 'cobol']
```

Fig 3.5

3. Now you want to print all elements in the list one by one, you can do this by using 'for' loop as shown in below example.

```
In [2]:  language_list = ['python','c','cobol']
         for language in language_list:
             print("language is: ", language)

         language is:  python
         language is:  c
         language is:  cobol
```

Fig 3.6

4. Let's check how many elements are there in our language list using list's **len()** method.

```
In [3]:  language_list = ['python','c','cobol']
         print("elements in the list: ", len(language_list))

         elements in the list:  3
```

Fig 3.7

5. Now you want to add a new language or item in your list, let's do this using list's **append()** method.

```
In [4]:  language_list = ['python','c','cobol']
         language_list.append('java')
         print("updated list is:", language_list)

         updated list is: ['python', 'c', 'cobol', 'java']
```

Fig 3.8

6. What about if you want to add a new element in a specific position? You have guessed it right, we can use index here with **insert()** method. In below example I am adding a new language '.net' in 3rd position or after the 'c' language.

```
In [5]:  language_list = ['python','c','cobol','java']
         language_list.insert(2, '.net')
         print("modified list is:", language_list)

         modified list is: ['python', 'c', '.net', 'cobol', 'java']
```

Fig 3.9

7. Sometimes you want to remove some element from your list. This can be done by three ways- either to remove the element by it's name using **remove()** method or by it's index using **pop()** method or by **del()** method. In below example, first I am removing the *'cobol'* language from my list and then from updated list I am removing *'java'* language by its index.

```
In [8]:  language_list = ['python','c','.net','cobol','java']
         # remove element by name
         language_list.remove('cobol')
         print("updated list:", language_list)
         # remove element by index
         language_list.pop(3)
         print("latest list:", language_list)

         updated list: ['python', 'c', '.net', 'java']
         latest list: ['python', 'c', '.net']
```

Fig 3.10

del() method use case is different to other ones. It also remove the element on specified index but it's syntax is different to **pop()** or **remove()** methods . Let's create a new list with duplicate elements to understand the difference between **remove()**, **del()** and **pop()** methods.

In below example digit 1 is repeated two times. When we apply remove() method, it's is removing the element 4 from the list. Pop() method is removing the 4th index of the list which is digit at last position whereas del() method is removing the 4th index element with a different syntax structure.

```
In [11]:  number_list = [1,2,3,4,1]
          number_list.remove(4)
          print("list after remove() example:", number_list)

          number_list = [1,2,3,4,1]
          number_list.pop(4)
          print("list after pop() example:", number_list)

          number_list = [1,2,3,4,1]
          del(number_list[4])
          print("list after del() example:", number_list)
```

```
list after remove() example: [1, 2, 3, 1]
list after pop() example: [1, 2, 3, 4]
list after del() example: [1, 2, 3, 4]
```

Fig 3.11

8. Now you want to sort your list in ascending or descending order. This can be done by sort() method of list as shown in below example-

```
In [18]:  language_list = ['python','c','.net','cobol','java']
          language_list.sort()
          print("sort in ascending order:", language_list)
          languages_list = ['python','c','.net','cobol','java','c#']
          language_list.sort(reverse=True)
          print("sort in descending order:", language_list)
```

```
sort in ascending order: ['.net', 'c', 'cobol', 'java', 'python']
sort in descending order: ['python', 'java', 'cobol', 'c', '.net']
```

Fig 3.12

Difference between Lists and Tuples

In Python there is a data type- Tuples similar to lists and often confuses which one to use in which condition. There are two main quality of a tuple which distinguish it to the list- first is the structure of a tuple means Tuples are initialized with small brackets () rather than square brackets [] in lists and second major difference is that tuples are immutable means neither we can change or delete it's value nor we add any new item after the declaration of a tuple. It means there is no append(), remove() or pop() methods in tuples.

A tuple looks like below.

```
tuple_example = ('CS','IT','EC','ME')
print("tuple example: ", tuple_example)
print("data type of the example is", type(tuple_example))

tuple example:  ('CS', 'IT', 'EC', 'ME')
data type of the example is <class 'tuple'>
```

Fig3.13

What is Dictionary?

In Python, dictionaries are made up of key-value pairs. Key is used to identify the item and the value holds the value of the item. The main concept of dictionaries is that for every value you have a unique key. Dictionary is initialized by defining key-value in curly {} bracket where they are separated by colon : sign. Unlike the list, a dictionary is a collection which is unordered in nature which means order of its element is not guaranteed when you get or print the dictionary.

How to create a dictionary?

A dictionary is a collection of key-value pairs. Let's create a dictionary to store the information of a car like where in key we store the car's property name and in value we will store its name or value like below.

```
In [19]: dict_example = {
             'brand':'Hyundai',
             'model':'Creta',
             'type':'SUV',
             'year':'2017'
         }
         print("dictionary example: ", dict_example)

         dictionary example:  {'brand': 'Hyundai', 'model': 'Creta', 'type': 'SUV', 'year': '2017'}
```

Fig 3.14

Some operations with dictionary

1. Once you created a dictionary and now you want to access any item in that dictionary. This can be done by two way- one is to use key and second is to use **get()** method. Let's do the both in our newly create car information dictionary.

In [22]:
```
# access the brand value by key
car_brand_by_key = dict_example['brand']
print("car brand by key:", car_brand_by_key)
# access the brand value by get()
print("car brand by method:", dict_example.get('brand'))
```

```
car brand by key: Hyundai
car brand by method: Hyundai
```

Fig 3.15

2. There may be a situation where you want to change any value in your dictionary, this can be done by referring to the key name as shown in below where we are changing the car manufacture year from 2017 to 2018.

In [24]:
```
dict_example['year'] = '2018'
print("updated dict: ", dict_example)
```

```
updated dict:  {'brand': 'Hyundai', 'model': 'Creta', 'type': 'SUV', 'year': '2018'}
```

Fig 3.16

3. Sometimes you need the keys or values from a dictionary. You can print all key names or values with the for loop as shown in below example.

In [26]:
```python
# printing all keys
for car_property in dict_example:
    print("key in dict:", car_property)

# printing all values
for car_property_value in dict_example.values():
    print("value in dict:", car_property_value)
```

```
key in dict: brand
key in dict: model
key in dict: type
key in dict: year
value in dict: Hyundai
value in dict: Creta
value in dict: SUV
value in dict: 2018
```

Fig 3.17

4. What about if business owner wants you to display car details in a key-value pair. No issue we can do that like below.

In [27]:
```python
for car_property, car_property_value in dict_example.items():
    print(car_property, car_property_value)
```

```
brand Hyundai
model Creta
type SUV
year 2018
```

Fig 3.18

Rest other methods in dictionary are same as we used in list earlier; instead of index we need to use key here.

Conclusion

List and Dictionary are the two most used data types towards efficiently working with huge amounts of data. In your daily data clean-up process you will need to store some information in variables and there this chapter learning will come in action. After practicing notebook examples in your notebook you will gain confidence and will not confuse which data structure to use in which condition. In the next chapter will learn about Python functions and packages.

## CHAPTER 4

Function and Packages

Functions provide better modularity for your application and a high degree of code reusing. For your daily to daily Data Science work you don't need to reinvent the wheel or write some code from scratch. Remember in previous chapters example we have already used print() and type() functions. Python developers have written mostly used functionalities which you can leverage easily in terms of functions. In this chapter we will learn some other built in Python functions and how to use them to organise, make our code reusable.

Structure

- Help() function in Python
- How to import a Python package?
- How to create and call a function?
- Passing parameter in a function
- Default parameter in a function
- How to use unknown parameters in a function?
- Global and Local variable in a function
- What is Lambda function?
- Understanding main in Python

Objective

After studying the chapter, you will be able to use inbuilt Python functions and packages and write your own function.

Help() function in Python

You must have already used and know the name of Python inbuilt functions, but sometimes you still have to figure out how to use it. To know more about a function Python provides us another function named as **help()**. In your Jupyter notebook you can simply type help(<function_name>) and once you run this it will give you all information about that function.

For example if I want to know about the inbuilt **len()** function, I will use help() function as below.

```
help(len)
```

Help on built-in function len in module builtins:

len(obj, /)
    Return the number of items in a container.

Fig 4.1

How to import a Python package?

To use some inbuilt functionalities first you need to import such package and for that you just need to use **Import** keyword. For example, you are working as a junior Data Scientist in an agriculture firm and you need to calculate the area of a circular land. You know it well that area of a circle can be calculated from the formula pi*r^2 where r is the radius of the circle, but you don't remember the value of the pi. No need to worry, Python provides a math package to help you in this scenario as shown in the next example.

```
import math
```

```
# define area as variable area
area = 0
# define radius as variable r
r = 5.89
# calculate area
area = math.pi * r**2
print("area of the land is: ", area)
```

area of the land is: 108.98844649760245

Fig 4.2

Here we have imported math package but if we know the specific package then we can also import only that sub package from its package. For our example we don't need to import math package completely, in fact we can import only pi from math package like below example.

```
from math import pi
# define radius as variable r
r = 5.89
# calculate area
area = math.pi * r**2
print("area of the land is: ", area)
```

area of the land is: 108.98844649760245

Fig 4.3

How to create and call a function?

In Python we define a function using the 'def' keyword followed by function name and colon. For example if you want to print hello world in a function; first we define the function and then write the print() inside that function then we will see how to call that function. In below example notice the space before the print(), it's called Python's **indentation** and required to make ensure that this code is a part of the function. You don't need to explicitly give space; your notebook already knows it and once you press enter key after the colon sign, it will automatically add a space.

```
# defining my own function
def my_function():
    print("Hello World")
```

```
# calling my function
my_function()
```

```
Hello World
```

Fig 4.4

Passing parameter in a function

We have written a simple function, sometimes you need to pass some information also in your function and that we do in the form of parameters or arguments. For example, you want to get the sum of the two numbers with the help of a function so we will write a function which will take two parameters- a and b considering both are integers and we will give the sum of both numbers by using **return** statement as shown in the next example.

```
# defining a function to return sum of two numbers
def add_two_numbers(a,b):
    return a + b
# call the function
add_two_numbers(9,8)
```

17

Fig 4.5

Default parameter in a function

Sometimes you need to pass a default value to a parameter in your function. For example, you want to return sum of two numbers where second number value is pre- defined as it is 6 here. You can do this as below.

```
# defining a function with default parameter
def add_function(a,b = 6):
  return a + b
# call `add_function()` with only `a` parameter
add_function(a=1)
```

7

Fig 4.6

Note In the *MyFirstNotebook,*I have shared an example to help you understand how to pass parameters to a function in runtime and determine the output value based on condition.

How to use unknown parameters in a function?

In previous examples you know there are only two parameters passed but sometimes you don't know the number of arguments to pass in a function. In such situation you can pass ***args** parameter in your function as shown in below example. Here we are adding three numbers with the help of inbuilt sum() function-

```
# Define `add_function()` function to accept any no.of parameters
def add_function(*args):
  return sum(args)
# Calculate the sum of the numbers
add_function(9,4,8)
```

21

Fig 4.7

Note In above example instead of **args** you can give any name but * sign is important to place before any name. Try replacing *args with another name that includes the asterisk. You'll see that the above code keeps working!

Global and Local variable in a function

We use variables to store some values before using them in function. But use of declared variables in Python has some limits. We can define them as a global or as a local variable. Main difference between both of them is that the local variables are defined within a function block and can only be accessed inside that function, while global variables can be accessed by all functions that might be in your script. In the next example we have created a global scoped variable *my_text*- outside of the functions and accessing the same in both two functions.

```python
# define a Global scope variable
my_text = "I am learning Python for Data Science"

def first_function():
    """ This function uses global scope variable"""
    print(my_text)
first_function()

def second_function():
    """ This function alse uses global scope variable"""
    print(my_text)
second_function()
```

```
I am learning Python for Data Science
I am learning Python for Data Science
```

Fig 4.8

Now let us try first to print the value of global scoped variable just after the function declaration as shown in the example below. Point to notice here is that *my_text* variable is defined outside of the function. If we run the program it will show *UnboundLocalError* because it is treating *my_text* as local variable.

```
def my_function():
    print(my_text)
    my_text = "I am also learning"
    print(my_text)

# define a Global scope variable
my_text = "I am learning Python for Data Science"
my_function()
print(my_text)
```

```
---------------------------------------------------------------------
UnboundLocalError                           Traceback (most recent call last)
<ipython-input-14-45a9008ed554> in <module>()
      6 # define a Global scope variable
      7 my_text = "I am learning Python for Data Science"
----> 8 my_function()
      9 print(my_text)

<ipython-input-14-45a9008ed554> in my_function()
      1 def my_function():
----> 2     print(my_text)
      3     my_text = "I am also learning"
      4     print(my_text)
      5

UnboundLocalError: local variable 'my_text' referenced before assignment
```

Fig 4.9

Now let us comment the first print line just after the function declaration, our program will run without any error giving you the desired output as shown in the next screenshot.

```
def my_function():
    #print(my_text)
    my_text = "I am also learning"
    print(my_text)

# define a Global scope variable
my_text = "I am learning Python for Data Science"
my_function()
print(my_text)
```

```
I am also learning
I am learning Python for Data Science
```

Fig 4.10

What is Lambda function?

Lambda function is also known as Anonyms function in Python. For declaring a lambda function we **don't** use **def** keyword instead we use **lambda** keyword in a different way. In below example I am going to write a normal function to multiply by 5 and then we will write the same functionality with lambda function.

```
def multiply(x):
    return x*5
multiply(2)
```

```
10
```

```
#same functionality with lambda function
multiply = lambda x: x*5
multiply(2)
```

```
10
```

Fig 4.11

Below is an another example of adding two numbers with the help of inbuilt **sum()** function.

```
def sum(x, y):
    return x+y
sum(9,8)
```

```
17
```

```
# same example with lambda function
sum = lambda x, y: x + y;
sum(9,8)
```

```
17
```

Fig 4.12

It's quite clear now that we use lambda functions when we require a nameless function for a short period of time and that is created at runtime.

Understanding main in Python

Python doesn't have a defined entry point like main() method in other languages i.e. Java. Rather Python executes a source file line by line. Before executing the code, it will define a few special variables. For example, if the Python interpreter is running that module (the source file) as the main program, it sets the special __name__ variable to have a value "__main__". If this file is being imported from another module, __name__ will be set to the module's name.

Sometimes you write a module (a python file with .py extension) where it can be executed directly. Alternatively, it can also be imported and used in another module. Here you can put main check (**if __name__ == "__main__":**), so that you can have that code only execute when you want to run the module as a program and not have it execute when someone just wants to import your module and call your functions themselves.

Let's understand above concept with an example. We will use a Python IDE to create python files. You can download and install this IDE by following this link:- https:// www.jetbrains.com/help/pycharm/install-and-set-up-pycharm.html

After installing the PyCharm, open the IDE and create a new project as shown below.

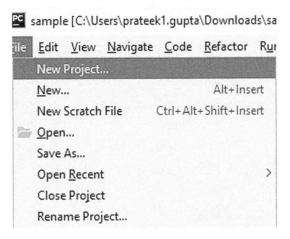

Fig 4.13

After creating the project ceate a python file with name my_module.py and put following line of code there-

```
 my_module.py ×
1     def hello():
2         print("This is from my_module.py file!")
3
4  ▶  if __name__ == "__main__":
5         print("Executing as main program")
6       💡 print("Value of __name__ is: ", __name__)
7         hello()|
```

Fig 4.14

You can run above created module by right clicking on the file and clicking on Run 'my_module' as shown below-

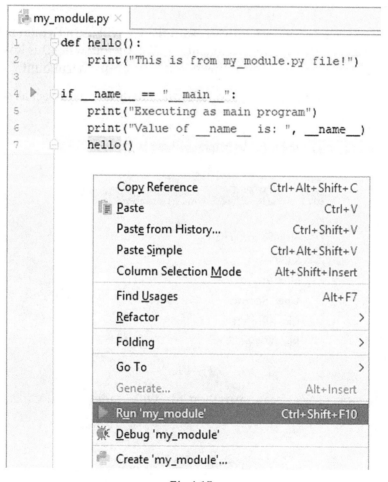

Fig 4.15

This will generate following result in console-

```
Run:   my_module
       C:\Users\prateek1.gupta\Downloads\sample\venv\Scripts\python.exe C:/Users/prateek1.gupta/Downloads/sample/my_module.py
       Executing as main program
       Value of __name__ is:  __main__
       This is from my_module.py file!

       Process finished with exit code 0
```

Fig 4.16

As you can see in the result, we have created a new module and executed it as main program so the value of __name__ is set to '__main__' . As a result if condition satisfies and hello() function gets called. Now create a new file called using_module. py and import my_module there by writing the following code-

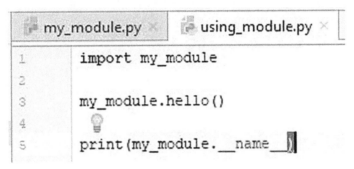

Fig 4.17

Now run this file and you will see following outcome-

```
Run:   using_module
       C:\Users\prateek1.gupta\Downloads\sample\venv\Scripts\python.exe C:/Users/prateek1.gupta/Downloads/sample/using_module.py
       This is from my_module.py file!
       my_module

       Process finished with exit code 0
```

Fig 4.18

As you can see now if statement in my_module fails to execute because the value of __name__ is set to 'my_module'. From this small program you can understand that every module in python has a special attribute called __name__ . The value of __name__ attribute is set to '__main__' when module run as main program. Otherwise the value of __name__ is set to contain the name of the module.

Conclusion

As an aspiring Data Scientist, you'll constantly need to write your own functions to solve problems that your data poses to you. In your daily work you will import various packages, you will write your functions for different tasks i.e. a function for data cleaning, another function for modelling and another for evaluating your model etc. Till then go chase your dreams, have an awesome day, make every second count and see you later In next chapter where we will learn first fundamental package of Python used for scientific computing- NumPy.

## CHAPTER 5

NumPy Foundation

NumPy is the fundamental package for scientific computing with Python. Most of the other packages such as *pandas, statsmodels* are built on top of it. NumPy is short name for "Numeric Python" or "Numerical Python". This package contains powerful N-dimensional array object and useful linear algebra capabilities. In this chapter we will learn about this N-dimensional array- a more powerful alternative to the list and we will see how to use this in data manipulation.

Structure

- Importing a NumPy package
- Why NumPy array over List?
- NumPy array attributes
- Creating NumPy arrays
- Accessing element of an NumPy array
- Slicing in NumPy array

Objective

After studying the chapter, you will be able to use NumPy array effectively.

Importing a NumPy package

The NumPy package comes preinstalled in Anaconda distribution so we don't need to install this package in fact for using it we just need to import it. We can import this package in following way.

```
# importing numpy package
import numpy as np
```

Fig 5.1

| **Note** | In above import statement **np** is an **alias** pointing to NumPy. This alias we can use with any import to short the package name in further uses. |

Why use NumPy array over List?

Say for example you have weather data, telling about the distance and the wind speed. Now you are supposed to calculate and generate a new feature from the data - the time. Ideally, we would go ahead with using the list and calculate by applying the formula to the list of distance and speed as shown in the example below.

```
distance = [55,60,45]
speed = [6,10,7]
time = distance/speed
print("time:", time)
```

Fig 5.2

But once you run your code you see unexpected result.

```
---------------------------------------------------------------
TypeError                              Traceback (most recent call last)
<ipython-input-2-3554454633bc> in <module>()
      1 distance = [55,60,45]
      2 speed = [6,10,7]
----> 3 time = distance/speed
      4 print("time:", time)

TypeError: unsupported operand type(s) for /: 'list' and 'list'
```

Fig 5.3

You must be confused and thinking, what I have done wrong with the list operations, but no clue!

List has some limitations. You cannot perform some mathematical operations directly on list and that's why Python has NumPy array to solve such problem. To solve this issue, we need to import the NumPy package first then we need to convert our list into NumPy array and then we need to perform our operation like below.

```python
import numpy as np
distance = [55,60,45]
speed = [6,10,7]
dist = np.array(distance)
spd = np.array(speed)
time= dist/spd
print(time)
```

```
[9.16666667 6.          6.42857143]
```

Fig 5.4

Note	In above example dist and speed variables are of type numpy array. Since time variable is associated with dist and speed numpy arrays, its type is automatically assigned as numpy array.

NumPy array Attributes

NumPy array has its own attributes like dimension, size, shape. We can know these attributes by using it's **ndim**, **shape** and **size** attributes as shown in below with our wind speed example –

```python
# data type
print("data type of array:", time.dtype)
# no. of dimensions
print("no. of dimensions:", time.ndim)
# size of each dimension
print("size of each dimension:", time.shape)
# total size of array
print("total size of array:", time.size)
```

```
data type of array: float64
no. of dimensions: 1
size of each dimension: (3,)
total size of array: 3
```

Fig 5.5

Creating NumPy arrays

An array can be one, two or three dimensions. Based on the problem you are solving you need to create any dimension array so let's create array using random numbers. For generating random numbers in our case it's integer numbers we will use **NumPy's random function** and then we will check individual array attributes as shown below.

```
# creating arrays with random values
np.random.seed(0)  # seed for reproducibility

x1 = np.random.randint(10, size=6)  # One-dimensional array
x2 = np.random.randint(10, size=(3, 4))  # Two-dimensional array
x3 = np.random.randint(10, size=(3, 4, 5))  # Three-dimensional array

print("x1 ndim: ", x1.ndim)
print("x1 shape:", x1.shape)
print("x1 size: ", x1.size)

print("x2 ndim: ", x2.ndim)
print("x2 shape:", x2.shape)
print("x2 size: ", x2.size)

print("x3 ndim: ", x3.ndim)
print("x3 shape:", x3.shape)
print("x3 size: ", x3.size)
```

```
x1 ndim:   1
x1 shape: (6,)
x1 size:   6
x2 ndim:   2
x2 shape: (3, 4)
x2 size:   12
x3 ndim:   3
x3 shape: (3, 4, 5)
x3 size:   60
```

Fig 5.6

As noted, **np.random.seed(0)** sets the random seed to 0, so the pseudo random numbers you get from random will start from the same point and **np.random. randint()** function Return random integers from the "discrete uniform" distribution of the specified dtype in the "half-open" interval [low, high). If high is None (the default), then results are from [0, low).

Let's create an another array using NumPy **arrange**() function which basically returns evenly spaced values within a given interval. In below example we are creating a sequence of integers from 0 to 20 with steps of 5-

```
f = np.arange(0, 20, 5)
print ("sequential array with steps of 5:\n", f)

sequential array with steps of 5:
 [ 0  5 10 15]
```

Fig 5.7

Accessing element of a NumPy array

For analyzing and manipulating an array you need to access the elements. we will use indexes of every element in an array as we did in list. In a one-dimensional array, the i'th value (counting from zero) can be accessed by specifying the desired index in square brackets, just as with Python lists. As shown below we are accessing the elements of the arrays we have created above using np.**random**() earlier.

```
print("1-d array:", x1)
print("second element of first array:", x1[1])
print("last element of first array:", x1[-1])
print("first element of first array:", x1[0])

1-d array: [5 0 3 3 7 9]
second element of first array: 0
last element of first array: 9
first element of first array: 5
```

Fig 5.8

What about other dimensions array? It's quite simple. We just need to use comma separated tuple of indices as shown in below where we are accessing the first elements of a 2-d and 3-d arrays-

```
print("2-d array:\n", x2)
print("first elements of 2-d array:\n", x2[0,0])
print("3-d array:\n", x3)
print("first element of 3-d array:\n", x3[0,0,0])
```

```
2-d array:
 [[3 5 2 4]
 [7 6 8 8]
 [1 6 7 7]]
first elements of 2-d array:
 3
3-d array:
 [[[8 1 5 9 8]
  [9 4 3 0 3]
  [5 0 2 3 8]
  [1 3 3 3 7]]

 [[0 1 9 9 0]
  [4 7 3 2 7]
  [2 0 0 4 5]
  [5 6 8 4 1]]

 [[4 9 8 1 1]
  [7 9 9 3 6]
  [7 2 0 3 5]
  [9 4 4 6 4]]]
first element of 3-d array:
 8
```

Fig 5.9

Multi-dedimensional array has its own importance while handling data. For example, let's take a look at how one might store a movie related data. A movie is nothing more than a time-varying sequence of images -- i.e., an array of images. Each image is a two-dimensional array, with each element of the array representing a color. A color has three components: Red, Green, Blue. So a movie can be modeled as a multidimensional array.

Slicing in NumPy array

As we used square brackets to access individual array elements, we can also use them to access subarrays with the slice notation, marked by the colon (:) character. Slicing is an important concept to access the element of an array or list. But unlike list in array slicing, they return views rather than copies of the array data. It means if we create a sub-array for an array and then modify any element then the original array will also be modified. In below examples we will create a 1-d array and then we will access its elements using slicing –

```python
# create an array
x = np.arange(10)
print("our array:", x)
print("first five elements:", x[:5])
print("elements after index 5:", x[5:])
print("middle sub-array:", x[4:7])
print("every other element:", x[::2])
print("every other element, starting at index 1:", x[1::2])
print("elements in reversed order:", x[::-1])
```

```
our array: [0 1 2 3 4 5 6 7 8 9]
first five elements: [0 1 2 3 4]
elements after index 5: [5 6 7 8 9]
middle sub-array: [4 5 6]
every other element: [0 2 4 6 8]
every other element, starting at index 1: [1 3 5 7 9]
elements in reversed order: [9 8 7 6 5 4 3 2 1 0]
```

Fig 5.10

Again, for the multi-dimensional array we need to use multiple slices with comma as shown in below example.

```python
print("2-d array:\n", x2)
print("two rows, three columns:\n", x2[:2, :3])
```

```
2-d array:
 [[3 5 2 4]
 [7 6 8 8]
 [1 6 7 7]]
two rows, three columns:
 [[3 5 2]
 [7 6 8]]
```

Fig 5.11

As I mentioned above, if we create a sub array form an array and make any changes in the sub-array then it will also change the original array. So how can we ensure data integrity of an array? In such cases, make a copy of the original array using **copy()** and then can modify without affecting the original array as shown in below example-

```
# original array
print("original 2-d array:\n", x2)
# creating a 2X2 subarray from the original array
x2_sub = x2[:2, :2]
print("sub-array:\n", x2_sub)
# modifying sub-array
x2_sub[0, 0] = 88
print("modified sub array:\n", x2_sub)
# original array after sub-array changes
print("original array after changes in sub-array:\n", x2)
print("making a copy of the original array")
x2_sub_copy = x2[:2, :2].copy()
print("copy of the orinal array:\n", x2_sub_copy)
# modifying copied array
x2_sub_copy[0, 0] = 42
print("copied array after changes:\n", x2_sub_copy)
print("original array:\n", x2)
```

Fig 5.12

```
original 2-d array:
 [[3 5 2 4]
 [7 6 8 8]
 [1 6 7 7]]
sub-array:
 [[3 5]
 [7 6]]
modified sub array:
 [[88  5]
 [ 7  6]]
original array after changes in sub-array:
 [[88  5  2  4]
 [ 7  6  8  8]
 [ 1  6  7  7]]
making a copy of the original array
copy of the orinal array:
 [[88  5]
 [ 7  6]]
copied array after changes:
 [[42  5]
 [ 7  6]]
original array:
 [[88  5  2  4]
 [ 7  6  8  8]
 [ 1  6  7  7]]
```

Fig 5.13

Array Concatenation

In some scenarios you may need to combine two arrays into a single one. For this situation NumPy has different methods- **np.concatenate(), np.vstack()** and **np.hstack().**

np.concatenate() is useful for combining arrays of same dimensions while np.vstack() and np.hstack() are good when you are working with arrays of mixed dimensions. For understanding each uses we will first see how to combine two same dimension arrays and then we will see how to add different dimensions arrays into one as shown in below example-

```python
# creating two sample arrays
x = np.array([1, 2, 3])
y = np.array([3, 2, 1])
# combining both arrays using concatenate
np.concatenate([x, y])
```

```
array([1, 2, 3, 3, 2, 1])
```

Fig 5.14

```python
# creating a sample array
x = np.array([1, 2, 3])
# creating a 2-d array
grid = np.array([[9, 8, 7],
                 [6, 5, 4]])

# vertically stack the arrays
np.vstack([x, grid])
```

```
array([[1, 2, 3],
       [9, 8, 7],
       [6, 5, 4]])
```

```python
# horizontally stack the arrays
y = np.array([[99],
              [99]])
np.hstack([grid, y])
```

```
array([[ 9,  8,  7, 99],
       [ 6,  5,  4, 99]])
```

Fig 5.15

Note	For seeing different NumPy inbuilt features in your notebook just press tab key after the dot sign of numpy alias (np.)

Conclusion

In this chapter we understood how to perform standard mathematical operations on individual elements or complete array using NumPy. The range of functions covered is linear algebra, statistical operations, and other specialized mathematical operations. For our purpose, we just need to know about N-dimentional array or ndarray and the range of mathematical functions that are relevant to our research purpose. In the next chapter where we will learn the second most important python package– Pandas.

## CHAPTER 6

Pandas and DataFrame

Pandas is a popular Python package for data science. It offers powerful, expressive and flexible data structures that make data manipulation and analysis easy, among many other things. Pandas DataFrame is one of the very powerful and useful data structure among these. Pandas library is one of the most preferred tools for data scientists to do data manipulation and analysis, next to matplotlib for data visualization and NumPy, the fundamental library for scientific computing in Python on which Pandas was built.

Structure

- Importing Pandas
- Pandas Data Structures
- .loc[] and .iloc[]
- Some useful DataFrame Functions
- Handling missing values in DataFrame

Objective

After studying this chapter, you will be able to create, manipulate and access the information you need from your data with the help of Pandas data structures

Importing Pandas

Importing Pandas in your notebook is quite simple. Pandas is preinstalled with Anaconda distribution, so you don't need to install it. In any case if it is not installed you can install it by typing following command in Anaconda Prompt-

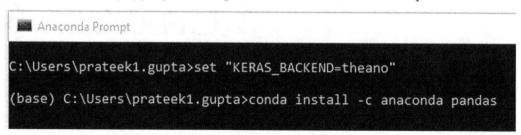

Fig 6.1

Once you installed the pandas, you can import it as below-

```
# importing Pandas package using alias
import pandas as pd
```

Fig 6.2

Pandas Data Structures

Pandas has two main data structures widely used in Data Science-

1. Series
2. DataFrame

Series in Pandas is a one-dimensional labelled array capable of holding any data type such as integers, floats and strings. It is similar to a NumPy 1-dimensional array. In addition to the values that are specified by the programmer, pandas assigns a label to each of the values. If the labels are not provided by the programmer, then pandas assigns labels (0 for first element, 1 for second element and so on). A benefit of assigning labels to data values is that it becomes easier to perform manipulations on the dataset as the whole dataset becomes more of a dictionary where each value is associated with a label.

A pandas Series can be constructed using the **pd.Series()** as shown in below example.

```
# creating an empty Series
x = pd.Series()
print("empty series example: ", x)
```

```
empty series example:  Series([], dtype: float64)
```

Fig 6.3

In output cell you can see it is showing the default data type of the Series as float. Let's create another example of Series from list of numbers.

```
# series example
series1 = pd.Series([10,20,30,50])
print(series1)
```

```
0    10
1    20
2    30
3    50
dtype: int64
```

Fig 6.4

In above code example you can see the output is in tabular form with two columns-first one is showing indexes starting from zero and second one is showing the elements. This index column is generated by Series and if you want to re-index this with your own index name then you can do it in using index parameter as shown in following way-

```
# re-indexing the default index column
series2 = pd.Series([10,20,30,50], index=['a','b','c','d'])
print(series2)
```

```
a    10
b    20
c    30
d    50
dtype: int64
```

Fig 6.5

The ways of accessing elements in a Series object are similar to what we have seen in NumPy. You can perform NumPy operations on Series data arrays as shown in the next screenshot.

```
# accessing a Series element
series2['b']
```

20

Fig 6.6

Data manipulation with Series is also an easy task. We can apply mathematical calculations as we did in NumPy like below example-

```
# data manipulation with Series
print("adding 5 to a Series:\n", series2 + 5)
print("filtering series with greater than 30:\n", series2[series2>30])
print("square root of Series elements:\n", np.sqrt(series2))
```

```
adding 5 to a Series:
 a    15
b    25
c    35
d    55
dtype: int64
filtering series with greater than 30:
 d    50
dtype: int64
square root of Series elements:
 a    3.162278
b    4.472136
c    5.477226
d    7.071068
dtype: float64
```

Fig 6.7

Remember the Dictionary data structure we have seen in earlier chapter! We can convert this data structure to a Series so that dictionary' key and value can be transformed into a tabular form as shown below.

```
# a sample dictionary
data = {'abc': 1, 'def': 2, 'ghi': 3}
print("dictionary example:\n", data)
# converting dictionary to series
pd.Series(data)
```

```
dictionary example:
 {'abc': 1, 'def': 2, 'ghi': 3}

abc    1
def    2
ghi    3
dtype: int64
```

Fig 6.8

DataFrame in Pandas is a two-dimensional labelled data structure with columns of potentially different types. You can imagine a DataFrame containing three components- index, rows and columns. A DataFrame is a tabular data structure in which data is laid out in rows and column format (similar to a CSV and SQL file), but it can also be used for higher dimensional data sets. The DataFrame object can contain homogenous and heterogenous values and can be thought of as a logical extension of Series data structures.

In contrast to Series, where there is one index, a DataFrame object has one index for column and one index for rows. This allows flexibility in accessing and manipulating data.

We can create a DataFrame using **pd.DataFrame()** as shown in below example-

```
# creating an empty dataframe
df = pd.DataFrame()
print("dataframe example:\n", df)
```

```
dataframe example:
 Empty DataFrame
Columns: []
Index: []
```

Fig 6.9

Let's create a DataFrame from a list where the list contains the name and age of a person. We will also rename the column names of our DataFrame using columns parameter as shown below-

```
# a sample list containing name and age
data = [['Tom',10],['Harry',12],['Jim',13]]
# creating a dataframe form given list with column names
df = pd.DataFrame(data,columns=['Name','Age'])
df
```

	Name	Age
0	Tom	10
1	Harry	12
2	Jim	13

Fig 6.10

Selecting a column in a DataFrame is as same as we have seen earlier with other data structure. For example, if you want to know all names under the 'Name' column from above DataFrame then we you can access them in two ways as shown in the next sreenshot.

```
# accessing a dataframe column- first way
df['Name']
```

```
0        Tom
1      Harry
2        Jim
Name: Name, dtype: object
```

```
# accessing a dataframe column- second way
df.Name
```

```
0        Tom
1      Harry
2        Jim
Name: Name, dtype: object
```

Fig 6.11

Let us suppose you want to add a new column to your DataFrame which will store the birth year of a person. You can do it easily as shown in below example.

```
# adding a column in existing dataframe
df['Year'] = 2008
df
```

	Name	Age	Year
0	Tom	10	2008
1	Harry	12	2008
2	Jim	13	2008

Fig 6.12

Next, deleting of a column is also an easy task. You can sue **del** or **.pop()** to delete a column. Look in the below example-

```
print("original dataframe:\n", df)
del df['Year']
print("dataframe after del:\n", df)
df.pop('Age')
print("dataframe after pop:\n", df)
```

```
original dataframe:
        Name  Age  Year
0       Tom   10  2008
1     Harry   12  2008
2       Jim   13  2008
dataframe after del:
        Name  Age
0       Tom   10
1     Harry   12
2       Jim   13
dataframe after pop:
        Name
0       Tom
1     Harry
2       Jim
```

Fig 6.13

.loc[] and .iloc[]

Selecting a row or an index in a DataFrame is quite different but very easy if you know how to used the .loc[] and .iloc[] functions. For understanding both let's first create a DataFrame to store the company stock price like below-

```
# a sample dataframe containing compaany stock data
data = pd.DataFrame({'price':[95, 25, 85, 41],
                    'ticker':['AXP', 'CSCO', 'DIS', 'MSFT'],
                    'company':['American Express', 'Cisco', 'Walt Disney','Microsoft']})
data
```

	company	price	ticker
0	American Express	95	AXP
1	Cisco	25	CSCO
2	Walt Disney	85	DIS
3	Microsoft	41	MSFT

Fig 6.14

> **Note** DataFrames by default do not preserve order of columns when it is created. Hence, in the above screenshot your may see the order of column display different from the order of order in which it was created.

To access the value that is at index 0, in column 'company', you can do it either using the label or by indicating the position. For label based indexing you can use .loc[] and for position based indexing you can use .iloc[] as shown below-

```
# access the value that is at index 0, in column 'company' using loc
print(data.loc[0]['company'])
# access the value that is at index 0, in column 'company' using iloc
print(data.loc[0][0])

American Express
American Express
```

Fig 6.15

From above example it is quite clear that *.loc[]* works on labels of your index. This means that if you give in loc[3], you look for the values of your DataFrame that have an index labeled 3.

On the other hand, *.iloc[]* works on the positions in your index. This means that if you give in iloc[3], you look for the values of your DataFrame that are at index '3`.

Some Useful DataFrame Functions

DataFrame is a very useful data structure which you will use often in your daily task. Storing data in a DataFrame has various benefits and it's quite simple for data analysis. Let's see some quite useful functions of a DataFrame -

```
# inspecting top 5 rows of a dataframe
print("top five data:\n", data.head())
# inspecting below 5 rows of a dataframe
print("below 5 data:\n", data.tail())
```

```
top five data:
              company  price ticker
0   American Express     95    AXP
1              Cisco     25   CSCO
2        Walt Disney     85    DIS
3          Microsoft     41   MSFT
below 5 data:
              company  price ticker
0   American Express     95    AXP
1              Cisco     25   CSCO
2        Walt Disney     85    DIS
3          Microsoft     41   MSFT
```

Fig 6.16

.head() and **.tail()** are useful when you have thousands of rows and columns in your data and you want to inspect it in a quick view as shown in the above screenshot.

Next, if you want to check data type of each columns in your data, you can do so by using **.dtypes** like below-

```
# check data type of columns
data.dtypes
```

```
company     object
price        int64
ticker      object
dtype: object
```

Fig 6.17

Pandas DataFrame has also one unique method which can give you descriptive statistics (mean, median, count etc) of your dataset. For knowing this statistics you can use **.describe()** as below. From this description we can easily say the highest stock price is 95 and minimum stock price is 25 and total no of stocks are 4. Imagine if this data contains records of million companies! Without Pandas it will be much more difficult to know the statistics of the data.

```
# descriptive statistics of the data
data.describe()
```

	price
count	4.000000
mean	61.500000
std	33.798422
min	25.000000
25%	37.000000
50%	63.000000
75%	87.500000
max	95.000000

Fig 6.18

Note If you have non-numeric data, then applying describe function would produce statistics such as count, unique, frequency. In addition to this, you can also calculate skewness (skew), kurtosis (kurt), percent changes, difference, and other statistics.

Next, important function of a Pandas DataFrame is to check the information of your data including column data type, non-null values and memory usage. This can be achieved using **.info()** as shown below-

```
# information of the dataframe
data.info()

<class 'pandas.core.frame.DataFrame'>
RangeIndex: 4 entries, 0 to 3
Data columns (total 3 columns):
company    4 non-null object
price      4 non-null int64
ticker     4 non-null object
dtypes: int64(1), object(2)
memory usage: 176.0+ bytes
```

Fig 6.19

Similarly there is shape, columns, corr(), cov() functions which you will see in later chapters of this book. Try these functions in your notebook and explore what information you get from them.

Handling missing values in DataFrame

As a Data Scientist you will come across uncleaned data with missing values most of the times. Here missing means data is not available (NA) for any reason. You cannot simply ignore those missing data. In fact, before applying any machine learning algorithm you need to handle such values. Pandas provides a flexible way to handle missing data. Pandas uses **NaN** (Not a number) or sometimes **NaT** as the default missing value marker with the help of it you can detect it easily using **isnull()** function. Let's understand this function by first creating a dataframe with missing values as shown in below example-

```
# a sample dataframe
df = pd.DataFrame(np.random.randn(5, 3), index=['a', 'c', 'e', 'f', 'h'],
                  columns=['one', 'two', 'three'])
# creating a data with missing values by reindexing
df2 = df.reindex(['a', 'b', 'c', 'd', 'e', 'f', 'g', 'h'])
df2
```

	one	two	three
a	-1.282674	1.081757	-0.559330
b	NaN	NaN	NaN
c	1.009585	0.876217	0.830863
d	NaN	NaN	NaN
e	1.308541	-0.434903	-1.224001
f	1.995670	1.199008	-0.671072
g	NaN	NaN	NaN
h	0.032248	-1.083125	-0.679454

Fig 6.20

You can see missing values as NaN. We can check the missing values using isnull() function and then count the sum of the missing values using sum() function as shown below. The isnull() function return a Boolean same-sized object indicating if the values are missing and sum() function counts the True values of the Boolean-

```
# checking missing values using isnull()
print(df2.isnull())
missing_values_count = df2.isnull().sum()
print("count of missing values:\n", missing_values_count)
```

```
    one     two   three
a   False   False   False
b   True    True    True
c   False   False   False
d   True    True    True
e   False   False   False
f   False   False   False
g   True    True    True
h   False   False   False
count of missing values:
 one      3
two      3
three    3
dtype: int64
```

Fig .21

Once you know the total count of missing values, you can now think how to handle those. One simple way when you don't have any clue why there are missing values, you can simply drop them using .**dropna()** function as shown below-

```
# remove all the rows that contain a missing value
df2 = df2.dropna()
print(df2)
```

```
         one        two      three
a  -1.282674   1.081757  -0.559330
c   1.009585   0.876217   0.830863
e   1.308541  -0.434903  -1.224001
f   1.995670   1.199008  -0.671072
h   0.032248  -1.083125  -0.679454
```

Fig 6.22

Dropna() can also be applied on columns basis. You can remove all columns with at least one missing value using **axis=1** parameter in dropna() function. For example, let's apply this approach on original df2 dataframe . You need to rerun the dataframe df2 creation cell before running the below cell otherwise you will get wrong output

```
# remove all columns with at least one missing value
columns_with_na_dropped = df2.dropna(axis=1)
columns_with_na_dropped.head()
```

___

a

b

c

d

e

Fig 6.23

Using column based removal of NaN values could be risky as you may risk losing all the columns if every column has NaN values. Instead dropna() with rows approach is useful in this case.

Second approach to handle missing values is to fill them either by zero or by the mean/median or by the occurrence of a word. Let's see how we can fill missing values-

```
# filling NaN with zeros
df3 = df2.fillna(0)
df3
```

	one	two	three
a	2.000749	-0.256641	-0.041130
b	0.000000	0.000000	0.000000
c	-0.074203	-1.090353	-0.066285
d	0.000000	0.000000	0.000000
e	1.088535	-1.029808	0.553896
f	1.316821	0.125611	-0.627532
g	0.000000	0.000000	0.000000
h	-0.623504	-1.266855	1.043820

Fig 6.24

```
# replace all NA's the value that comes directly after it in the same column
# then replace all the reamining na's with 0
df4 = df2.fillna(method = 'bfill', axis=0).fillna(0)
df4
```

	one	two	three
a	2.000749	-0.256641	-0.041130
b	-0.074203	-1.090353	-0.066285
c	-0.074203	-1.090353	-0.066285
d	1.088535	-1.029808	0.553896
e	1.088535	-1.029808	0.553896
f	1.316821	0.125611	-0.627532
g	-0.623504	-1.266855	1.043820
h	-0.623504	-1.266855	1.043820

Fig 6.25

In above code cell , we are filling the missing values using the backward filling method of Pandas DataFrame. Similarly you can use forward filling using **ffil()** method.

Conclusion

The fast, flexible, and expressive Pandas data structures are designed to make real-world data analysis significantly easier, but this might not be immediately the case for those who are just getting started with it. There is so much functionality built into this package that learning the options in just one go could be overwhelming. It is highly recommended to practice the functionalities with suitable case-studies. So, open your notebook, apply the learnings of this chapter and explore more. In the next chapter we will learn how to interact with different databases in Python.

CHAPTER 7

Interacting with Databases

As a Data Scientist, you will interact with the databases constantly. For this purpose, you need to know how to query, build and write to different databases. Knowledge of SQL (Structured Query Language) is a perfect fit for this. SQL is all about Data. SQL is really used for three things- it used to Read/Retrieve Data – so Data is often stored in a Database. It is also used to Write Data in a Database and finally, it is used to Update and insert new data. Python has its own toolkit- SQLAlchemy which provides an accessible and intuitive way to query, build & write to SQLite, MySQL and Postgresql databases (among many others). We will cover all required database details specific to Data Science here.

Structure

- What is SQLAlchemy?
- Installing SQLAlchemy Package
- How to use SQLAlchemy?
- SQLAlchemy Engine Configuration
- Creating A Table In Database
- Inserting Data In Table
- Update a record
- How to join two tables

Objective

After studying the chapter, you will become familiar with the fundamentals of Relational Databases and the Relational Model. You will learn how to connect to a database and interact with it by writing basic SQL queries, both in raw SQL as well as with SQLAlchemy.

What is SQLAlchemy?

SQLAlchemy is the Python SQL toolkit and Object Relational Mapper that gives you the full power and flexibility of SQL. It provides a nice "Pythonic" way of interacting with databases. Rather than dealing with the differences between specific dialects of traditional SQL such as MySQL or PostgreSQL or Oracle, you can leverage the Pythonic framework of SQLAlchemy to streamline your workflow and more efficiently query your data.

Installing SQLAlchemy Package

Let's start our journey by first installing the SQLAlchemy package in our notebook. You can install this package from the Anaconda Distribution using command (**conda install -c anaconda sqlalchemy)** in Anaconda Prompt as shown below.

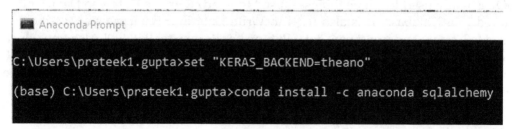

Fig 7.1

Once this package is installed, you can import it in your notebook as shown in the next screenshot.

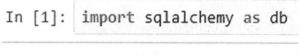

Fig 7.2

How to use SQLAlchemy?

Before using our toolkit there should be a database to whom you want to connect first. We can use SQLAlchemy to connect with PostgreSQL, MySQL, Oracle, Microsoft

SQL, SQLite and many others. For our learning purpose we will use MySQL db. You can download and install the MYSQL db from their official website-

https://dev.mysql.com/downloads/installer/ and for creating database, tables etc ypu can install workbench from following link- https://dev.mysql.com/downloads/workbench/

After installing the MySQL workbench, you need to first create a connection there. For this open the workbench and click on the + icon as highlighted in below screen shot-

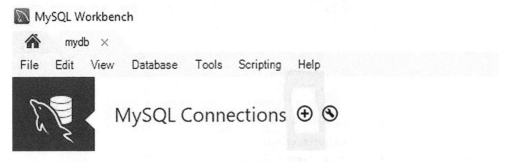

Fig 7.3

Once you click on + icon, a pop-up screen will come. Here you need to give connection name, username and password for creating the connection. Note down the connection name, hostname, port and password because we will need this information later. Once you complete this step, your connection is ready to be used

Setup New Connection			— □ ×
Connection Name:			Type a name for the connection
Connection Method:	Standard (TCP/IP)	˅	Method to use to connect to the RDBMS
Parameters SSL	Advanced		
Hostname:	127.0.0.1	Port: 3306	Name or IP address of the server host - and TCP/IP port.
Username:	root		Name of the user to connect with.
Password:	Store in Vault ... Clear		The user's password. Will be requested later if it's not set.
Default Schema:			The schema to use as default schema. Leave blank to select it later.
Configure Server Management...		Test Connection Cancel OK	

Fig 7.4

After the successful creation of connection, next step is to create a schema. For this right click in the SCHEMAS menu and select option Create Schema-

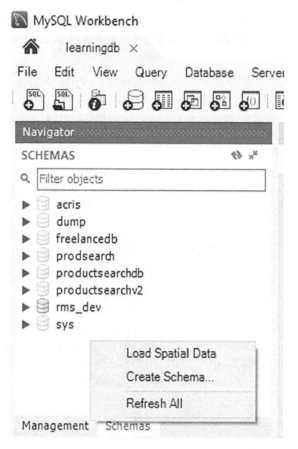

Fig 7.5

In above screen shot it is showing many schemas I have created earlier. Once you click on Create Schema option follow the screen by entering schema name and then selecting default options. In the above example, I have saved the schema with name *rms_dev*.

SQLAlchemy Engine Configuration

Once you know your database information, next step is to interact with the database. For this purpose, SQLAlchemy uses **Engine.** Creating an Engine with SQLAlchemy is quite simple. You need to use it's **create_engine** api. You can import this api with following import: **from sqlalchemy import create_engine** .This create_engine() api uses following syntax to store the db information as parameters-

```
dialect+driver://username:password@host:port/database
```

Fig 7.6

Here, dialect names include the identifying name of the SQLAlchemy dialect, a name such as sqlite, mysql, postgresql, oracle, or mssql. The driver name is the name of the DBAPI to be used to connect to the database using all lowercase letters. If not specified, a "default" DBAPI will be imported if available - this default is typically the most widely known driver available for that backend. You can check name of the DBAPI in following link- https://docs.sqlalchemy.org/en/latest/core/engines.html#mysql

In below example I am going to use my MySQL db connection details in the Jupyter notebook for creating an engine.

```
engine = db.create_engine('mysql://root:admin@127.0.0.1:3306/rms_dev')
```

```
connection = engine.connect()
```

Fig 7.7

Here I am passing my db details (with username as root and password as admin) in required format of create_engine() api then I am connecting with the database using engine's **connect()**. Since we have created a new schema, there is no any table. So let's create a new table/data there first.

| **Note** | If you face 'No module named 'MySQLdb'' error, it means you need to install mysqlclient that you can install from the anaconda prompt using 'pip install mysqlclient' command. |

Creating A Table In Database

Since we have connected to our engine, let's create a table by using **execute()** method of Engine. In this example I am creating a table to hold customer specific data- name and address. SQL syntax for creating a table is as below-

```
CREATE TABLE [IF NOT EXISTS] `TableName` (`fieldname` dataType [optional parameters]) ENGINE = sto
rage Engine;
```

Fig 7.8

In our case we have already connected to our engine so no need to use ENGINE parameter. First I am storing my create table sql query in a variable named as 'query' then I am passing this query to Engine's execute() method. To check if my table is created or not, I am printing table name and in the last I am closing my database connection-

```
query = "CREATE TABLE customers (name VARCHAR(255), address VARCHAR(255))"
```

```
connection.execute(query)
print("Table Name:", engine.table_names())
connection.close()
```

```
Table Name: ['customers']
```

Fig 7.9

Note	Always remember to close the database connection after any operation just like we did with *connection.close()*

Inserting Data In a Table

Once you have created a table, it's time to insert some data in it. For adding new data to an existing table we will use sql insert query which syntax is like below-

```
INSERT INTO table_name ( field1, field2,...fieldN )

    VALUES

    ( value1, value2,...valueN );
```

Fig 7.10

In our customers table let us add a customer name and address as shown in the next screenshot-

```
engine = db.create_engine('mysql://root:admin@127.0.0.1:3306/schemaexample')
connection = engine.connect()
sql = "INSERT INTO customers (name, address) VALUES ('Prateek', 'India')"
connection.execute(sql)
connection.close()
```

Fig 7.11

Now to check the existing records of the table we can use select query of sql and then we can fetch all rows using **fetchall()** of sqlalchemy api as below-

```
engine = db.create_engine('mysql://root:admin@127.0.0.1:3306/schemaexample')
connection = engine.connect()
sql = "SELECT * from customers"
result = connection.execute(sql)
print("table data:", result.fetchall())
connection.close()
```

```
table data: [('Prateek', 'India')]
```

Fig 7.12

In this way you are now able to read the data from a database easily. You will be writing similar codes which will help you fetch thousands of the data from a db for analysis.

Update a record

Updating an existing record is a daily task and you must know how to run updates on your records in case a record was wrongly inserted into the db. In below example we are going to update our existing customer's address using update sql query.

```
engine = db.create_engine('mysql://root:admin@127.0.0.1:3306/schemaexample')
connection = engine.connect()
sql = "UPDATE customers SET address = 'Singapore' WHERE address = 'India'"
connection.execute(sql)
print("record(s) is updated")
q = "SELECT * from customers"
result = connection.execute(q)
print("table data:", result.fetchall())
connection.close()
```

```
record(s) is updated
table data: [('Prateek', 'Singapore')]
```

Fig 7.13

For **deleting** a record you can use WHERE clause to delete a record based on a column as shown in the next screenshot-

```
engine = db.create_engine('mysql://root:admin@127.0.0.1:3306/schemaexample')
connection = engine.connect()
sql = "DELETE FROM customers WHERE address = 'Singapore'"
connection.execute(sql)
print("record is deleted!")
connection.close()
```

```
record is deleted!
```

Fig 7.14

How to join two tables

In relational database there may be many tables and in those tables, there may be a relationship between their columns. In such condition you need to join tables. A real-world example of this scenario is from e-commerce domain where product related data is in a table, user specific data is in another table and inventory is in another one, here you need to fetch product details based on user or inventory. Joining of table can be done by three ways- inner join, left join and right join. Let's understand each of these joining-

Inner Join

We can join or combine rows from two or more tables based on a related column by using a JOIN statement. Let's create two tables- users and products in our db to understand this type of joining first. Don't forget to create and then connect your db connection before running below code-

```
query = "CREATE TABLE IF NOT EXISTS users (id INT, name VARCHAR(255), prod_id INT)"
connection.execute(query)
sql = "INSERT INTO users (id, name, prod_id) VALUES (1, 'Prateek', 11),(2,'John',12),(3,'Tom',13)"
connection.execute(sql)
query2 = "CREATE TABLE IF NOT EXISTS products (id INT, name VARCHAR(255))"
connection.execute(query2)
sql2 = "INSERT INTO products (id, name) VALUES (11, 'Apple'),(12,'Samsung'),(15,'Vivo')"
connection.execute(sql2)
connection.close()
```

Fig 7.15

Once you run above code, you can also verify the outcome in your workbench. Go to your workbench and select the schema you have created in the starting and then expand that schema. You will see new table which you have just created from above cell as shown in below image-

Fig 7.16

Since in our example users and products tables have product id as a common column so we can join users and products tables based on the product id to see which user has bought which product as below.

```
engine = db.create_engine('mysql://root:admin@127.0.0.1:3306/schemaexample')
connection = engine.connect()
join_query = "SELECT \
  users.name AS user, \
  products.name AS favorite \
  FROM users \
  INNER JOIN products ON users.prod_id = products.id"
result = connection.execute(join_query)
myresult = result.fetchall()
for bought_product in myresult:
    print(bought_product)
```

```
('Prateek', 'Apple')
('John', 'Samsung')
```

Fig 7.17

| **Note** | INNER JOIN only shows the records where there is a match. |

Left Join

The LEFT JOIN returns all the rows from the table on the left even if no matching rows have been found in the table on the right. Where no matches have been found in the table on the right, none is returned as shown in below example-

```
left_join = "SELECT \
  users.name AS user, \
  products.name AS favorite \
  FROM users \
  LEFT JOIN products ON users.prod_id = products.id"
result = connection.execute(left_join)
myresult = result.fetchall()
for bought_product in myresult:
    print(bought_product)
```

```
('Prateek', 'Apple')
('John', 'Samsung')
('Tom', None)
```

Fig 7.18

Don't forget to create and connect the db connection before executing any query as we have done in earlier normal join example.

Right Join

RIGHT JOIN is the opposite of LEFT JOIN. The RIGHT JOIN returns all the columns from the table on the right even if no matching rows have been found in the table on the left. Where no matches have been found in the table on the left, none is returned as shown in below example-

```
right_join = "SELECT \
  users.name AS user, \
  products.name AS favorite \
  FROM users \
  RIGHT JOIN products ON users.prod_id = products.id"
result = connection.execute(right_join)
myresult = result.fetchall()
for bought_product in myresult:
    print(bought_product)
```

```
('Prateek', 'Apple')
('John', 'Samsung')
(None, 'Vivo')
```

Fig 7.19

Don't forget to create and connect the db connection before executing any query as we have done in earlier normal join example.

Conclusion

SQL proficiency is a basic requirement for many data science jobs, including data analyst, business intelligence developer, programmer analyst, database administrator, and database developer. You'll need SQL to communicate with the database and work with the data. Learning SQL will give you a good understanding of relational databases, which are the bread and butter of data science. It will also boost your professional profile, especially compared to those with limited database experience. So keep practicing the python skills of interfacing with sql shared in the chapter by creating your own databases/schemas. In the next chapter, we will learn core concepts of statistics often used in Data Science.

CHAPTER 8

Thinking Statistically in Data Science

Statistics plays an important role in data science. If it is used wisely you can extract knowledge from the vague, complex, and difficult real world. A clear understanding of statistics and the meanings of various statistical measures is important to distinguishing between truth and misdirection. In this chapter you will learn important statistics concepts and Python-based statistics tools that will help you to understand the data focused on data science.

Structure

- Statistics in Data Science
- Types of Statistical data/variables?
- Mean, Median and Mode
- Basics of Probability
- Statistical Distributions
- Pearson Correlation Coefficient
- Probability Density Function
- Real World Example
- Statistical Inference and Hypothesis Testing

Objective

After studying the chapter, you will be able to apply statistics in Pythonic way to analyze the data.

Statistics in Data Science

Statistics is the discipline of analyzing data. In data science you will use two types of statistics-**Descriptive** and **Inference** statistics. **Descriptive statistics** includes exploratory data analysis, unsupervised learning, clustering and basic data summaries. Descriptive statistics have many uses, most notably helping us get familiar with a data set. Descriptive statistics usually are the starting point for any analysis therefore enables us to present the data in a more meaningful way, which allows simpler interpretation of the data.

Inference is the process of making conclusions about populations from samples. Inference includes most of the activities traditionally associated with statistics such as: estimation, confidence intervals, hypothesis tests and variability. Inference forces us to formally define targets of estimations or hypotheses. It forces us to think about the population that we're trying to generalize to from our sample. In statistics, population refers to the total set of observations that can be made. For example, if we are studying the weight of adult women, the population is the set of weights of all the women in the world. If we are studying the grade point average (GPA) of students at Harvard, the population is the set of GPA's of all the students at Harvard.

Types of Statistical data/variables?

When working with statistics, it's important to recognize the different types of data. Most data fall into one of two groups: **numerical** or **categorical**. Example of **Numerical or Quantitative data** is a measurement, such as a person's height, weight, IQ, or blood pressure; or they're a count, such as the number of stocks shares a person owns, how many teeth a dog has, or how many pages you can read of your favorite book before you fall asleep. **Categorical or Qualitative data** represent characteristics such as a person's gender, marital status, hometown, or the types of movies they like. Categorical data can take on numerical values (such as "1" indicating male and "2" indicating female), but those numbers don't have mathematical meaning. You couldn't add them together, for example. (Other names for categorical data are qualitative data, or Yes/No data).

These two types of variables in statistics can be divided further as shown in in the following diagram-

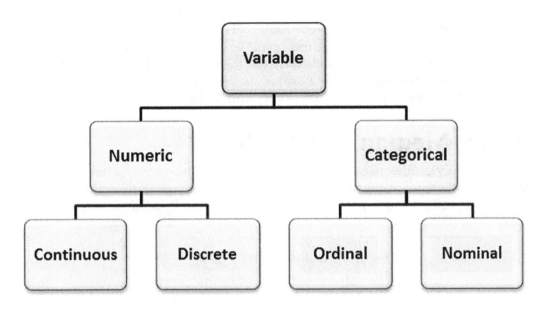

Fig 8.1

Let's understand these categorization-

1. **Discrete Variables:-** Discrete variables are countable in a finite amount of time. For example, you can count the change in your pocket. You can count the money in your bank account. You could also count the amount of money in everyone's bank account.

2. **Continuous Variables:-** Continuous Variables would take forever to count. In fact, you would never finish counting them. For example, take an example of person's age. You can't count "age" because it could be: 25 years, 10 months, 2 days, 5 hours, 4 seconds, 4 milliseconds, 8 microseconds, 9 nanoseconds… and so on. You could turn age into a discrete variable and then you could count it; for example: A person's age in years.

3. **Nominal Variables:-** Nominal Variables are variables that have two or more categories, but which do not have an intrinsic order. For example, a real estate agent could classify their types of property into distinct categories such as houses, condos, co-ops or bungalows. So "type of property" is a nominal variable with 4 categories called houses, condos, co-ops and bungalows.

4. **Ordinal Variables:-** Ordinal Variables are variables that have two or more categories just like nominal variables only the categories can also be ordered or ranked. So if you asked someone if they liked the policies of the RepublicanParty and they could answer either "Not very much", "They are

OK" or "Yes, a lot" then you have an ordinal variable. Because you have 3 categories, namely "Not very much", "They are OK" and "Yes, a lot" and you can rank them from the most positive (Yes, a lot), to the middle response (They are OK), to the least positive (Not very much). However, we can rank the levels, we cannot place a "value" to them; we cannot say that "They are OK" is twice as positive as "Not very much" for example.

Mean, Median and Mode

Mean is simply another name for **average**. To calculate the mean of a data set, divide the sum of all values by the number of values. We can compute the arithmetic mean along the specified axis using Numpy. Following is the Pythonic way to calculate the mean-

```
import pandas as pd
import numpy as np
a = np.array([[1, 2], [3, 4]])
print(np.mean(a))
print(np.mean(a, axis=0))
print(np.mean(a, axis=1))
```

```
2.5
[2. 3.]
[1.5 3.5]
```

Fig 8.2

Median is the number that lies in the middle of a list of ordered numbers. The numbers may be in the ascending or descending order. The median is easy to find when there are odd number of elements in the data set. When there are even number of elements, you need to take the average of the two numbers that fall in the center of the ordered list. Following is the way to calculate median-

```
a = np.array([[10, 7, 4], [3, 2, 1]])
print(np.median(a))
print(np.median(a, axis=0))
print(np.median(a, axis=1))
```

```
3.5
[6.5 4.5 2.5]
[7. 2.]
```

Fig 8.3

Mode is that value which appears most number of times in a data. To calculate mode, we need another package named as stats from scipy along with numpy-

```
from scipy import stats
a = np.array([[1, 3, 4, 2, 2, 7],
              [5, 2, 2, 1, 4, 1],
              [3, 3, 2, 2, 1, 1]])
m = stats.mode(a)
print(m[0])
```

```
[[1 3 2 2 1 1]]
```

Fig 8.4

Now the question arises when to use mean, median or mode? Answer is it depends on your dataset.

Mean is a good measure of the average when a data set contains values that are relatively evenly spread with no exceptionally high or low values. Median is a good measure of the average value when the data include exceptionally high or low values because these have little influence on the outcome. It is the most suitable measure of average for data classified on an ordinal scale. Lastly, mode is the measure of average that can be used with nominal data. For example, late-night users of the library were classified by faculty as: 14% science students, 32% social science students, and 54% biological sciences students. No median or mean can be calculated but the mode is biological science students as students from this faculty were the most common.

Basics of Probability

We all must agree that our lives are full of uncertainties. We don't know the outcomes of a situation until it happens. Will it rain today? Will I pass the next math test? Will my favorite team win the toss? Will I get a promotion in next 6 months? All these questions are examples of uncertain situations we live in. If you understand these uncertain situations, you can plan thing accordingly. That's why probability plays an important role in analysis.

We must know following terminology related to probability- **Experiment** is the uncertain situation which could have multiple outcomes, **Outcome** is the result of a single trail, **Event** is one or more outcome from an experiment and **Probability** is a measure of how likely an event is.

Statistical Distributions

One of the most important things you need to know while arming yourself with prerequisite Statistics for Data Science is the distributions. While the concept of probability gives us the mathematical calculations, distributions help us visualize what's happening underneath. Following are some important distributions we must know-

1. **Poisson Distribution-** Poisson Distribution is used to calculate the number of events that might occur in a continuous time interval. For instance, how many phone calls will be received at any time period or how many people might show up in a queue. The Poisson distribution is a discrete function, meaning that the event can only be measured as occurring or not as occurring, meaning the variable can only be measured in whole numbers.

To calculate this function in Python we can use scipy's stats package and to visualize samples we can use matplotlib library as shown in below example-

```python
from scipy.stats import poisson
import matplotlib.pyplot as plt
plt.title('Probability Distribution Example')
arr = []
rv = poisson(25)
for num in range(0,40):
    arr.append(rv.pmf(num))
prob = rv.pmf(28)
plt.grid(True)
plt.plot(arr, linewidth=2.0)
plt.plot([28], [prob], marker='o', markersize=6, color="red")
plt.show()
```

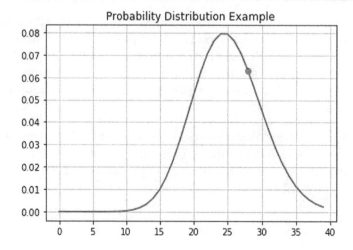

Fig 8.5

In above code cell first we have imported the Poisson package from the scipy.stats api with matplotlib library to plot the distribution. Then we have created a Poisson discrete random variable named as 'rv'. Next, we have calculated the "probability mass function(pmf)' which is a function that can predict or show the mathematical probability of a value occurring of a certain data point. In the end we just plotted the graph using matplotlib's plot() and show() functions.

2. **Binomial Distribution-** A distribution where only two outcomes are possible, such as success or failure, gain or loss, win or lose and where the probability of success and failure is same for all the trials is called a Binomial Distribution. We can use the matplotlib python library which has in-built functions to create such probability distribution graphs. Also, the scipy package helps in creating the binomial distribution as shown below-

```python
from scipy.stats import binom
import matplotlib.pyplot as plt
fig, ax = plt.subplots(1, 1)
x = range(7)
n, p = 6, 0.5
rv = binom(n, p)
ax.vlines(x, 0, rv.pmf(x), colors='k', linestyles='-', lw=1,label='Probablity of Success')
ax.legend(loc='best', frameon=False)
plt.show()
```

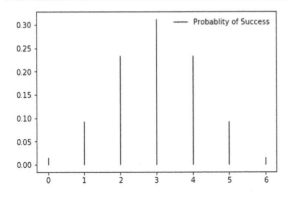

Fig 8.6

In above code cell, we have imported the binom package from the scipy.stats api. Then we have create a binomial discrete random variable named as 'rv'. Now to plot vertical lines at each x from ymin to ymax we have used matplotlib's vlines() function where we are passing our probability mass function (pmf) as one argument and then we are plotting and displaying the distribution as we did earlier.

3. **Normal Distribution-** Any distribution is known as Normal distribution if it has the following characteristics:

    a. The mean, median and mode of the distribution coincide,

b. The curve of the distribution is bell-shaped and symmetrical about the line, Exactly half of the values are to the left of the center and the other half to the right.

You can calculate and draw the same using Python's scipy and matplotlib packages as shown in the next example.

```
import numpy as np
import matplotlib.pyplot as plt
from scipy.stats import norm

range = np.arange(-3,3,0.001)
plt.plot(range, norm.pdf(range, 0, 1))
plt.show()
```

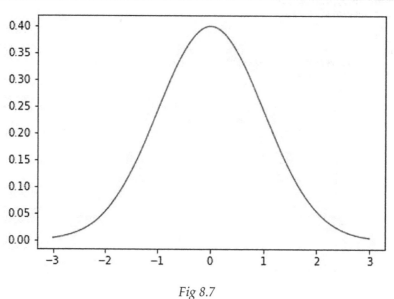

Fig 8.7

In above code cell we imported the norm package form scipy.stats api. Later We have passed the probability density function (pdf) of normal continuous discrete variable as an argument in plot() function. Here a probability density function (pdf) is a function that can predict or show the mathematical probability of a value occurring between a certain interval in the function. You will know more about this function later of this chapter.

Pearson Correlation Coefficient

In real world data problem, you may face hundreds of attributes and you cannot include all of them for your analysis. That's why you need to find a relationship between each variable. The Pearson correlation coefficient is a measure of the strength of a linear association between two variables and is denoted by r. Basically, it attempts to draw a line of best fit through the data of two variables, and the Pearson correlation coefficient, r, indicates how far away all these data points are to this line of best fit (i.e., how well the data points fit this new model/line of best fit).

The Pearson correlation coefficient can take a range of values from +1 to -1. A value of 0 indicates that there is no association between the two variables. A value greater than 0 indicates a positive association; that is, as the value of one variable increases, so does the value of the other variable. A value less than 0 indicates a negative association; that is, as the value of one variable increases, the value of the other variable decreases. The stronger the association of the two variables, the closer the Pearson correlation coefficient.

Following is a guideline (depend on what you are measuring) to interpret the Pearson's correlation coefficient-

Strength of Association	Coefficient, r	
	Positive	Negative
Small	.1 to .3	-0.1 to -0.3
Medium	.3 to .5	-0.3 to -0.5
Large	.5 to 1.0	-0.5 to -1.0

Fig 8.8

Pythonic way to interpret Pearson's correlation coefficient where **r_row** denotes Pearson's correlation coefficient and **p_value** denotes the probability of an uncorrelated system producing datasets that have a Pearson correlation at least as extreme as the one computed from these datasets. The p-values are not entirely reliable but are probably reasonable for datasets larger than 500 or so.

```
import scipy
from scipy.stats import pearsonr
x = scipy.array([-0.65499887,  2.34644428, 3.0])
y = scipy.array([-1.46049758,  3.86537321, 21.0])
r_row, p_value = pearsonr(x, y)
print(r_row)
print(p_value)
```

0.7961701483197555
0.41371200873701036

Fig 8.9

Probability Density Function (PDF)

Probability Density Function or PDF is used to specify the probability of the random variable falling within a range of values, as opposed to taking on any one value. The probability density function is nonnegative everywhere, and its integral over the entire space is equal to one.

In Python we can interpret the PDF in following way- first import **norm** package from **scipy.stats** library to create a normalized probability density function with NumPy and matplotlib libraries. In this example we are creating a variable, x, and assign it to, **np.arange(-4,4,0.001)** that range from -4 to 4 with an increment of 0.001 then we plot a normalized probability density function with the line, **plt.plot(x, norm.pdf(x))-**

```
from scipy.stats import norm
import numpy as np
import matplotlib.pyplot as plt
x= np.arange(-4,4,0.001)
plt.plot(x, norm.pdf(x))
plt.show()
```

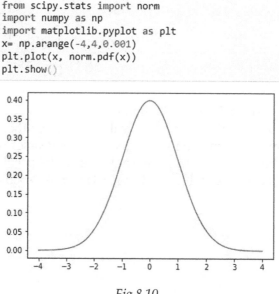

Fig 8.10

Real World Example

Pearson correlation is used in thousands of real-life situations. One recent example is- Scientists in China wanted to know if there was a relationship between how weedy rice populations are different genetically. The goal was to find out the evolutionary potential of the rice. Pearson's correlation between the two groups were analyzed. It showed a positive Pearson Product Moment correlation of between 0.783 and 0.895 for weedy rice populations. This figure is quite high, which suggested a fairly strong relationship.

Statistical Inference and Hypothesis Testing

Statistical inference is the process of deducing properties of an underlying distribution by analysis of data. Inferential statistical analysis infers properties about a population: this includes testing hypotheses and deriving estimates. Statistics prove helpful in analysing most collections of data. **Hypothesis testing** can justify conclusions even when no scientific theory exists. A statistical hypothesis, sometimes called confirmatory data analysis, is a hypothesis that is testable on the basis of observing a process that is modelled via a set of random variables. Whenever we want to make claims about the distribution of data or whether one set of results are different from another set of results in applied machine learning, we must rely on statistical hypothesis tests.

In simple words, we can interpret data by assuming a specific structure our outcome and use statistical methods to confirm or reject the assumption. The assumption is called a hypothesis and the statistical tests used for this purpose are called statistical hypothesis tests. In statistics, a hypothesis test calculates some quantity under a given assumption. The result of the test allows us to interpret whether the assumption holds or whether the assumption has been violated.

Following are two concrete examples that we will use a lot in machine learning are:

- A test that assumes that data has a normal distribution.
- A test that assumes that two samples were drawn from the same underlying population distribution.

The assumption of a statistical test is called the **null hypothesis**, or **hypothesis 0** (H0 for short). It is often called the default assumption, or the assumption that nothing has changed. A violation of the test's assumption is often called the first hypothesis, **hypothesis 1** or H1 for short. H1 is really a short hand for "some other hypothesis," as all we know is that the evidence suggests that the H0 can be rejected.

The process of distinguishing between the null hypothesis and the alternative hypothesis is aided by identifying two conceptual types of errors (type 1 & type 2), and by specifying parametric limits on e.g. how much type 1 error will be permitted.

Let's understand these statistics concepts based on a real-world example. In this exercise we will aim to study how accurately can we characterize the actual average participant experience (population mean) from the samples of data (sample mean). We can quantify the certainty of outcome through the confidence intervals. In this exercise we will first create an array of total experience in data science specialization batch of a class and store it in a variable named as *dss_exp*

```
%matplotlib inline
import matplotlib.pyplot as plt
import numpy as np
import pandas as pd

# array containing no of total experience
dss_exp = np.array([12, 15, 13, 20, 19, 20, 11, 19, 11, 12, 19, 13,
                    12, 10, 6, 19, 3, 1, 1, 0, 4, 4, 6, 5, 3, 7,
                    12, 7, 9, 8, 12, 11, 11, 18, 19, 18, 19, 3, 6,
                    5, 6, 9, 11, 10, 14, 14, 16, 17, 17, 19, 0, 2,
                    0, 3, 1, 4, 6, 6, 8, 7, 7, 6, 7, 11, 11, 10,
                    11, 10, 13, 13, 15, 18, 20, 19, 1, 10, 8, 16,
                    19, 19, 17, 16, 11, 1, 10, 13, 15, 3, 8, 6, 9,
                    10, 15, 19, 2, 4, 5, 6, 9, 11, 10, 9, 10, 9,
                    15, 16, 18, 13])
```

Fig 8.11

Next, we will plot a histogram to see the distribution of experiences. For histogram plotting we will use matplotlib's hist() function. In this function we are using bins parameter that tells us the number of bins that our data will be divided into -

```
#Understanding the Underlying distribution of Experience
# Plot the distribution of Experience
plt.hist(dss_exp, range = (0,20), bins = 21)
# Add axis labels
plt.xlabel("Experience in years")
plt.ylabel("Frequency")
plt.title("Distribution of Experience in Data Science Specialization")
# Draws the red vertical line in graph at the average experience
plt.axvline(x=dss_exp.mean(), linewidth=2, color = 'r')
plt.show()
# Statistics of DSS Batch experience
print("Mean Experience of DSS Batch: {:4.3f}".format(dss_exp.mean()))
print("Std Deviation of Experience of DSS Batch: {:4.3f}".format(dss_exp.std()))
```

Fig 8.12

Above cell will draw following histogram-

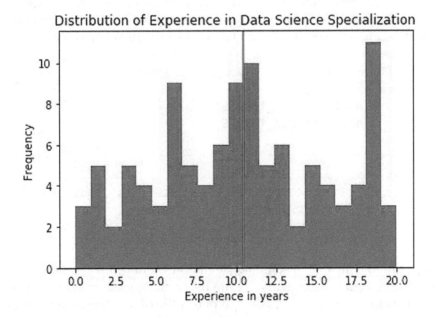

Mean Experience of DSS Batch: 10.435
Std Deviation of Experience of DSS Batch: 5.665

Fig 8.13

After this we will estimate the experiences by taking the mean and standard deviation-

```
# Set the parameters for sampling
n = 10
NUM_TRIALS = 1000
#Estimating DSS Experience from samples
samp = np.random.choice(dss_exp, size = n, replace = True)#Just try for 1 iteration
samp_mean = samp.mean()
samp_sd = samp.std()
print("Samp_mean = {:4.3f} Sample_SD = {:4.3f}".format(samp_mean, samp_sd))
print("sample values:", samp)
```

Samp_mean = 10.900 Sample_SD = 5.665
sample values: [10 1 19 9 3 13 19 15 11 9]

Fig 8.14

Now to see how the distribution of sample mean look like we are now drawing samples for 1000 times (NUM_TRIALS) and compute the mean each time. The distribution is plotted to identify range of values it can take. The original data has experience raging between 0 years and 20 years and spread across it-

```
#How will the distribution of Sample Mean look like
np.random.seed(100)
mn_array = np.zeros(NUM_TRIALS)
sd_array = np.zeros(NUM_TRIALS)

# Extract Random Samples and compute mean & standard deviation
for i in range(NUM_TRIALS):
    samp = np.random.choice(dss_exp, size = n, replace = True)
    mn_array[i] = samp.mean()
```

Fig 8.15

For computing the mean and standard deviation we have used mean() and std() function. For computing percentile we are using numpy library's percentile() function. This function computes the qth percentile of the data along the specified axis and returns the qth percentile(s) of the array elements.

```
mn = mn_array.mean()
sd = mn_array.std()
x5_pct = np.percentile(mn_array, 5.0)
x95_pct = np.percentile(mn_array, 95.0)
print("Mean = {:4.3f}, Std Dev = {:4.3f}, 5% Pct = {:4.3f}, 95% Pct = {:4.3f}".format(mn, sd, x5_pct, x95_pct))
# Plot Sampling distribution of Mean
plt.hist(mn_array, range=(0,20), bins = 41)
# Add axis labels
plt.xlabel("Avg Experience with n={}".format(n))
plt.ylabel("Frequency")
plt.title("Sampling Distribution of Mean")
plt.axvline(x=x5_pct, linewidth=2, color = 'r')
plt.axvline(x=x95_pct, linewidth=2, color = 'r')
plt.show()
```

Fig 8.16

The above code will plot following histogram which tell that the original experience of students of Data science is in no way appears to be normal distribution. It has peaks around 5 years, 10 years and 19 years' experience. The below plot is histogram of mean of samples for any given n-

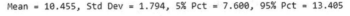

Mean = 10.455, Std Dev = 1.794, 5% Pct = 7.600, 95% Pct = 13.405

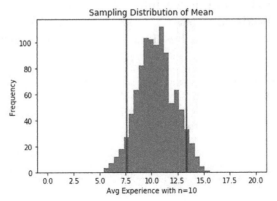

Fig 8.17

Now to find an estimated range of values which is likely to include an unknown population parameter, that is the estimated range being calculated from a given set of sample data, we will select the confidence interval of our samples.In below code cell we are creating a function for selecting confidence interval. Always remember that the selection of a confidence level for an interval determines the probability that the confidence interval produced will contain the true parameter value. Common choices for the confidence level are 0.90, 0.95, and 0.99. These levels correspond to percentages of the area of the normal density curve. For example, a 95% confidence interval covers 95% of the normal curve -- the probability of observing a value outside of this area is less than 0.05-

```
# Function to check if the true mean lies within 90% Confidence Interval
def samp_mean_within_ci(mn, l_5pct, u_95pct):
    out = True
    if (mn < l_5pct) | (mn > u_95pct):
        out = False
    return out
```

```
# Estimation and Confidence Interval
samp = np.random.choice(dss_exp, size = n, replace = True)
samp_mean = samp.mean()
samp_sd = samp.std()
#  divided by sqrt(n) is done so as to compensate for the reduction in std. dev due to sample size of n
sd_ci = samp_sd/np.sqrt(n)
# Lower 90% confidence interval (This is approximate version to build intution)
samp_lower_5pct = samp_mean - 1.645 * sd_ci
# Upper 90% confidence interval (This is approximate version to build intution)
samp_upper_95pct = samp_mean + 1.645 * sd_ci
print("Pop Mean: {:4.3f} | Sample: L_5PCT = {:4.3f} | M = samp_mean = {:4.3f}  | H_95PCT = {:4.3f}".format(dss_exp.mean(),
# Checking if the population mean lies within 90% Confidence Interval (CI)
mn_within_ci_flag = samp_mean_within_ci(dss_exp.mean(), samp_lower_5pct, samp_upper_95pct)
print("True mean lies with the 90% confidence Interval = {}".format(mn_within_ci_flag))
```

```
Pop Mean: 10.435 | Sample: L_5PCT = 7.408 | M = samp_mean = 8.800  | H_95PCT = 10.192
True mean lies with the 90% confidence Intervel = False
```

Fig 8.18

This shows us that given the sample size n, we can estimate the sample mean and confidence interval. The confidence interval is estimated assuming normal distribution which really holds good when n >= 30. When n is increased, confidence interval becomes smaller which implies that results are obtained with higher certainty.

```
Pop Mean: 10.435 | Sample: L_5PCT = 7.408 | M = samp_mean = 8.800  | H_95PCT = 10.192
True mean lies with the 90% confidence Intervel = False
```

Fig 8.19

Let's apply the same concept to an array of old batch experienced so that we can perform Hypothesis testing. Firstly, let's define the Hypotheses as follows for our example:

- **H0** : Average Experience of Current Batch & Previous batch are same

- **H1** : Average Experience of Current Batch & Previous batch are different

The process of distinguishing between the null hypothesis and the alternative hypothesis is aided by identifying two conceptual types of errors (type 1 & type 2), and by specifying parametric limits on e.g. how much type 1 error will be permitted.

```
# Previous Batch Data for working experience
dss_exp_prev = np.array([1, 14,  6,  7, 10, 10, 19, 15, 19, 15,
                 2,  2, 14, 14, 14,  3,  0,  4, 11,  7,
                 1,  2,  0,  1,  2,  2,  2,  1,  1,  2,
                 4,  4,  3,  3,  3,  4,  3,  3,  7,
                 8,  6,  6,  6,  7, 8, 8, 8, 8, 7,
                 8,  0,  0,  7,  6, 9, 10, 9, 9, 11,
                 11, 9, 10, 10, 11, 10, 11, 9, 9, 9,
                 12, 14, 13, 14, 18, 14, 11, 10, 17, 20,
                 18, 5, 13, 4, 2, 4, 3, 12, 12, 14,
                 12, 12, 10, 14, 4, 11, 9])
```

```
avg_exp_prev = dss_exp_prev.mean()
std_exp_prev = dss_exp_prev.std()
print("Previous DSS Batch: Avg Exp - {:4.3f} Std Dev - {:4.3f}".format(avg_exp_prev, std_exp_prev))

plt.hist(dss_exp_prev, range=(0,20), bins = 21)
plt.axvline(x=dss_exp_prev.mean(), linewidth=2, color = 'r')
plt.show()
```

```
Previous DSS Batch: Avg Exp - 8.041 Std Dev - 5.034
```

Fig 8.20

From the output you can see easily that the previous batch average experience is around 8 while new batch has average experience of 10 years. Thus, our first

Hypothesis(H1) is fulfilled in our example which means we can reject the null Hypothesis.

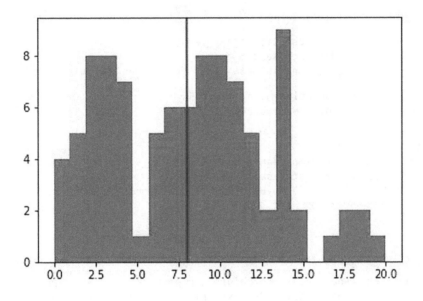

Fig 8.21

The results of a statistical hypothesis test may cause a lot of confusion to decide whether to take the result or reject it. To understand this, we need to interpret the **'p-value'**. P-value is a quantity that we can use to interpret or quantify the result of the test and either reject or fail to reject the null hypothesis. This is done by comparing the p-value to a threshold value chosen beforehand called the significance level. The significance level is often referred to by the Greek lower-case letter alpha. A common value used for alpha is 5% or 0.05. A smaller alpha value suggests a more robust interpretation of the null hypothesis, such as 1% or 0.1%.

In the next examples, we'll do hypothesis testing based on the intuition from Sampling distribution of mean and then we will interpret the p-value-

```
np.random.seed(100)
n = 20

dss_mean = dss_exp.mean()
dss_sd   = dss_exp.std()
print("Current DSS Batch : Population Mean - {:4.3f}".format(dss_mean))

dss_prev_samp = np.random.choice(dss_exp_prev, size = n, replace = True)
dss_prev_samp_mean = dss_prev_samp.mean()
print("Previous DSS Batch Sample Mean: {:4.3f}".format(dss_prev_samp_mean))
```

```
Current DSS Batch : Population Mean - 10.435
Previous DSS Batch Sample Mean: 8.250
```

```
from scipy import stats
t_statistic = (dss_prev_samp_mean - dss_mean)/(dss_sd/np.sqrt(n))
p_val = 2 * stats.t.cdf(t_statistic, df= (n-1))
print("T-Statistic : {:4.2f}, p-Value = {:4.2f}".format(t_statistic,p_val))
```

```
T-Statistic : -1.72, p-Value = 0.10
```

```
# For 2-tailed hypothesis testing
from scipy import stats
dss_exp_prev_samp = np.random.choice(dss_exp_prev, size = 20, replace = True)
dss_exp_samp = np.random.choice(dss_exp, size = 20, replace = True)
stats.ttest_ind(dss_exp_prev_samp, dss_exp_samp)
```

```
Ttest_indResult(statistic=-0.24857316405070548, pvalue=0.80502950101657478)
```

Fig 8.22

In above code cell after calculating the average experiences of previous and current batches, we are performing the **t test** using stats.ttest_ind() function. The t test (also called Student's T Test) compares two averages (means) and tells us if they are different from each other. The t test also tells us how significant the differences are; In other words, it lets us know if those differences could have happened by chance. This test gives us a t score. The t score is a ratio between the difference between two groups and the difference within the groups. A large t-score tells you that the groups are different. A small t-score tells you that the groups are similar.

Every t-value has a **p-value** to go with it. A p-value is the probability that the results from our sample data occurred by chance. P-values are from 0% to 100%. They are usually written as a decimal. For example, a p value of 5% is 0.05. **Low p-values are good**; They indicate our data did not occur by chance. So in our example, p-value is greater than 0.05 or 1.0 so we cannot reject the null hypothesis.Since the p-value is probabilistic; when we interpret the result of a statistical test, we do not know what is true or false, only what is likely. Rejecting the null hypothesis means that there is sufficient statistical evidence that the null hypothesis does not look likely. Otherwise, it means that there is not sufficient statistical evidence to reject the null hypothesis. If we say that we "accept" the null hypothesis, the language suggests that the null hypothesis is true. Instead, it is safer to say that we "fail to reject" the null hypothesis, as in, there is insufficient statistical evidence to reject it.

Conclusion

We have covered some core concepts of statistics in this chapter and we will cover more statistical concepts related to machine learning during the course of later chapters in this book. Statistics is important in data analysis and we cannot ignore it. Framing questions statistically allows researchers to leverage data resources to extract knowledge and obtain better answers. It also allows them to establish methods for prediction and estimation, to quantify their degree of certainty, and to do all of this using algorithm that exhibit predictable and reproducible behavior. So, practice and implement learnings from this chapter. In the next chapter, we will learn importing various forms of data and working with data in next chapter.

## CHAPTER 9

How to import data in Python?

Data importing is the first step you will do before analysing. Since data is present in various forms - .txt, .csv,. excel,. json etc.; importing or reading of such data is also different but quite simple in Pythonic way. While importing external data you need to check various points i.e. whether header row exists in data or not, is there any missing values there, data type of each attributes etc. In this chapter with the help of Pandas I/O API you will not only learn to read the data but also how to write data into various formats of files.

Structure

- Importing txt data
- Importing csv data
- Importing Excel data
- Importing JSON data
- Importing pickled data
- Importing a compressed data

Objective

After studying the chapter, you will become expert to import, read and refine various forms of data.

Importing txt data

The simplest form of flat data you will see is in .txt files. To import a txt data, we need a dataset in this format. For this purpose, we are going to import a real-world dataset. In the next example, I have made use of consumer price index data obtained from the US Labor department. You can download the data from following URL.

https://catalog.data.gov/dataset/consumer-price-index-average-price-data

Once you copy and save the above data in a txt file in your system and provide the path to read it. We will use **Pandas read_table()** function to read the txt file as shown below with indicating the path where the file is stored in your system (I have stored the file in my E:/pg/docs/BPB/data folder) as shown below.

```
import pandas as pd
cpi_data = pd.read_table('E:/pg/docs/BPB/data/cpi_us.txt')
cpi_data.head()
```

	series_id	year	period	value	footnote_codes
0	APU0000701111	1995	M01	0.238	
1	APU0000701111	1995	M02	0.242	
2	APU0000701111	1995	M03	0.242	
3	APU0000701111	1995	M04	0.236	
4	APU0000701111	1995	M05	0.244	

Fig 9.1

Isn't that simple! The **pd.read_table()** function imports all data in a variable cpi_data. If you check the type of this variable, you will notice this is a pandas dataframe. Pandas imports the data in DataFrame format which basically denotes row and column with index. This data type is easy to manipulate data further-

```
type(cpi_data)
```

```
pandas.core.frame.DataFrame
```

Fig 9.2

We can inspect the data using. head() function. Pandas read_table() function has an inbuilt functionality to filter blank columns which you can use by passing as arguments separated by comma. For example, in above cpi data there is a blank column footnote_codes. By using the **usecols** argument as below we can filter the unwanted columns.

```
cpi_data = pd.read_table('E:/pg/docs/BPB/data/cpi_us.txt',
                    usecols=['series_id', 'year', 'period', 'value'])
cpi_data.head()
```

	series_id	year	period	value
0	APU0000701111	1995	M01	0.238
1	APU0000701111	1995	M02	0.242
2	APU0000701111	1995	M03	0.242
3	APU0000701111	1995	M04	0.236
4	APU0000701111	1995	M05	0.244

Fig 9.3

Note

1) Always provide correct file location to the *read_table()* function.

2) Pandas read_table() function has a lot of arguments which are very helpful in data cleaning as per your need. You can check these in below link-

https://pandas.pydata.org/pandas-docs/stable/generated/pandas.read_table.html

Importing csv data

CSV or comma-separated values is the favourite format for saving data. You will see most of the publicly available datasets for analysis/machine learning are in .csv format. In the next example, I have made use of crime data to analyse the crime incidents occurred in Chicago city. You can download this data from the following link.

https://catalog.data.gov/dataset?res_format=CSV

Similar to our previous example of reading data from .txt file, you can import and read this csv data using Pandas **read_csv()** function as shown in the next screenshot. This function has also in built features which you can find in following official link-
https://pandas.pydata.org/pandas-docs/stable/generated/pandas.read_csv.html

```
crime_data = pd.read_csv('E:\pg\docs\BPB\data\Crimes_-_2001_to_present.csv')
crime_data.head()
```

	ID	Case Number	Date	Block	IUCR	Primary Type	Description	Location Description	Arrest	Domestic	...
0	10000092	HY189866	03/18/2015 07:44:00 PM	047XX W OHIO ST	041A	BATTERY	AGGRAVATED: HANDGUN	STREET	False	False	...
1	10000094	HY190059	03/18/2015 11:00:00 PM	066XX S MARSHFIELD AVE	4625	OTHER OFFENSE	PAROLE VIOLATION	STREET	True	False	...
2	10000095	HY190052	03/18/2015 10:45:00 PM	044XX S LAKE PARK AVE	0486	BATTERY	DOMESTIC BATTERY SIMPLE	APARTMENT	False	True	...
3	10000096	HY190054	03/18/2015 10:30:00 PM	051XX S MICHIGAN AVE	0460	BATTERY	SIMPLE	APARTMENT	False	False	...
4	10000097	HY189976	03/18/2015 09:00:00 PM	047XX W ADAMS ST	031A	ROBBERY	ARMED: HANDGUN	SIDEWALK	False	False	...

Fig 9.4

Sometimes, csv files can be loaded with numerous rows of datasets (our dataset if approximately of 1.47GB). Please be patient while the importing of data is in process. You will notice a clock icon on the top of browser tab of your notebook indicating the system is busy.

Importing Excel data

Excel is another most widely used dataset format which contains numbers of sheet in form of tab. You can use Pandas **read_excel()** function with its **sheet_name** argument to read the data from a particular sheet of an excel data. In the next example, I have used a Superstore excel sheet with three tabs-Orders, Returns, People which you can download from the link - https://community.tableau.com/docs/DOC-1236

```
order_data = pd.read_excel('E:\pg\docs\BPB\data\Sample - Superstore.xls', sheet_name='Orders')
order_data.head()
```

	Row ID	Order ID	Order Date	Ship Date	Ship Mode	Customer ID	Customer Name	Segment	Country	City	...	Postal Code	Region	Product ID
0	1	CA-2016-152156	2016-11-08	2016-11-11	Second Class	CG-12520	Claire Gute	Consumer	United States	Henderson	...	42420	South	FUR-BO-10001798
1	2	CA-2016-152156	2016-11-08	2016-11-11	Second Class	CG-12520	Claire Gute	Consumer	United States	Henderson	...	42420	South	FUR-CH-10000454
2	3	CA-2016-138688	2016-06-12	2016-06-16	Second Class	DV-13045	Darrin Van Huff	Corporate	United States	Los Angeles	...	90036	West	OFF-LA-10000240

Fig 9.5

In the above example, we have just imported data from the 'Orders' sheet of the Superstore.xls.

Importing JSON data

JSON format is most preferred form of data exchange in today's world of API. To deal with a json structured data, you can use Pandas **read_json()** function to read and with its **orient** argument as shown in below example-

```
glossary_data = pd.read_json('E:\pg\docs\BPB\data\glossary.json', orient='table')
glossary_data.head()
```

	glossary
GlossDiv	{'title': 'S', 'GlossList': {'GlossEntry': {'I...
title	example glossary

Fig 9.6

Here the orient parameter can take values as 'split', 'records', 'index', 'columns'. Try these in your notebook and see the difference in output. Please note if you are facing error like **keyerror: 'schema'**, update your pandas version to v0.23 since orient="table' parameter has some issues in older version of pandas.

Importing pickled data

Any object in python can be pickled so that it can be saved on disk. What pickle does is that it "serialises" the object first before writing it to file. The idea is, this character stream contains all the information necessary to reconstruct the object in another python script. When you will work on Machine learning then you will need to train your model many times and there picking will help you by saving the training time. Once you pickled your trained model, you can share this trained model to others and they don't need to waste their time in retraining of the model. We will cover that part later; let's learn how to read a pickled file using Pandas-

```
import pandas as pd
unpickled_data = pd.read_pickle("E:/pg/docs/BPB/data/mnist.pkl")
print("data type::", type(unpickled_data))
for index, digit in enumerate(unpickled_data):
    print(index, ":", digit)

data type:: <class 'tuple'>
0 : (array([[0., 0., 0., ..., 0., 0., 0.],
       [0., 0., 0., ..., 0., 0., 0.],
       [0., 0., 0., ..., 0., 0., 0.],
       ...,
```

Fig 9.7

Importing a compressed data

Our next type of data is in compressed form. The ZIP file format is a common archive and compression standard. So how can you unzip a file so that you can read the data? For this purpose, Python has **zipfile** module which provides tools to create, read, write, append, and list a ZIP file. In this example we will unzip soil data from Africa region which you can download from our repository-

https://rebrand.ly/ab68d

```
import zipfile
Dataset = "africa_soil_train_data.zip"
with zipfile.ZipFile("E:/pg/bpb/BPB-Publications/Datasets/"+Dataset,"r") as z:
    z.extractall("E:/pg/bpb/BPB-Publications/Datasets")
```

Fig 9.8

Above code will unzip the file in your given path; in our example the unzipped file is in csv format that you can easily read using Pandas read_csv() function. There are various inbuilt parameters for this zipfile which you can try in your notebook from this link https://docs.python.org/3.6/library/zipfile.html

Conclusion

Data importing is the first step to get the data. In this chapter we have learned various formats of data importing. Without loading dataset in an appropriate data type you cannot move further. As a data scientist you will mostly find datasets in csv format so Pandas read_csv() function will be your best friend in data importing process. The more you practice in your notebook the more you will learn. So explore the data importing with different -different parameters and see the result. In next chapter we will learn about the data cleaning process.

CHAPTER 10

Cleaning of Imported Data

Before starting your analysis, you need to transform the raw data into a clean form. As a data scientist you will spend 80% of your time cleaning and manipulating of data. This process is also known as data wrangling. A machine learning model's accuracy depends on the data it is applied. Hence, data cleaning is a vital step for any data scientist. In this chapter you will work on an a couple of case studies and apply learnings from the previous chapter's to clean the data.

Structure

- Know your data
- Analysing Missing Values
- Dropping Missing Values
- How to scale and normalize data?
- How to Parse Dates?
- How to apply character encoding
- Cleaning inconsistent data

Objective

After studying this chapter, you will have an applied knowledge of data cleaning process

Know your data

As a first step, you must understand the business problem and then look upon the data given by business team or client. In this first case study we are going to work on National Football league(NFL) data. You can access the data from our repository. As a data scientist your first task is to read the data in your notebook.

Since the data is in zip format, our first step will be to unzip this data and read it using Pandas .zipfile() function by providing the correct location of file stored in the system as shown below.

```
# unzipping nfl zip data
import zipfile
Dataset = "NFL Play by Play 2009-2017 (v4).csv.zip"
with zipfile.ZipFile("E:/pg/bpb/BPB-Publications/Datasets/"+Dataset,"r") as z:
    z.extractall("E:/pg/bpb/BPB-Publications/Datasets")
```

```
# unzipping building permit zip data
import zipfile
Dataset2 = "Building_Permits.csv.zip"
with zipfile.ZipFile("E:/pg/bpb/BPB-Publications/Datasets/"+Dataset2,"r") as z:
    z.extractall("E:/pg/bpb/BPB-Publications/Datasets")
```

```
# import required modules
import pandas as pd
import numpy as np
```

```
# reading NFL data
nfl_data = pd.read_csv("E:/pg/bpb/BPB-Publications/Datasets/NFL Play by Play 2009-2017 (v4).csv", low_memory=False)
building_permits = pd.read_csv("E:/pg/bpb/BPB-Publications/Datasets/Building_Permits.csv", low_memory=False)
```

Fig 10.1

Please note, while reading the data using Pandas **read_csv()** function I am passing **low_memory** parameter.Otherwise you will get the low_**memory warning** because guessing dtypes (data type) for each column is very memory demanding and Pandas tries to determine what dtype to set by analyzing the data in each column. Pandas can only determine what dtype a column should have after reading the entire file. This means none of the data can really be parsed before the whole file is read unless you risk having to change the dtype of that column when you read the last value. For now, it's ok to use **low_memory** parameter with setting the parameter value to False .

After reading the data we can now look at it so that we get an idea about it's attributes. For this we can use **.head()** or **.sample()** function. Since you have already come across how to use the *.head()* function, I will use *.sample()* function viewing the data as shown below.

```
# Looking up the data
nfl_data.sample(5)
```

	Date	GameID	Drive	qtr	down	time	TimeUnder	TimeSecs	PlayTimeDiff	SideofField	...	yacEPA	Home_WP_pre
219237	2013-12-15	2013121507	20	4	NaN	03:07	4	187.0	0.0	NO	...	NaN	0.955040
113588	2011-11-13	2011111302	20	4	1.0	11:16	12	676.0	1.0	HOU	...	NaN	0.010379
214092	2013-12-05	2013120500	13	3	2.0	14:20	15	1760.0	19.0	HOU	...	0.228558	0.783278
299928	2015-11-26	2015112601	17	4	NaN	04:17	5	257.0	4.0	DAL	...	NaN	NaN
277934	2015-09-27	2015092703	16	3	1.0	11:45	12	1605.0	5.0	TB	...	NaN	0.482456

5 rows × 102 columns

Fig 10.2

Tada ! the data is displayed in tabular form with some columns having **NaN** values, these values are called **missing values.** Let's apply the same function in building_permits dataframe as shown below-

```
building_permits.sample(5)
```

	Permit Number	Permit Type	Permit Type Definition	Permit Creation Date	Block	Lot	Street Number	Street Number Suffix	Street Name	Street Suffix	...	E: Constr
106029	201511162641	8	otc alterations permit	11/16/2015	1744	006	1237	NaN	06th	Av	...	
98590	201509116784	8	otc alterations permit	09/11/2015	0690	116	1	NaN	Daniel Burnham	Ct	...	
45517	201404213721	8	otc alterations permit	04/21/2014	1081	048	2549	NaN	Post	St	...	
136805	201609157776	8	otc alterations permit	09/15/2016	6534	010A	454	NaN	Fair Oaks	St	...	
74940	201502057581	8	otc alterations permit	02/05/2015	3538	040	63	NaN	Noe	St	...	

5 rows × 43 columns

Fig 10.3

Analysing Missing Values

After reading the data, we have found out that both datasets have missing values. Our **next step** will be to **calculate how many missing values we have in each column**. For counting the null values Pandas has **.isnull()** function. Since nfl_data has 102 columns we will analyse the first ten columns containing missing values as shown in following example-

```
# getting the number of missing values per column
missing_values_count = nfl_data.isnull().sum()
# looking at first 10 columns missing values in nfl dataset
missing_values_count[0:10]
```

```
Date                 0
GameID               0
Drive                0
qtr                  0
down             61154
time               224
TimeUnder            0
TimeSecs           224
PlayTimeDiff       444
SideofField        528
dtype: int64
```

Fig 10.4

Each coloumn name and the associated number indicates the number of missing values- That seems like a lot! We cannot ignore such a high number of missing values. It might be helpful to see **what percentage of the values in our dataset were missing** to give us a better sense of the scale of this problem. For this percentage calculation we will take help of combination of **NumPy's .prod() and Pandas shape** functions as shown below-

```
# how many total missing values do we have in nfl_data
total_cells = np.prod(nfl_data.shape)
total_missing = missing_values_count.sum()
# percent of data that is missing
(total_missing/total_cells) * 100
```

```
24.87214126835169
```

Fig 10.5

That's amazing right, almost a quarter of the cells in this dataset are empty! Now it's your turn to apply the same steps in the **building_permits** dataset and check percentage of missing values there.

In the next step, we're going to take a closer look at some of the columns with missing values and try to figure out what might be going on with them. This process in data science means closely looking at your data and trying to figure out why it is the way it is and how that will affect your analysis. **For dealing with missing values, you'll need to use your intuition to figure out why the value is missing**.

To help figure this out the next question that a data scientist must himself/herself - **Is this value missing because it wasn't recorded or because it doesn't exist?**

In the first case, if a value is missing because it doesn't exist (for example the height of the oldest child of someone who doesn't have any children) then it doesn't make any sense to try and guess what it might be. These values you probably do want to keep as NaN. In the second case, if a value is missing because it wasn't recorded, then you can try to guess what it might have been based on the other values in that column and row. This is called "**imputation**" that you will learn in next.

In our nfl_data dataset, if you check the **TimeSecs** column, it has total 224 missing values because they were not recorded, rather than thinking if the data in these columns ever existed. So, it would make sense for us to try and guess what they should be rather than just leaving them as NA's or NaN's. On the other hand, there are other fields, like **PenalizedTeam** that also have lot of missing fields. In this case, though, the field is missing because if there was no penalty then it doesn't make sense to say which team was penalized. For this column, it would make more sense to either leave it empty or to add a third value like "noone" and use that to replace the NA's.

Till now you must have understood that reading and understanding through your data can be a tedious process. Imagine doing such careful data analysis daily where you have to look at each column individually until you figure out the best strategy for filling those missing values. **Now it's your turn to look at the columns Street Number Suffix and Zipcode from the building_permits datasets with a similar approach.** Both contain missing values. Which, if either, of these are missing because they don't exist? Which, if either, are missing because they weren't recorded?

Dropping Missing Values

If you don't have any reason to figure out why your values are missing, the last option you could be left with is to just remove any rows or columns that contain missing values. But this is not recommended for important projects! It's usually worth taking out some time to go through your data and carefully look at all the columns with missing values one-by-one and understand your dataset. It could be frustrating at the beginning but you'll get used to eventually helping you evolve as a better data scientist.

For dropping missing values, Pandas does have a handy function, **dropna()** to help you do this. **Stay alert**! When using this function if you don't pass any parameter, **it will remove all of the data even if every row in your dataset has at least one missing value**. For saving from this situation we can use **axis** parameter having column value with this function. We will also check before and after effect of missing values dropping in dataset as shown below-

```
# remove all columns with at least one missing value
columns_with_na_dropped = nfl_data.dropna(axis=1)
columns_with_na_dropped.head()

# checking how much data did we lose?
print("Columns in original dataset:", nfl_data.shape[1])
print("Columns with missing values dropped:", columns_with_na_dropped.shape[1])

Columns in original dataset: 102
Columns with missing values dropped: 41
```

Fig 10.6

By passing *axis=1* as parameter we were able to drop columns with one or more missing values.

We've lost quite a bit of data, but at this point we have successfully removed all the NaN's from our NFL data. Now it's your turn to try removing all the rows from the building_permits dataset that contain missing values and see how many are left and then try to remove all the columns with empty values and check, how much of your data is left?

Automatically Fill Missing Values

Instead of dropping missing values, we have another option to fill these values. For this purpose Pandas has **fillna()** function with an option of replacing the NaN values with value of our choice. In the case of our example data set, I am going to replace all the NaN values with 0 in *nfl_data* dataset. Since I have already removed/dropped columns with NaN values. Before applying this function, I am going to pick a small subset view of data in the columns from *EPA* to *Season* so that it will print well in notebook. For this sub setting you can use **.loc()** function and pass the range indexes of columns after the comma inside the function. The single colon before the comma in the .loc() function indicates data from all rows for the sub-setting.

```
# get a small subset of the NFL dataset
subset_nfl_data = nfl_data.loc[:, 'EPA':'Season'].head()
subset_nfl_data
# replace all NA's with 0
subset_nfl_data.fillna(0)
```

	EPA	airEPA	yacEPA	Home_WP_pre	Away_WP_pre	Home_WP_post	Away_WP_post	Win_Prob	WPA	airWPA	yacWPA	Season
0	2.014474	0.000000	0.000000	0.485675	0.514325	0.546433	0.453567	0.485675	0.060758	0.000000	0.000000	2009
1	0.077907	-1.068169	1.146076	0.546433	0.453567	0.551088	0.448912	0.546433	0.004655	-0.032244	0.036899	2009
2	-1.402760	0.000000	0.000000	0.551088	0.448912	0.510793	0.489207	0.551088	-0.040295	0.000000	0.000000	2009
3	-1.712583	3.318841	-5.031425	0.510793	0.489207	0.461217	0.538783	0.510793	-0.049576	0.106663	-0.156239	2009
4	2.097796	0.000000	0.000000	0.461217	0.538783	0.558929	0.441071	0.461217	0.097712	0.000000	0.000000	2009

Fig 10.7

In the code file, I have prepared and shared another example to check the sum and percentage of missing values in the nfl_data. I hope you'll be surprised to see the changes in dataset after the example operations we performed in our previous examples. The second option of filling missing values automatically is by replacing missing values with the value that follows (in the next row) it in the same column. This makes a lot of sense for datasets where the observations have some sort of logical order to them-

```
# replace all NaN's the value that comes directly after it in the same column,
# then replace all the reamining NaN's with 0
subset_nfl_data.fillna(method = 'bfill', axis=0).fillna(0)
```

	EPA	airEPA	yacEPA	Home_WP_pre	Away_WP_pre	Home_WP_post	Away_WP_post	Win_Prob	WPA	airWPA	yacWPA	Season
0	2.014474	-1.068169	1.146076	0.485675	0.514325	0.546433	0.453567	0.485675	0.060758	-0.032244	0.036899	2009
1	0.077907	-1.068169	1.146076	0.546433	0.453567	0.551088	0.448912	0.546433	0.004655	-0.032244	0.036899	2009
2	-1.402760	3.318841	-5.031425	0.551088	0.448912	0.510793	0.489207	0.551088	-0.040295	0.106663	-0.156239	2009
3	-1.712583	3.318841	-5.031425	0.510793	0.489207	0.461217	0.538783	0.510793	-0.049576	0.106663	-0.156239	2009
4	2.097796	0.000000	0.000000	0.461217	0.538783	0.558929	0.441071	0.461217	0.097712	0.000000	0.000000	2009

Fig 10.8

Try the same steps in building_permits dataset and explore the automatic filling missing values!

How to scale and normalize data?

Most of the machine learning algorithms do not take raw numerical attributes of your dataset. You need to fit the numerical values within the specific scale. For example, you might be looking at the prices of some products in both Rupee and US Dollars. One US Dollar is worth about 70 Rupee, but if you don't scale your prices methods like some machine learning algorithms will consider a difference in price of 1 Rupee as important as a difference of 1 US Dollar! This clearly doesn't fit with our intuitions of the world. With currency, you can convert between currencies. But what if you're looking at something like height and weight? It's not entirely clear how many pounds should equal one inch (or how many kilograms should equal one meter).

In this second case study of this chapter you will work on a Kickstarter Project dataset - *ks-projects-201612.csv*, which you can download from our repository. Kickstarter is a community of more than 10 million people comprising of creative, tech enthusiasts who help in bringing creative project to life. Till now, more than $3 billion dollars have been contributed by the members in fueling creative projects. The projects can be literally anything – a device, a game, an app, a film etc. Kickstarter works on all or nothing basis i.e if a project doesn't meet it goal, the project owner gets nothing. For example: if a projects's goal is $500. Even if it gets funded till $499, the project won't be a success. In this dataset you are going to transform the values of numeric variables so that the transformed data points have specific helpful properties.

These transforming techniques are known as **Scaling** and **Normalization.** One difference between these two techniques is that, in scaling, you're changing the range of your data while in normalization you're changing the shape of the distribution of your data. To understand the output of both techniques we will need visualization also, so we will use some visualization libraries also. Let's understand each of them one by one –

For **Scaling,** you will first need to install **mlxtend** library which is a Python library of useful tools for the day-to-day data science tasks. For this installation open Anaconda Prompt and run the following command: **conda install -c conda-forge mlxtend** follow the instructions.

After installing the required library, read the download data-

```python
import pandas as pd
import numpy as np

# for Box-Cox Transformation
from scipy import stats

# for min_max scaling
from mlxtend.preprocessing import minmax_scaling

# for visualization
import seaborn as sns
import matplotlib.pyplot as plt

# reading kickstarters project data
kickstarters_2017 = pd.read_csv("E:/pg/bpb/BPB-Publications/Datasets/ks-projects-201801.csv")
# set seed for reproducibility
np.random.seed(0)
kickstarters_2017.head()
```

Fig 10.9

	ID	name	category	main_category	currency	deadline	goal	launched	pledged	state	backers	country	usd pledged
0	1000002330	The Songs of Adelaide & Abullah	Poetry	Publishing	GBP	2015-10-09	1000.0	2015-08-11 12:12:28	0.0	failed	0	GB	0.0
1	1000003930	Greeting From Earth: ZGAC Arts Capsule For ET	Narrative Film	Film & Video	USD	2017-11-01	30000.0	2017-09-02 04:43:57	2421.0	failed	15	US	100.0
2	1000004038	Where is Hank?	Narrative Film	Film & Video	USD	2013-02-26	45000.0	2013-01-12 00:20:50	220.0	failed	3	US	220.0
3	1000007540	ToshiCapital Rekordz Needs Help to Complete Album	Music	Music	USD	2012-04-16	5000.0	2012-03-17 03:24:11	1.0	failed	1	US	1.0
4	1000011046	Community Film Project: The Art of Neighborhoo	Film & Video	Film & Video	USD	2015-08-29	19500.0	2015-07-04 08:35:03	1283.0	canceled	14	US	1283.0

Fig 10.10

By scaling your variables, you can help compare different variables on equal footing. To help solidify what scaling looks like. Let's start by scaling the goals of each campaign in our dataset, which is how much money they were asking for-

```
# select the usd_goal_real column
usd_goal = kickstarters_2017.usd_goal_real

# scale the goals from 0 to 1
scaled_data = minmax_scaling(usd_goal, columns = [0])

# plot the original & scaled data together to compare
fig, ax=plt.subplots(1,2)
sns.distplot(kickstarters_2017.usd_goal_real, ax=ax[0])
ax[0].set_title("Original Data")
sns.distplot(scaled_data, ax=ax[1])
ax[1].set_title("Scaled data")
plt.show()
```

Fig 10.11

Once you run the above shell following plots will be displayed-

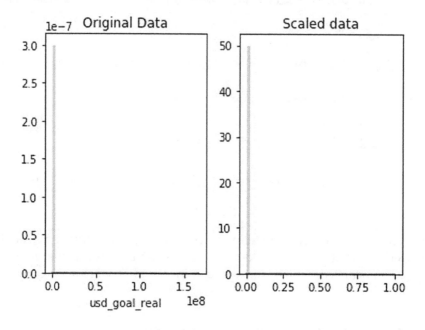

Fig 10.12

You can see that scaling changed the scales of the plots dramatically but not the shape of the data and we can conclude that **it looks like most campaigns have small goals but a few have very large ones.**

Scaling just changes the range of your data. **Normalization** is a more radical transformation. The point of normalization is to change your observations so that they can be described as a normal distribution. Remember here that normal distribution is a specific statistical distribution where a roughly equal observations fall above and below the mean, the mean and the median are the same, and there are more observations closer to the mean. The normal distribution is also known as the Gaussian distribution.

The method we are using to normalize here is called the **Box-Cox Transformation**. In the kickstarter data example, we're going to normalize the amount of money pledged for each campaign-

```
# get the index of all positive pledges (Box-Cox only takes postive values)
index_of_positive_pledges = kickstarters_2017.usd_pledged_real > 0

# get only positive pledges (using their indexes)
positive_pledges = kickstarters_2017.usd_pledged_real.loc[index_of_positive_pledges]

# normalize the pledges (w/ Box-Cox)
normalized_pledges = stats.boxcox(positive_pledges)[0]

# plot both together to compare
fig, ax=plt.subplots(1,2)
sns.distplot(positive_pledges, ax=ax[0])
ax[0].set_title("Original Data")
sns.distplot(normalized_pledges, ax=ax[1])
ax[1].set_title("Normalized data")
plt.show()
```

Fig 10.13

Once you run the above shell, you will see following plots-

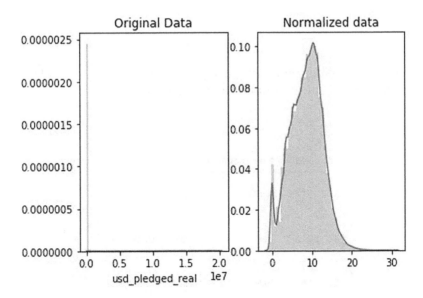

Fig 10.14

It's not perfect- it looks like a lot pledges got very few pledges but it is much closer to normal! Now it's your turn to apply same with the "pledged" column. Does it has the same info?

How to Parse Dates?

Many datasets have a date column and sometimes you may have to deal with requirements like fetching transactional data for a particular month or dates of a month. In such cases, you must know how to parse date. For this you are going to work on a case study where you will work on natural disaster dataset and will learn how to parse data. Let's import required modules and load our datasets-

```
import pandas as pd
import numpy as np
import seaborn as sns
import datetime

# read in our data
earthquakes = pd.read_csv("E:/pg/bpb/BPB-Publications/Datasets/database.csv")
landslides = pd.read_csv("E:/pg/bpb/BPB-Publications/Datasets/catalog.csv")
volcanos = pd.read_csv("E:/pg/bpb/BPB-Publications/Datasets/database.csv")

# set seed for reproducibility
np.random.seed(0)
```

Fig 10.15

If you check the landslides dataframe using .head() function you will see that there is a date column on which we will build our example.

```
landslides.head()
```

	id	date	time	continent_code	country_name	count
0	34	3/2/07	Night		NaN	United States
1	42	3/22/07	NaN		NaN	United States
2	56	4/6/07	NaN		NaN	United States
3	59	4/14/07	NaN		NaN	Canada
4	61	4/15/07	NaN		NaN	United States

5 rows × 23 columns

Fig 10.16

Looking at the data, we can tell that date column contains dates, but does Python know that they're dates? Let's verify it the data types of each column with the .info() function.

```
landslides.info()

<class 'pandas.core.frame.DataFrame'>
RangeIndex: 1693 entries, 0 to 1692
Data columns (total 23 columns):
id                      1693 non-null int64
date                    1690 non-null object
time                    629 non-null object
continent_code          164 non-null object
```

Fig 10.17

Shocked to see a strange data type of the date column! Pandas by default uses the "object" dtype for storing various types of data types. When you see a column with the dtype "object" it will have strings in it. To convert dtype object into date object, we will use **Pandas to_datetime()** function for parsing date value as shown below.

```
# create a new column, date_parsed, with the parsed dates
landslides['date_parsed'] = pd.to_datetime(landslides['date'], format = "%m/%d/%y")
# print the first few rows
landslides['date_parsed'].head()
```
```
0    2007-03-02
1    2007-03-22
2    2007-04-06
3    2007-04-14
4    2007-04-15
Name: date_parsed, dtype: datetime64[ns]
```

Fig 10.18

The dtype object is now converted into the datetime64 format which is a standard one for storing dates. If you want to extract day of the month from the date_parsed column use the **.dt.day** function as shown in the next screenshot.

```
# get the day of the month from the date_parsed column
day_of_month_landslides = landslides['date_parsed'].dt.day
day_of_month_landslides
```

```
0      2.0
1     22.0
2      6.0
3     14.0
4     15.0
5     20.0
```

Fig 10.19

Apply the same approach with and try your hand at fetching the day of the month from the volcanos dataset.

How to apply character encoding?

Character encodings are specific sets of rules for mapping from raw binary byte strings (that look like this: 0110100001101001) to characters that make up human-readable text (like "hello"). There are many different techniques used to encode such binary datasets and if you try converting such data in text without knowing the encoding technique it was originally written in, you will end up with scrambled text.

While working with text in Python 3, you'll come across two main data types. One is the string, which is what text is by default. The other data is the bytes data type, which is a sequence of integers. Most datasets will probably be encoded with UTF-8. This is what Python expects by default, so most of the time you won't run into problems. However, sometimes you'll get an error like this:

UnicodeDecodeError: 'utf-8' codec can't decode byte 0x99 in position 11: invalid start byte

To understand this let's work on the kickstarts project again but this time try to read 2016 csv file-

```
# try to read in a file not in UTF-8
kickstarter_2016 = pd.read_csv("E:/pg/bpb/BPB-Publications/Datasets/ks-projects-201612.csv")
--------------------------------------------------------------
UnicodeDecodeError                      Traceback (most recent call last)
pandas/_libs/parsers.pyx in pandas._libs.parsers.TextReader._convert_tokens (pandas\_libs\parsers.c:14858)()

pandas/_libs/parsers.pyx in pandas._libs.parsers.TextReader._convert_with_dtype (pandas\_libs\parsers.c:17119)()
```

Fig 10.20

To solve this error, you need to pass correct encoding while reading the file. We can check the encoding of this project's 2018 version file which you have already downloaded using **chardet** module shown as below-

```
# helpful character encoding module
import chardet

# Look at the first ten thousand bytes to guess the character encoding
with open("E:/pg/bpb/BPB-Publications/Datasets/ks-projects-201801.csv", 'rb') as rawdata:
    result = chardet.detect(rawdata.read(10000))

# check what the character encoding might be
print(result)
```

```
{'encoding': 'Windows-1252', 'confidence': 0.73, 'language': ''}
```

Fig 10.21

Encoding is "Windows-1252" having 73% confidence value. Let's see if that's correct-

```
# read in the file with the encoding detected by chardet
kickstarter_2016 = pd.read_csv("E:/pg/bpb/BPB-Publications/Datasets/ks-projects-201612.csv",
                    encoding='Windows-1252', low_memory=False)

# Look at the first few lines
kickstarter_2016.head()
```

	ID	name	category	main_category	currency	deadline	goal	launched	pledged	state	ba
0	1000002330	The Songs of Adelaide & Abullah	Poetry	Publishing	GBP	2015-10-09 11:36:00	1000	2015-08-11 12:12:28	0	failed	
1	1000004038	Where is Hank?	Narrative Film	Film & Video	USD	2013-02-26 00:20:50	45000	2013-01-12 00:20:50	220	failed	

Fig 10.22

Cleaning inconsistent data

Sometimes, you may come across duplicate data entry in your dataset like 'Karachi' and 'Karachi ' where there is a space in second or same name with case issues as shown in the next example. These types of inconsistency need to be removed. To understand this type of situation we will work on a sample dataset where suicide attacks held in Pakistan. Let's understand this situation by importing the suicide attack dataset and explore the inconsistent column as below-

```
# read in our dat
suicide_attacks = pd.read_csv("E:/pg/bpb/BPB-Publications/Datasets/PakistanSuicideAttacks Ver 11 (30-November-2017).csv",
                    encoding='Windows-1252')
suicide_attacks.head()
```

S#	Date	Islamic Date	Blast Day Type	Holiday Type	Time	City	Latitude	Longitude	Province	...	Targeted Sect if any	Killed Min	Killed Max	Injured Min	Injured Max	N Su B
0 1	Sunday-November 19-1995	25 Jumaada al-THaany 1416 A.H	Holiday	Weekend	NaN	Islamabad	33.7180	73.0718	Capital	...	None	14.0	15.0	NaN	60	
1 2	Monday-November 6-2000	10 SHa'baan 1421 A.H	Working Day	NaN	NaN	Karachi	24.9918	66.9911	Sindh	...	None	NaN	3.0	NaN	3	

Fig 10.23

Since our focus is on inconsistency, move on to the city name column-

```
# get all the unique values in the 'City' column
cities = suicide_attacks['City'].unique()

# sort them alphabetically and then take a closer look
cities.sort()
cities
```

```
array(['ATTOCK', 'Attock ', 'Bajaur Agency', 'Bannu', 'Bhakkar ', 'Buner',
       'Chakwal ', 'Chaman', 'Charsadda', 'Charsadda ', 'D. I Khan',
       'D.G Khan', 'D.G Khan ', 'D.I Khan', 'D.I Khan ', 'Dara Adam Khel',
       'Dara Adam khel', 'Fateh Jang', 'Ghallanai, Mohmand Agency ',
       'Gujrat', 'Hangu', 'Haripur', 'Hayatabad', 'Islamabad',
       'Islamabad ', 'Jacobabad', 'KURRAM AGENCY', 'Karachi', 'Karachi ',
```

Fig 10.24

Let us format the each cell data by converting every letter in lower case and by removing white spaces from the beginning and end of cells. You can easily do this using **str** module's **lower() and strip()** functions. Inconsistencies in capitalizations and trailing white spaces are very common in text data and you can fix a good 80% of your text data entry inconsistencies by doing this-

```
# convert to lower case
suicide_attacks['City'] = suicide_attacks['City'].str.lower()
# remove trailing white spaces
suicide_attacks['City'] = suicide_attacks['City'].str.strip()
```

Fig 10.25

Conclusion

If you have read this chapter carefully and applied the learning in your notebook then at the end of this chapter you have gained practical knowledge of data cleaning process. There are many techniques to learn when it comes to mastering data science subject. After practising the techniques covered in this chapter on different data sets you'll gain competitive skills to stay ahead in data science role. So, keep practicing and explore more techniques day by day. In the next chapter we will learn visualization in detail.

## CHAPTER 11

Data Visualization

Data is very powerful. It's not easy to completely understand large data sets by looking at lots of numbers and statistics. For the ease of understanding, data needs to be classified and processed. It is well known fact that the human brain process visual content better than it processes plain text. That's why data visualization is one of the core skills in data science. In simple words- Visualization is nothing but, representing data in a visual form. This visual form can be a chart, graphs, lists or a map etc. In this chapter you will work on a case study and learn different types of charts to plot with the help of Python's matplotlib and seaborn libraries along with Pandas.

Structure

- Bar Chart
- Line Chart
- Histograms
- Scatter Plot
- Stacked Plot
- Box Plot

Objective

After studying the chapter, you will become expert in visualization using Pandas.

Bar Chart

Bar charts or Bar graphs is the simplest form of data visualization method. They map categories to numbers, that's why Bar graphs are good to present the data of different groups that are being compared with each other. To understand how to plot a bar chart you are going to work on **Wine Reviews Points dataset** which you can download in zip form from our repository. In this dataset, **wine-producing provinces of the world (category) is compared to the number of labels of wines they produce (number).** Let's load this zip file, unzip it and read the file with following the same steps learnt in the previous chapter.

```
import zipfile
Dataset = "winemag-data_first150k.csv.zip"
with zipfile.ZipFile("E:/pg/bpb/BPB-Publications/Datasets/"+Dataset,"r") as z:
    z.extractall("E:/pg/bpb/BPB-Publications/Datasets")
```

Fig 11.1

The csv file is now extracted and stored in the location mentioned in the .extractall() function. Read the csv file and store data in a Pandas' DataFrame variable as shown below-

```
import pandas as pd
reviews_df = pd.read_csv("E:/pg/bpb/BPB-Publications/Datasets/winemag-data_first150k.csv", index_col=0)
reviews_df.head(5)
```

	country	description	designation	points	price	province	region_1	region_2	variety	winery
0	US	This tremendous 100% varietal wine hails from ...	Martha's Vineyard	96	235.0	California	Napa Valley	Napa	Cabernet Sauvignon	Heitz
1	Spain	Ripe aromas of fig, blackberry and cassis are ...	Carodorum Selección Especial Reserva	96	110.0	Northern Spain	Toro	NaN	Tinta de Toro	Bodega Carmen Rodríguez
2	US	Mac Watson honors the memory of a wine once ma...	Special Selected Late Harvest	96	90.0	California	Knights Valley	Sonoma	Sauvignon Blanc	Macauley
3	US	This spent 20 months in 30% new French oak, an...	Reserve	96	65.0	Oregon	Willamette Valley	Willamette Valley	Pinot Noir	Ponzi

Fig 11.2

Suppose, you want to understand which province produces more wine than any other province of the world. For this comparison you can use Bar Chart as shown below-

```
import matplotlib.pyplot as plt
reviews_df['province'].value_counts().head(10).plot.bar()
plt.xlabel('Province')
plt.ylabel('No of Wines')
plt.title('Provice with Wine Production Data')
plt.show()
```

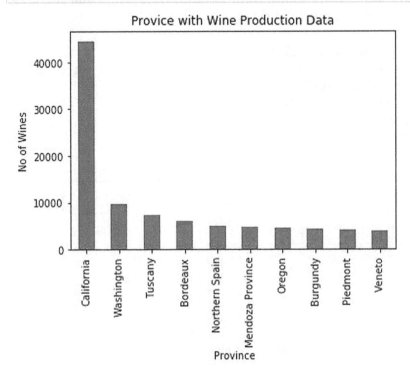

Fig 11.3

Isn't it easy to clearly say that California produces more wine than any other province of the world! From this visualization you can demonstrate a chart instead of showing statistics code to your client. That's is the beauty of data visualization. Now coming back to the actual code, we are using **matplotlib.pyplot** as our main plotting library. Next, we are using **value_counts()** function to find the frequency of the values present in province column in descending order. For denoting the x and y axis with a name we are using **xlabel()** and **ylabel()** functions of pyplot. Lastly, we have used the **show()** function to display the plots.

Line Chart

A line chart or line graph is a type of chart which displays information as a series of data points called 'markers' connected by straight line segments. Line Graphs are used to display quantitative values over a continuous interval or time period. A Line Graph is most frequently used to show trends and analyse how the data has changed over time. In our example let us a draw line graph to plot and understand wine reviews points using **plot.line()** function as shown in below example-

```
import matplotlib.pyplot as plt
reviews_df['points'].value_counts().sort_index().plot.line()
plt.xlabel('points')
plt.ylabel('No of Wines')
plt.title('points with Wine Production Data')
plt.show()
```

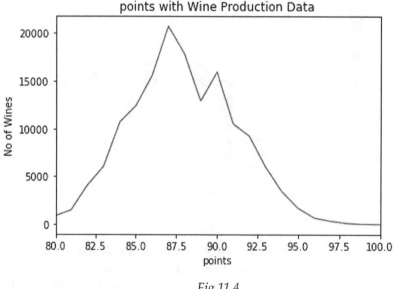

Fig 11.4

Here points in wine review dataset denotes the number of points WineEnthusiast rated the wine on a scale of 1-100. From the above line chart you can easily say that almost 20000 wines got 87 points in their reviews.

Histograms

A histogram looks like a bar plot. In fact, a histogram is special kind of bar plot that splits your data into even intervals and displays how many rows are in each interval with bars. The only analytical difference is that instead of each bar representing a single value, it represents a range of values. However, histograms have one major shortcoming. Because they break space up into even intervals, they don't deal very well with skewed data (meaning it tends to have a long tail on one side or the other). For example, let us check number of wines which are priced less than $200 as shown in the following screenshot.

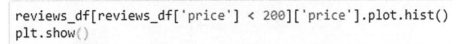

```python
reviews_df[reviews_df['price'] < 200]['price'].plot.hist()
plt.show()
```

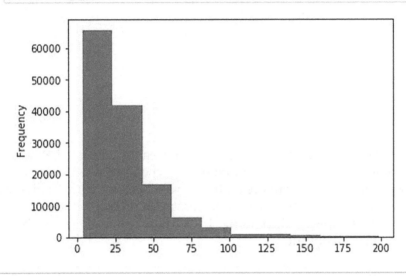

Fig 11.5

If you run the same code but price with greater than $200, then the plot will not break up Iin even interval. This is also one of technique to deal with skewness of the data. Histograms work best for interval variables without skew as well as for ordinal categorical variables.

Scatter Plot

Scatter plot is a bivariate plot which simply maps each variable of interest to a point in two-dimensional space. If you want to see the relationship between two numerical variables, then you can use scatter plot. In our wine dataset suppose you want to check the relationship between 'price' and 'points then to visualize a scatter plot with best fitting in our output cell, instead of taking all prices we will take sample like all the wines which have price below $100 and then we plot the relationship using *scatter()* function

```
reviews_df[reviews_df['price'] < 100].sample(100).plot.scatter(x='price', y='points')
plt.show()
```

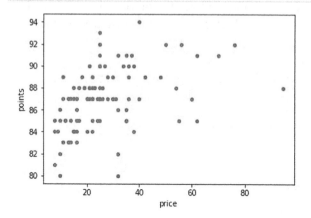

Fig 11.6

The above plot shows us that price and points are weakly correlated, it means that more expensive wines generally earn more points when reviewed. Scatter plot has one weakness- over plotting therefore scatter plots work best with relatively small datasets, and with variables which has large number of unique values. That's why I have taken only 100 sample while plotting. Try without using sample in above code and see the difference in output.

Stacked Plot

A stacked chart is one which plots the variables one on top of the other. It is like a bar graph or line chart, but it is subdivided into its components so that the comparisons as well as the totals can be seen. To plot a stacked plot, we will have to work on another dataset which represents the top five wine reviews-

```
wine_count_df = pd.read_csv("E:/pg/bpb/BPB-Publications/Datasets/top-five-wine-score-counts.csv", index_col=0)
wine_count_df.head()
```

points	Bordeaux-style Red Blend	Cabernet Sauvignon	Chardonnay	Pinot Noir	Red Blend
80	5.0	87.0	68.0	36.0	72.0
81	18.0	159.0	150.0	83.0	107.0
82	72.0	435.0	517.0	295.0	223.0
83	95.0	570.0	669.0	346.0	364.0
84	268.0	923.0	1146.0	733.0	602.0

Fig 11.7

In this dataset, the review score of top five wines is mentioned which is a perfect example to visualize each component as stacked plot.. Let's plot a stacked plot-

```python
wine_count_df.plot.bar(stacked=True)
plt.show()
```

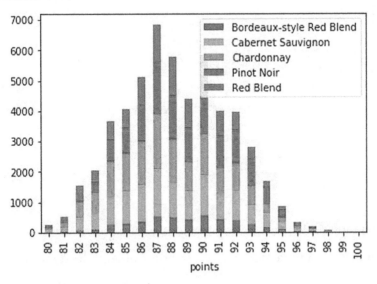

Fig 11.8

Doesn't it look beautiful? But this plot has following two limitations-

- The first limitation is that the second variable in a stacked plot must be a variable with a very limited number of possible values.

- The second limitation is one of interpretability. As easy as they are to make and pretty to look at, stacked plots sometimes make it hard to distinguish concrete values. For example, looking at the plots above, can you tell which wine got a score of 87 more often: Red Blends (in purple), Pinot Noir (in red), or Chardonnay (in green)?

Box Plot

If you want to visualize statistics summary of a given dataset then Box Plot is your friend. As shown in following diagram, the left and right of the solid-lined box are always the first and third quartiles (i.e 25% and 75% of the data), and the band inside the box is always the second quartile (the median). The whiskers (i.e the blue lines with the bars) extend from the box to show the range of the data-

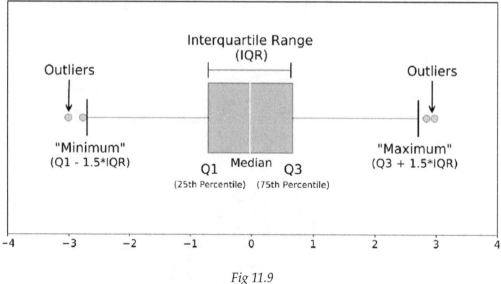

Fig 11.9

Let's understand first these five statistics terms-

1. median (Q2/50th Percentile): the middle value of the dataset.

2. first quartile (Q1/25th Percentile): the middle number between the smallest number (not the "minimum") and the median of the dataset.

3. third quartile (Q3/75th Percentile): the middle value between the median and the highest value (not the "maximum") of the dataset.

4. interquartile range (IQR): 25th to the 75th percentile.

5. whiskers (shown in blue)

6. outlier: the data point that is located outside the fences ("whiskers")

7. "maximum": Q3 + 1.5*IQR

8. "minimum": Q1 -1.5*IQR

Let's see how to utilize a box plot on a real-world dataset- Breast Cancer Diagnostic which you can download from our repository and read it as shown below-

```
import pandas as pd
cancer_df = pd.read_csv("E:/pg/bpb/BPB-Publications/Datasets/breast_cancer.csv")
cancer_df.head()
```

	id	diagnosis	radius_mean	texture_mean	perimeter_mean	area_mean	smoothness_mean	compactness_mean	concavity_mean	concave points_mean
0	842302	M	17.99	10.38	122.80	1001.0	0.11840	0.27760	0.3001	0.14710
1	842517	M	20.57	17.77	132.90	1326.0	0.08474	0.07864	0.0869	0.07017
2	84300903	M	19.69	21.25	130.00	1203.0	0.10960	0.15990	0.1974	0.12790
3	84348301	M	11.42	20.38	77.58	386.1	0.14250	0.28390	0.2414	0.10520
4	84358402	M	20.29	14.34	135.10	1297.0	0.10030	0.13280	0.1980	0.10430

5 rows × 33 columns

Fig 11.10

Next task is to analyse the relationship between malignant or benign tumour (a categorical feature) and area_mean (continuous feature).

For this task, first you need to separate the malignant or benign tumour data from the complete dataset based on the mean area. This time I will use seaborn library to plot my boxplot and save the plot as an image . For plotting a box plot we will use *boxplot()* function of seaborn library as shown below-

```
import seaborn as sns
malignant_tumour  = cancer_df[cancer_df['diagnosis']=='M']['area_mean']
benign_tumour  = cancer_df[cancer_df['diagnosis']=='B']['area_mean']
sns.boxplot(x='diagnosis', y='area_mean', data=cancer_df)
plt.savefig('E:/pg/bpb/BPB-Publications/Datasets/cancer_area_mean_diagnosis.png')
plt.show()
```

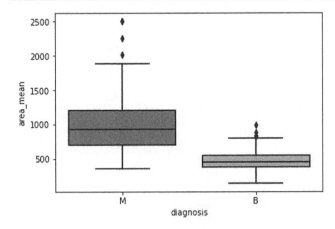

Fig 11.11

Using above graph, we can compare the range and distribution of the area mean for malignant and benign diagnosis. We observe that there is a greater variability for malignant tumour area mean as well as larger outliers. Also, since the notches in the boxplots do not overlap, you can conclude that with 95% confidence, that the true medians do differ.

Conclusion

Data visualization is one of the core skills in data science. In order to start building useful models, we need to understand the underlying dataset. Effective data visualization is the most important tool in your arsenal for getting this done, and hence a critical skill for you to master. There are various readymade visualization tools like Tableau and QlikView present in the market but you must know the basic plotting skills as we did in this chapter. The more you practice on actual datasets, the more you will gain your visualization knowledge so start practicing in your notebook and check what you can analyse from the output. In the next chapter you will learn data pre-processing steps.

## CHAPTER 12

Data Pre-processing

For achieving better results from the applied model in Machine Learning projects properly formatted of data is mandatory. Some Machine Learning model need information to be in a particular format, for example, some machine learning algorithm(s) do not support null values. For such algorithms null values have to be managed in the original raw data set. Another important reason for having formatted data is to evaluate it using more than one Machine Learning and Deep Learning algorithms and chose among the best fit algorithmic solution to the data problem . In this chapter, you will learn data pre-processing steps which will form the final step towards working with machine learning algorithms. You will learn **Feature Engineering** along with data cleaning and visualization with the help of a real-world case study.

Structure

- About the case-study
- Importing the dataset
- Exploratory Data Analysis
- Data cleaning & Pre-processing
- Feature Engineering

Objective

After studying this chapter, you will be equipped with the skills to make your data ready to start working with machine learning algorithms.

About the case-study

In this chapter we are going to analyze datasets of two pioneer e-retail merchants- ModCloth and RentTheRunWay. Both retailers want to improve their catalog size recommendation process and thus asked data scientists to help. Following type of information is available in the datasets:

- ratings and reviews

- fit feedback (small/fit/large)

- customer/product measurements

- category information

These datasets are highly sparse, with most products and customers having only a single transaction. Note that, here a 'product' refers to a specific size of a product, as your goal is to predict fitness for associated catalog sizes. Also, since different clothing products use different sizing conventions, you will standardize sizes into a single numerical scale preserving the order.

Importing the dataset

You can download the two datasets of each merchants from the link provided in the book for downloading dataset. Both datasets are in zip format. So before reading the actual file you need to unzip it first as shown in the following code block-

```
import zipfile
Dataset = "modcloth_final_data.json.zip"
with zipfile.ZipFile("E:/pg/bpb/BPB-Publications/Datasets/"+Dataset,"r") as z:
    z.extractall("E:/pg/bpb/BPB-Publications/Datasets")
```

Fig 12.1

Once you run the above code, it unzips thedata file which is in json format. Use Pandas **.read_json()** function to read this json file and store it in a dataframe for processing later and don"t forget to import the pandas library before running below code-

```
modcloth_df = pd.read_json('E:/pg/bpb/BPB-Publications/Datasets/modcloth_final_data.json', lines=True)
modcloth_df.head()
```

	bra size	bust	category	cup size	fit	height	hips	item_id	length	quality	review_summary	review_text	shoe size	shoe width	size	user_id	user_name	waist
0	34.0	36	new	d	small	5ft 6in	38.0	123373	just right	5.0	NaN	NaN	NaN	NaN	7	991571	Emily	29.0
1	36.0	NaN	new	b	small	5ft 2in	30.0	123373	just right	3.0	NaN	NaN	NaN	NaN	13	587883	sydneybraden2001	31.0
2	32.0	NaN	new	b	small	5ft 7in	NaN	123373	slightly long	2.0	NaN	NaN	9.0	NaN	7	395665	Ugggh	30.0
3	NaN	NaN	new	dd/e	fit	NaN	NaN	123373	just right	5.0	NaN	NaN	NaN	NaN	21	875643	alexmeyer626	NaN
4	36.0	NaN	new	b	small	5ft 2in	NaN	123373	slightly long	5.0	NaN	NaN	NaN	NaN	18	944840	dberrones1	NaN

Fig 12.2

Exploratory Data Analysis

From the above head view of our case-study dataset, you will notice the following points-

- There are **missing values** (NaN) across the dataframe, which need to be handled.

- **Cup-size** contains some **multiple preferences**- which will need handling, if we wish to define cup sizes as **'category'** datatype.

- **Height** column needs to be parsed for extracting the height in a numerical quantity, it looks like a string (**object**) right now.

Let's explore the columns and information of the dataset in details-

```
modcloth_df.columns
```
```
Index(['bra size', 'bust', 'category', 'cup size', 'fit', 'height', 'hips',
       'item_id', 'length', 'quality', 'review_summary', 'review_text',
       'shoe size', 'shoe width', 'size', 'user_id', 'user_name', 'waist'],
      dtype='object')
```

Fig 12.3

It looks like there are spaces between some column names. So let's rename the space with underscore as below-

```
modcloth_df.columns = ['bra_size', 'bust', 'category', 'cup_size', 'fit', 'height', 'hips',
    'item_id', 'length', 'quality', 'review_summary', 'review_text',
    'shoe_size', 'shoe_width', 'size', 'user_id', 'user_name', 'waist']
modcloth_df.columns
```

```
Index(['bra_size', 'bust', 'category', 'cup_size', 'fit', 'height', 'hips',
    'item_id', 'length', 'quality', 'review_summary', 'review_text',
    'shoe_size', 'shoe_width', 'size', 'user_id', 'user_name', 'waist'],
    dtype='object')
```

Fig 12.4

Let's move further and check the data types of each column so that you can make more observations-

```
modcloth_df.info()
```

```
<class 'pandas.core.frame.DataFrame'>
RangeIndex: 82790 entries, 0 to 82789
Data columns (total 18 columns):
bra_size          76772 non-null float64
bust              11854 non-null object
category          82790 non-null object
cup_size          76535 non-null object
fit               82790 non-null object
height            81683 non-null object
hips              56064 non-null float64
item_id           82790 non-null int64
length            82755 non-null object
quality           82722 non-null float64
review_summary    76065 non-null object
review_text       76065 non-null object
shoe_size         27915 non-null float64
shoe_width        18607 non-null object
size              82790 non-null int64
user_id           82790 non-null int64
user_name         82790 non-null object
waist             2882 non-null float64
dtypes: float64(5), int64(3), object(10)
memory usage: 11.4+ MB
```

Fig 12.5

Once again if you analyze the data type of each column you will find below points-

- There are total 18 columns but out of 18 only 6 columns have complete data (82790).

- There are a lot of data missing in various columns like- bust, shoe width, shoe size and waist.

- A lot of the columns have strings (object) datatype, which needs to be parsed into the category datatype for memory optimization.

Next, you can check the missing values in each column as shown in the following block of code-

```
missing_data = pd.DataFrame({'total_missing': modcloth_df.isnull().sum(),
                    'percentage_missing': (modcloth_df.isnull().sum()/82790)*100})
missing_data
```

Fig 12.6

	percentage_missing	total_missing
bra_size	7.268994	6018
bust	85.681846	70936
category	0.000000	0
cup_size	7.555260	6255
fit	0.000000	0
height	1.337118	1107
hips	32.281677	26726
item_id	0.000000	0
length	0.042276	35
quality	0.082136	68
review_summary	8.122962	6725
review_text	8.122962	6725
shoe_size	66.282160	54875
shoe_width	77.525063	64183
size	0.000000	0
user_id	0.000000	0
user_name	0.000000	0
waist	96.518903	79908

Fig 12.7

Further analyzing the output we can inder that **waist column surprisingly has a lot of NULL values(97%)** – but consider also that Modcloth is online retail merchant and most of the data from Modcloth comes from the 3 categories of 'dresses, tops and bottoms'.

Let's dig more into the data before you dive into performing the pre-processing tasks as below-

```
modcloth_df.describe()
```

	bra_size	hips	item_id	quality	shoe_size	size	user_id	waist
count	76772.000000	56064.000000	82790.000000	82722.000000	27915.000000	82790.000000	82790.000000	2882.000000
mean	35.972125	40.358501	469325.229170	3.949058	8.145818	12.661602	498849.564718	31.319223
std	3.224907	5.827166	213999.803314	0.992783	1.336109	8.271952	286356.969459	5.302849
min	28.000000	30.000000	123373.000000	1.000000	5.000000	0.000000	6.000000	20.000000
25%	34.000000	36.000000	314980.000000	3.000000	7.000000	8.000000	252897.750000	28.000000
50%	36.000000	39.000000	454030.000000	4.000000	8.000000	12.000000	497913.500000	30.000000
75%	38.000000	43.000000	658440.000000	5.000000	9.000000	15.000000	744745.250000	34.000000
max	48.000000	60.000000	807722.000000	5.000000	38.000000	38.000000	999972.000000	50.000000

Fig 12.8

From above statics description you can infer the following -:

- Most of the shoe sizes are around 5-9, but the maximum shoe size is 38! It is surprising because if you check their website (https://www.modcloth.com/shop) you will find that they use UK shoe sizing.

- Size has a minimum of 0 and maximum Size matches the maximum shoe size.

You have analyzed some quite interesting and important points till now! Keeping in mind the basic statistical analysis we have done till now, let's check the outliers in our dataset by plotting a box plot using numerical columns of the dataset. First make a list of numerical columns and then use boxplot() method to draw a plot like below-

```
num_cols = ['bra_size','hips','quality','shoe_size','size','waist']
plt.figure(figsize=(10,5))
modcloth_df[num_cols].boxplot()
plt.title("Numerical variables in Modcloth dataset", fontsize=20)
plt.show()
```

Fig 12.9

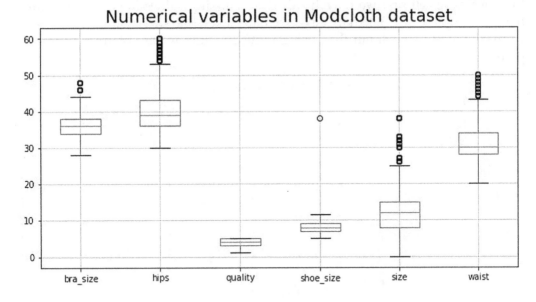

Fig 12.10

You can analyze following key points from above box plot-

- The single maximum value of shoe size (38) is an outlier and you should ideally remove that row or handle that outlier value. Since it is a single value in whole dataset, it could be wrongly entered by the customer or simple noise. As of now you can enter this as null value..

- In the bra-size you can see that boxplot shows 2 values as outliers, as per the IQR- Inter-Quartile Range. Thus you can visualize the distribution of bra_size vs size (bivariate) to arrive at an understanding about the values.

The next step will be to handle the null values in shoe size and then visualize the bra_size vs size-

```
modcloth_df.at[37313,'shoe_size'] = None
```

```
plt.figure(figsize=(10,5))
plt.xlabel("bra_size")
plt.ylabel("size")
plt.suptitle("Joint distribution of bra_size vs size")
plt.plot(modcloth_df.bra_size, modcloth_df['size'], 'ro', alpha=0.2)
plt.show()
```

Fig 12.11

In above code cell first we have handled the missing values in shoe_size column having a value of 37313 then in x-axis we have taken bra_size column and in y-axis we have taken size column then using plot() function we are plotting below like plot-

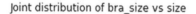

Joint distribution of bra_size vs size

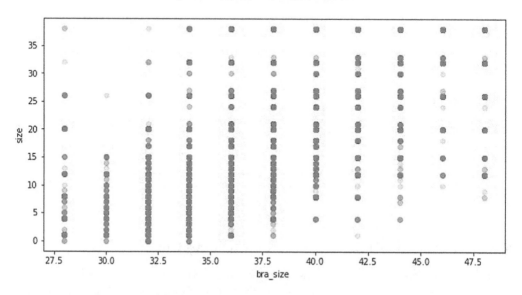

Fig 12.12

In above output cell, you see values scattered and from the plot we can't see any significant deviation from usual behavior for bra-size, in-fact for all other numerical variables as well- you can expect the 'apparent' outliers, from the boxplot, to behave similarly. Now, we 'll head to pre-processing the dataset for suitable visualizations.

Data Cleaning & Pre-processing

Let's handle the variables and change the data type to the appropriate type for each column. For this purpose, you will define a function first for creating the distribution plot of different variables. In this function we are passing two parameters- column and axis. Inside this function we will take care of missing values in column and then take the counts to plot a bar chart as shown below-

```
# function for initial distribution of features
def plot_features(col, ax):
    modcloth_df[col][modcloth_df[col].notnull()].value_counts().plot('bar', facecolor='b', ax=ax)
    ax.set_xlabel('{}'.format(col), fontsize=20)
    ax.set_title("{} on Modcloth Dataset".format(col))
    return ax

f, ax = plt.subplots(3,3, figsize = (20,13))
f.tight_layout(h_pad=9, w_pad=2, rect=[0, 0.03, 1, 0.93])
cols = ['bra_size','bust', 'category', 'cup_size', 'fit', 'height', 'hips', 'length', 'quality']
k = 0
for i in range(3):
    for j in range(3):
        plot_features(cols[k], ax[i][j])
        k += 1
__ = plt.suptitle("Initial Distributions of features")
plt.show()
```

Fig 12.13

Once you run the above function it will draw following looks like plot in your notebook-

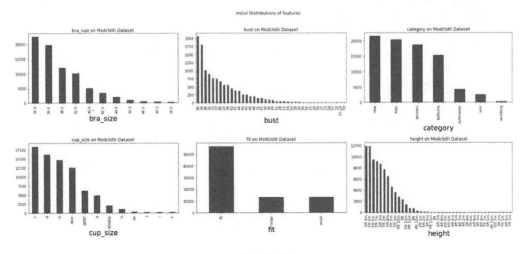

Fig 12.14

Looking at the individual plots from the output you can analyze and infer the following-

- bra_size- Although it looks numerical, it only ranges from 28 to 48, with most of the sizing lying around 34-38. You can see above that most of the buyers have a bra-sizing of 34 or 36. It makes sense to convert this to categorical data type. You can further refine the analysis by filling the NaN values into an 'Unknown' category..

- bust- You can see by looking at the values which are not null, that bust should be an integer data type. You can further refines the data where bust is given as - '37-39'and replace the entry of '37-39' with its mean, i.e.- 38, for analysis purposes. Later convert the data type to int.

- category- none missing; you can change it to data type category.

- cup size- Change the data type to category for this column. This column has around 7% missing values.

- fit- Change the data type to category for this column. You can see that a vast majority of customers gave a good 'fit' feedback for the items on Modcloth!

- height- You need to parse the height column as currently it is a string object, of the form - Xft. Yin. It will make sense to convert height to centimeters. We also take a look at the rows where the height data is missing.

Let's apply these observations one by one as below-

```
modcloth_df.cup_size.fillna('Unknown', inplace=True)
modcloth_df.cup_size = modcloth_df.cup_size.astype('category').cat.as_ordered()
modcloth_df.fit = modcloth_df.fit.astype('category')
```

Fig 12.15

```
def change_in_cms(x):
    # function to chnage height in cm
    if type(x) == type(1.0):
        return
    try:
        return (int(x[0])*30.48) + (int(x[4:-2])*2.54)
    except:
        return (int(x[0])*30.48)
modcloth_df.height = modcloth_df.height.apply(change_in_cms)
```

Fig 12.16

Feature Engineering

Creating new features from existing ones is called Feature engineering. This step improves your model accuracy amazingly. To extract a new feature, you must understand the actual business problem, it's dataset and you must think out of the box sometimes. In the given dataset we will try to do the same, so let's start this approach by creating a new feature of **first_time_user**-

You can use following logic to identify first time buyer:

1. If bra_size/cup_size have a value and height, hips, shoe_size, shoe_width and waist do not- it is a first time buyer of lingerie.

2. If shoe_size/shoe_width have a value and bra_size, cup_size, height, hips, and waist do not- it is a first time buyer of shoes.

3. If hips/waist have a value and bra_size, cup_size, height, shoe_size, and shoe_width do not- it is a first time buyer of a dress/tops.

You can verify above logic as below before creating the new feature-

1. Looking at the few rows where either bra_size or cup_size exists, but no other measurements are available.

2. Looking at the few rows where either shoe_size or shoe_width exists, but no other measurements are available.

3. Looking at the few rows where either hips or waist exists, but no other measurements are available.

Now we can add a new column to the original data- first_time_user, with boolean data type which will indicates if a user/a transaction, is a first-time user or not. This is based on the grounds that Modcloth has no previous information about the person, infact it is possible that the new user did multiple transactions in the first time!

```
lingerie_logic = (((modcloth_df.bra_size != 'Unknown') | (modcloth_df.cup_size != 'Unknown'))
            & (modcloth_df.height.isnull()) & (modcloth_df.hips.isnull()) &
            (modcloth_df.shoe_size.isnull()) & (modcloth_df.shoe_width.isnull()) & (modcloth_df.waist.isnull()))

shoe_logic = ((modcloth_df.bra_size == 'Unknown') & (modcloth_df.cup_size == 'Unknown') & (modcloth_df.height.isnull())
            & (modcloth_df.hips.isnull()) & ((modcloth_df.shoe_size.notnull()) | (modcloth_df.shoe_width.notnull()))
            & (modcloth_df.waist.isnull()))

dress_logic = ((modcloth_df.bra_size == 'Unknown') & (modcloth_df.cup_size == 'Unknown') &
            (modcloth_df.height.isnull()) & ((modcloth_df.hips.notnull()) | (modcloth_df.waist.notnull())) &
            (modcloth_df.shoe_size.isnull()) & (modcloth_df.shoe_width.isnull()))

modcloth_df['first_time_user'] = (lingerie_logic | shoe_logic | dress_logic)
print("Column is added!")
print("Total transactions by first time users who bought bra, shoes, or a dress: " + str(sum(modcloth_df.first_time_user)))
print("Total first time users: " + str(len(modcloth_df[(lingerie_logic | shoe_logic | dress_logic)].user_id.unique())))

Column is added!
Total transactions by first time users who bought bra, shoes, or a dress: 903
Total first time users: 565
```

Fig 12.17

Let's move further and observe other columns, you will find below analysis result-

*   hips- **Hips column has a lot of missing values ~ 32.28%!** May be Modcloth never got this data from the user. You **cannot remove** such a significant chunk

of the data, so you need another way of handling this feature. You will learn how to bin the data- on the basis of quartiles.

- length- **There are only 35 missing rows in length**. Most probably the customers did not leave behind the feedback or the data was corrupted in these rows. However, you should be able to impute these values using review related fields (if they are filled!). Or you could also simply choose to remove these rows. For the sake of this analysis, we will remove these rows.

- quality- **There are only 68 missing rows in quality**. Just like we assumed the possibility for length column, the customers did not leave behind the feedback or the data was corrupted in these rows. We will remove these rows and convert the data type to an ordinal variable (ordered categorical).

```
# cleaning hips column
modcloth_df.hips = modcloth_df.hips.fillna(-1.0)
bins = [-5,0,31,37,40,44,75]
labels = ['Unknown','XS','S','M', 'L','XL']
modcloth_df.hips = pd.cut(modcloth_df.hips, bins, labels=labels)

# cleaning length column
missing_rows = modcloth_df[modcloth_df.length.isnull()].index
modcloth_df.drop(missing_rows, axis = 0, inplace=True)

# cleaning quality
missing_rows = modcloth_df[modcloth_df.quality.isnull()].index
modcloth_df.drop(missing_rows, axis = 0, inplace=True)
modcloth_df.quality = modcloth_df.quality.astype('category').cat.as_ordered()
```

Fig 12.18

Let's analyze remaining columns-

- review_summary/ review_text- The NaN values are there because these reviews are simply not provided by customers. Let's just fill those as 'Unknown'.

- shoe_size - Roughly 66.3% of the shoe_size data is missing. We will have to change the shoe_size into category data type and fill the NaN values as 'Unknown'.

- shoe_width - Roughly 77.5% of the shoe_width data is missing. We will have to fill the Nan values as 'Unknown'

- waist- Waist column has the highest number of missing values - 96.5%! We will have to drop this column.

- bust- 85.6% missing values and highly correlated to bra_size. We'll have to remove them.

- user_name- user_name itself is not needed with the user_id given. We'll have to remove them.

Let's apply above analysis to our dataframe-

```
modcloth_df.review_summary = modcloth_df.review_summary.fillna('Unknown')
modcloth_df.review_text = modcloth_df.review_text.fillna('Unkown')
modcloth_df.shoe_size = modcloth_df.shoe_size.fillna('Unknown')
modcloth_df.shoe_size = modcloth_df.shoe_size.astype('category').cat.as_ordered()
modcloth_df.shoe_width = modcloth_df.shoe_width.fillna('Unknown')
modcloth_df.drop(['waist', 'bust', 'user_name'], axis=1, inplace=True)
missing_rows = modcloth_df[modcloth_df.height.isnull()].index
modcloth_df.drop(missing_rows, axis = 0, inplace=True)
```

Fig 12.19

Now if you check the dataset using .info(), you will find that now there are no more missing values! You can move onto visualizing and gaining more insight about the data.

Here, you will **visualize how the items of different categories fared in terms of - fit, length, and quality. This will tell Modcloth which categories need more attention!** For this you can plot 2 distributions in categories like below:

- **Unnormalized distributions** - viewing the frequency counts directly- for comparison across categories. We also include the best fit, length, or quality measure in this plot.

- **Normalized distributions** - viewing the distribution for the category after normalizing the counts, amongst the category itself- it will help us compare what was the major reason for return amongst the category itself. We exclude the best sizing & quality measures, to focus on the pre-dominant reasons of return per category (if any).

For the above purpose, I have used various functions in the next code block as shown below-

```
# functions for Unnormalized and Normalized distributions
def plot_barh(df,col, cmap = None, stacked=False, norm = None):
    df.plot(kind='barh', colormap=cmap, stacked=stacked)
    fig = plt.gcf()
    fig.set_size_inches(24,12)
    plt.title("Category vs {}-feedback -  Modcloth {}".format(col, '(Normalized)' if norm else ''))
    plt.ylabel('Category', fontsize = 18)
    plot = plt.xlabel('Frequency', fontsize=18)

def norm_counts(t):
    norms = np.linalg.norm(t.fillna(0), axis=1)
    t_norm = t[0:0]
    for row, euc in zip(t.iterrows(), norms):
        t_norm.loc[row[0]] = list(map(lambda x: x/euc, list(row[1])))
    return t_norm
```

Fig 12.20

In above code cell, I have defined two functions. First one is for the visualization as we did earlier and in second function we are using **numpy.linalg.norm()** function for calculating the vector lengths or magnitudes. This norm_counts(t) is a generic function and you can use it for calculating the vector lengths in any dataset which is highly sparse like in this case study' datasets.

Don't forget to import the numpy package before running these functions! Let's apply our functions to visualize the comparison of category and fit-

```
# Category vs. Fit
group_by_category = modcloth_df.groupby('category')
cat_fit = group_by_category['fit'].value_counts()
cat_fit = cat_fit.unstack()
cat_fit_norm = norm_counts(cat_fit)
cat_fit_norm.drop(['fit'], axis=1, inplace=True)
plot_barh(cat_fit, 'fit')
plt.show()
```

Fig 12.21

The output will look like below-

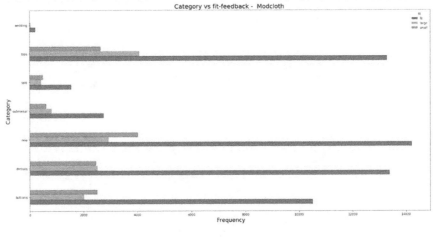

Fig 12.22

Analyze the above plot and you can find below observation-

1. **Best-fit response (fit)** has been **highest** for **new, dresses, and tops categories**.

2. Overall **maximum bad fit-feedback** has belonged mostly to 2 categories-**new and tops**! Dresses and bottoms categories follow.

3. **Weddings, outerwear**, and **sale are not prominent** in our visualization-mostly due to the lack of transactions in these categories.

Same plot you can draw to see the comparison between category and length, try at your end and analyze what observation you can make! There is another dataset of RentTheRunWay merchant which I have provided in the datasets for your own practice. Try implementing the learnings from this chapter to thedataset and see what observations you can make.

Conclusion

Feature Engineering and Visualization are very impactful skill in data analysis. If done in a right way they can push your machine learning modelling in a very positive way. Achieving expertise in skills like feature engineering and visualization requires practicing all the previous chapters as well as this chapter learning with different-different datasets. Don't just load the dataset in your notebook- try to understand the actual business problem first, explore each attributes of the dataset, think how you can extract a new feature from the existing one and what will be the impact of it on analysis. Keep practicing and in the next chapter you will start your machine learning journe and you will learn about Supervised machine learning.

CHAPTER 13

Supervised Machine Learning

In previous chapters of this book you have gained all required skills to jump into the machine learning (ML) world. Machine Learning is the field of teaching machines and computers to learn from existing data to make predictions on new data without being explicitly programmed. In this chapter, you will learn about different types of machine learning, deep dive in to some supervised machine learning techniques and how to use Python to perform supervised learning. You will also learn how to build predictive models, tune their parameters and how to tell how well they will perform on unseen data, all the while using real world datasets. You will do so using scikit-learn, one of the most popular and user-friendly machine learning libraries for Python.

Structure

- Some common ML Terms
- Machine Learning (ML) Introduction
- List of common ML Algorithms
- Supervised ML Fundamentals
- Solving a Classification ML Problem
- Solving a Regression ML Problem
- How to Tune your ML Model?
- How to handle categorical variable in Sklearn?
- Advance technique to handle missing data

Objective

After studying and practicing this chapter you will be an expert in solving supervised ml problems.

Some common ML Terms

1. **Dataset-** is a collection of data that is organized into some types of data structure.

2. **Model-** The representation of what an ML system has learned from the training data. To generate a machine learning model, you will need to provide training data to a machine learning algorithm to learn from.

3. **Training-** The process of determining the ideal parameters comprising a ML model.

4. **Learning-** The output of the training process is a machine learning model which you can then use to make predictions. This process is called-learning.

5. **Training Dataset-** The subset of the data set used to train a model.

6. **Validation Dataset-** A subset of the data set; disjunct from the training dataset that you use to adjust hyperparameters.

7. **Testing Dataset-** The subset of the data set that you use to test your model after the model has gone through initial vetting by the validation set.

8. **Hyperparameter-** is a parameter whose value is set before training a machine learning or deep learning model. Different models require different hyperparameters and some require none.

9. **Parameter-** A variable of a model that the ML system trains on its own.

10. **Target-** The target is the output of the input variables. A target variable is also called **dependent variable** or **response variable**.

11. **Feature-** are individual independent variables that act as the input in your system. You can consider one column of your data set to be one feature. Sometimes these are also called **predictor variables** or **independent variables** or **attributes** and the number of features is called **dimensions**.

12. **Label-** Labels are the final output. You can also consider the output classes to be the labels.

13. **Fit-** Capture patterns from provided data. This is the heart of modelling.

14. **Evaluate-** Determine how accurate the model's predictions are.

15. **Regularization-** is the method to estimate a preferred complexity of the machine learning model so that the model generalizes, and the over-fit/under-fit problem is avoided.

Introduction to Machine Learning (ML)

Machine Learning algorithms are divided into following four categories according to their purpose:

1. Supervised learning

2. Unsupervised Learning

3. Semi-supervised Learning

4. Reinforcement Learning

Supervised ML Learning algorithms try to model relationships and dependencies between the target prediction output and the input features such that we can predict the output values for new data based on those relationships which it learns from the original data set. Supervised ML algorithm is further divided into following two categories based on two types of problems-

- **Classification**: Classification problem can be defined as the problem that brings output variable which falls just in particular categories, such as the "red" or "blue", "male" or "female" or it could be "disease" and "no disease". Some examples are- A mail is spam or not? Is this picture of a car or a bus?

- **Regression**: Regression problem is when the output variable is a real value, such as "dollars", "Rupees" or it could be "weight". Some examples are- What is the price of a house in a specific city? What is the value of the stock?

Unsupervised ML Learning algorithms are used when computer/system is trained with unlabelled data - meaning the training data does not include Targets or in other sense we don't tell the system where to go. On the contrary, a system will arrive at an understanding by itself from the data we provide. These algorithms are useful in cases where the human expert doesn't know what to look for in the data. **Clustering** is the most important unsupervised ml problem where we group similar things together. For grouping of data we don't provide the labels, the system understands from data itself and clusters the data. Some examples are- Given a set of tweets, cluster data based on content of tweet or based on set of images or cluster into different objects.

Semi-supervised ML Learning algorithm falls in between the above two types of algorithms introduced above. In many practical situations, the cost to label is quite high, since it requires skilled human experts to do that. So, in absence of labels in most of the observations (but present in few), semi-supervised algorithms are the best candidates for the model building. Speech analysis and Web Content Classification are twos classic example of the semi-supervised learning models.

Reinforcement ML Learning algorithm allows machines/software agents to automatically determine the ideal behaviour within a specific context, in order to maximize its performance. In this process- Input state is observed by the agent; Decision making function is used to make the agent perform an action; After the action is performed, the agent receives reward or reinforcement from the environment and then the state-action pair information about the reward is stored. Some applications of the reinforcement learning algorithms are computer played board games (Chess, Go), robotic hands, and self-driving cars.

List of common ML Algorithms

1. Linear Regression

2. Logistic Regression

3. Decision Tree

4. SVM

5. Naive Bayes

6. kNN

7. K-Means

8. Random Forest

9. Dimensionality Reduction Algorithms

10. Gradient Boosting algorithms-

    1) GBM

    2) XGBoost

    3) LightGBM

    4) CatBoost

In the next few chapters we will learn to apply these algorithms like Logistic Rregression, Linear Discriminant Analysis,k Nearest Neighbours, Decision Trees, Gradient Boosting and Support Vector Machine to real-life case studies and understand how they help provide solutions.

Supervised ML Fundamentals

In Supervised ML problems we act as the teacher where we feed the computer with training data containing the input/predictors. We show the system correct answers (output) obtained from analyzing the data and from the analysis the computer should be able to learn the patterns to predict the output values for new input data based on relationships it learned by analyzing the original data sets. In more simple words- We first train the model with lots of training data (inputs & targets) then with new data and the logic we got before, we predict the output.

Always remember a thumb rule to distinguish between two types of supervised ml problems-

Classification: Target variable consists of categories

Regression: Target variable is continuous.

The first type of Supervised ML algorithm- **Classification** algorithms; are used when the desired output is a discrete label. In other words, they're helpful when the answer to your question about your business falls under a finite set of possible outcomes. Many use cases, such as determining whether an email is spam or not, have only two possible outcomes. This is called **binary classification**.

Multi-label classification captures everything else, and is useful for customer segmentation, audio and image categorization, and text analysis for mining customer sentiment.

Following is a list of some common **Classification** ML algorithms-

1. Linear Classifiers: Logistic Regression and Naive Bayes Classifier
2. Support Vector Machines
3. Decision Trees
4. Boosted Trees
5. Random Forest
6. Neural Networks
7. Nearest Neighbour

Second type of Supervised ML algorithm- **Regression;** is useful for predicting outputs that are continuous. That means the answer to your question is represented by a quantity that can be flexibly determined based on the inputs of the model rather than being confined to a set of possible labels. Linear Regression is one form of Regression algorithm. The representation of linear regression is an equation that describes a line that best fits the relationship between the input variables (x) and the output variables (y), by finding specific weightings for the input variables called coefficients (B). For example: $y = B0 + B1 * x$

We will predict y given the input x and the goal of the linear regression learning algorithm is to find the values for the coefficients B0 and B1.

> **Note** In machine learning, there's something called the "No Free Lunch" theorem. In a nutshell, it states that no one algorithm works best for every problem, and it's especially relevant for supervised learning (i.e. predictive modeling).

1. **Logistic Regression:** Don't confuse with the name, it is a classification model. Logistic regression (LR) is used to describe data and to explain the relationship between one dependent binary variable and one or more nominal, ordinal, interval or ratio-level independent variables. Behind the scene, Logistic regression algorithm uses a linear equation with independent predictors to predict a value. The predicted value can be anywhere between negative infinity to positive infinity. We need the output of the algorithm to be class variable, i.e 0-no, 1-yes. LR is based on the probability (p) so if the probability>0.5, the data is labelled as '1' otherwise data is labelled as '0'. By default, value of the probability threshold (p) in LR is 0.5.

2. **Decision Tree Classifier:** The decision tree classifiers organized a series of test questions and conditions in a tree structure. In the decision tree, the root and internal nodes contain attribute test conditions to separate records that have different characteristics. All the terminal node is assigned a class label- Yes or No. Once the decision tree has been constructed, classifying a test record is straightforward. Starting from the root node, we apply the test condition to the record and follow the appropriate branch based on the outcome of the test. It then lead us either to another internal node, for which a new test condition is applied, or to a leaf node. When we reach the leaf node, the class label associated with the leaf node is then assigned to the record. Various efficient algorithms have been developed to construct a reasonably accurate, albeit suboptimal, decision tree in a reasonable amount of time. For example, Hunt's algorithm, ID3, C4.5, CART, SPRINT are greedy decision tree induction algorithms.

3. **K-Nearest Neighbour Classifier:** The principle behind nearest neighbor classification consists in finding a predefined number, i.e. the 'k' - of training samples closest in distance to a new sample, which has to be classified. The label of the new sample will be defined from these neighbors. k-nearest neighbor classifiers have a fixed user defined constant for the number of neighbors which has to be determined. There are also radius-based neighbor learning algorithms, which has a varying number of neighbors based on the local density of points, all the samples inside of a fixed radius. The distance can, in general, be any metric measure: standard Euclidean distance

is the most common choice. Neighbors-based methods are known as non-generalizing machine learning methods, since they simply "remember" all of its training data. Classification can be computed by a majority vote of the nearest neighbors of the unknown sample.

4. **Linear Discriminant Analysis (LDA):**. Linear Discriminant Analysis is a dimensionality reduction technique but can be also used as linear classifier technique. Since Logistic regression can become unstable when the classes are well separated or when there are few examples from which to estimate the parameters; LDA is a better technique in such cases. LDA model consists of statistical properties of your data, calculated for each class. For a single input variable (x) this is the mean and the variance of the variable for each class. For multiple variables, this is the same properties calculated over the multivariate Gaussian, namely the means and the covariance matrix.

These statistical properties are estimated from your data and plug into the LDA equation to make predictions. These are the model values that you would save to file for your model.

5. **Gaussian Naive Bayes Classifier:** A Gaussian Naive Bayes (NB) algorithm is a special type of NB algorithm. It's specifically used when the features have continuous values. It's also assumed that all the features are following a gaussian distribution i.e, normal distribution. Remember that Bayes' theorem is based on conditional probability. The conditional probability helps us calculating the probability that something will happen, given that something else has already happened.

6. **Support Vector Classifier:** Support Vector Machine (SVM) is a supervised machine learning algorithm which can be used for both classification or regression challenges. In Support Vector Classifier algorithm, we plot each data item as a point in n-dimensional space (where n is number of features you have) with the value of each feature being the value of a particular coordinate. Then, we perform classification by finding the hyper-plane that differentiate the two classes very well. Support Vectors are simply the co-ordinates of individual observation. Support Vector Machine is a frontier which best segregates the two classes (hyper-plane/ line).

Solving a Classification ML Problem

For solving a Supervised Machine Learning problem, you need labelled data. You can get labelled data either in the form of the historical data with labels or can perform experiments like A/B testing to get labelled data or get from crowd sourcing labelled data. In all cases our goal is to learn from the data and then make prediction on new data based on the past learning. To understand this in our next example, we will use **Python's sci-kit learn or sklearn** library to solve a classification problem. Except sklearn there are TensorFlow and keras libraries also widely used in solving ML problems.

Note	Sklearn api expects inputs in numpy array so always check the data type of the data and convert it according. Also it expects that the data should not have missing values so handle the missing values before training of the model.

About the dataset- You will work on the best known and simple dataset named as Iris; to be found in the pattern recognition. Iris is a plant which have three species. This dataset was introduced by the British statistician Ronald Fisher in 1936. Based on the features of this plant Fisher developed a linear discriminant model to distinguish the Iris species with each other. The data set contains 3 classes of 50 instances each, where each class refers to a type of iris plant. One class is linearly separable from the other 2; the latter are NOT linearly separable from each other.

Attribute Information-

1. sepal length in cm
2. sepal width in cm
3. petal length in cm
4. petal width in cm
5. class-
   - Iris Setosa
   - Iris Versicolour
   - Iris Virginica

Goal- Your goal is to predict the class of an iris plant.

From the above description of the problem you can understand that sepal length/width and petal length/width are the **Features** whereas Species is the **Target variable.** Species has three possibilities- Versicolor, Virginica, Setosa. This is a **multi-class classification problem**. Along with many datasets, iris dataset is also present in Sklearn library, so you don't need to download it. The complete solution of this exercise has been done as a notebook for your reference with named as "Solving a classification ml problem.ipynb". Let's start our step by step to solve the problem-

1. Loading the dataset from sklearn library-

```
from sklearn import datasets
import pandas as pd
import numpy as np
import matplotlib.pyplot as plt
plt.style.use('ggplot')
```

```
#load the iris dataset
iris = datasets.load_iris()
```

Fig 13.3

2. After importing the dataset check the type of the dataset as shown below-

```
print(type(iris))
```

```
<class 'sklearn.utils.Bunch'>
```

Fig 13.4

It will show the data type is of class **Bunch** which is like a dictionary containing key-value Each key will be unique in the key-value pair and the values can be accessed if you know the keys. To find out the list of keys present in the dataset *iris* you can print the keys with .keys() function as shown below.

```
print(iris.keys())
```

```
dict_keys(['data', 'target', 'target_names', 'DESCR', 'feature_names'])
```

Fig 13.5

3. Further diagnosis of data key with the shape attribute, you will notice that there are total 150 samples (observations) and 4 features in iris data-

```
#check rows(samples) and columns(features) in iris data
iris.data.shape
```

```
(150, 4)
```

Fig 13.6

4. Let's look at the values associated with the target variable as shown below-

```
#check target variables
iris.target_names
```

```
array(['setosa', 'versicolor', 'virginica'], dtype='<U10')
```

Fig 13.7

5. In next step we will store iris plant's length/width and species in separate variables so that you can pass these two variables in further processing. Here you can also convert the iris data which is in n- dimensional array data type into a Pandas data frame using Pandas DataFrame() function-

```
X = iris.data
y = iris.target
#converting data in Pandas Dataframe
iris_df = pd.DataFrame(X, columns=iris.feature_names)
#check first five rows of iris dataframe
print(iris_df.head())
```

	sepal length (cm)	sepal width (cm)	petal length (cm)	petal width (cm)
0	5.1	3.5	1.4	0.2
1	4.9	3.0	1.4	0.2
2	4.7	3.2	1.3	0.2
3	4.6	3.1	1.5	0.2
4	5.0	3.6	1.4	0.2

Fig 13.8

6. Next to visualize the relationship between samples, we can plot a histogram plot as below-

```
#plotting histogram of features
_ = pd.plotting.scatter_matrix(iris_df, c=y, figsize=[8,8], s=150, marker='D')
plt.show()
```

Fig 13.9

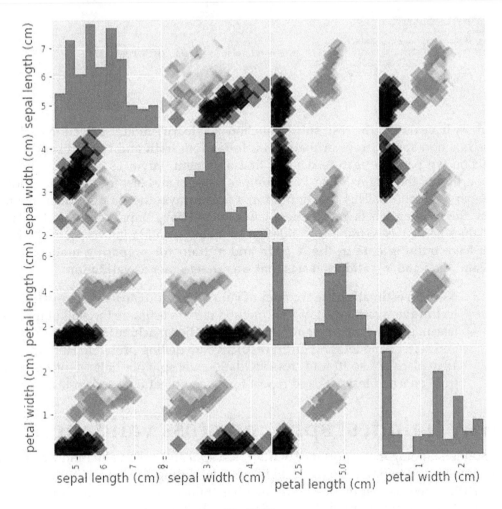

Fig 13.10

Here we have created a scatter plot matrix of our Iris datafarme using the scatter_ matrix method in pandas.plotting. In simple words, scatter matrix is plotting each of the columns specified against each other column which you can see as the diagonal of the matrix.

7. To know whether the selected model is any good or not, we are going to hold back some data that the algorithms will not get to see. Which means, we will use this data to get a second and independent idea of how accurate the best model could actually be. We will split the loaded dataset into two sets- 80% of which we will use to train our models and 20% that we will hold back as a validation dataset. Splitting a dataset is an important and highly recommended step while testing and applying a machine learning solution to a problem-

```
validation_size = 0.20
seed = 7
from sklearn import model_selection
X_train, X_validation, Y_train, Y_validation = model_selection.train_test_split(X, y,
                                                    test_size=validation_size,
                                                    random_state=seed)
```

Fig 13.11

Here we have used **train_test_split()** function of **sklearn's model_selection** package. This function **splits arrays or matrices into random train and test subsets.** In this function we pass the feature data as first argument, target as second argument, proportion of the original data for testing as *test_size* and last the seed for random number generations. This function returns four arrays- the training data, the test data, the training labels and the test labels so we have unpacked these four into variables named as X_train, X_validation, Y_train, Y_validation respectively. **Now you have training data in the X_train and Y_train for preparing models and a X_validation and Y_validation sets that we can use later as validation**.

8. Next, for **estimating the accuracy of your model** you can use **Cross-validation technique** which is a statistical method used to estimate the skill of machine learning models. It is commonly used in applied machine learning to compare and select a model for a given predictive modelling problem. Here we used 10 in place of k so 10-fold cross validation will split our dataset into 10 parts- train on 9 and test on 1 and repeat for all combinations of train-test splits.

Why train/test split and cross validation?

For understanding the importance of train/test split and cross validation we need to first understand two types of problem in ML- Overfitting and Underfitting a model. **Overfitting** means that model we trained has trained "too well" and is now, well, fit too closely to the training dataset. This usually happens when the model is too complex (i.e. too many features/variables compared to the number of observations). **This model will be very accurate on the training data but will probably be very not accurate on untrained or new data**. It is because this model is not generalized, meaning you can generalize the results and can't make any inferences on other data, which is, ultimately, what you are trying to do. In contrast to overfitting, **Underfitting** means when a model is underfitted, it means that the model does not fit the training data and therefore misses the trends in the data. It also means the model cannot be generalized to new data.

Train/test split and cross validation help to avoid overfitting more than underfitting. But train/test split does have its dangers—what if the split we make isn't random? In order to avoid this, we perform cross validation. It's very similar to train/test split, but it's applied to more subsets. Meaning, we split our data into k subsets, and train on k-1 one of those subsets. What we do is to hold the last subset for test. We're able to do it for each of the subsets.

9.   Next, we will use the **metric** of 'accuracy' to **evaluate** models. In classification, accuracy is a commonly used metric for measuring the performance of a model. This is a ratio of the number of correctly predicted instances in divided by the total number of instances in the dataset multiplied by 100 to give a percentage (e.g. 95% accurate). We will be using the scoring variable when we run build and evaluate each model next.

```
seed = 7
scoring = 'accuracy'
```

Fig 13.12

10.   Before testing out the any algorithm(s) we would not know which would be good to use for a problem or what configurations to use. We get an idea from the plots that some of the classes are partially linearly separable in some dimensions, so we are expecting generally good results. So here we will apply some classification algorithms and evaluate each model. For this purpose, we will reset the random number seed before each run to ensure that the evaluation of each algorithm is performed using exactly the same data splits. It ensures the results are directly comparable. Since we have to repeat the logic for all algorithms we are going to use, we will take help of 'for' loop in this case. Import the required algorithms like Logistic Regression, Linear Discriminant Analysis, K Nearest Neighbours, Decision Trees Classifier, Gaussian Naïve Bayes and Support Vector Classifier then follow below code cell-

```
#Check Algorithms
models = []
models.append(('LR', LogisticRegression()))
models.append(('LDA', LinearDiscriminantAnalysis()))
models.append(('KNN', KNeighborsClassifier()))
models.append(('CART', DecisionTreeClassifier()))
models.append(('NB', GaussianNB()))
models.append(('SVM', SVC()))
# evaluate each model in turn
results = []
names = []
for name, model in models:
    kfold = model_selection.KFold(n_splits=10, random_state=seed)
    cv_results = model_selection.cross_val_score(model, X_train, Y_train, cv=kfold, scoring=scoring)
    results.append(cv_results)
    names.append(name)
    msg = "%s: %f (%f)" % (name, cv_results.mean(), cv_results.std())
    print(msg)
```

```
LR: 0.966667 (0.040825)
LDA: 0.975000 (0.038188)
KNN: 0.983333 (0.033333)
CART: 0.975000 (0.038188)
NB: 0.975000 (0.053359)
SVM: 0.991667 (0.025000)
```

Fig 13.13

Code Explanation: Here we have first initialized an empty list where we can store our models. Next, we are adding six classification algorithms in these models so that we can compare result of each. For evaluating each model one by one and saving the result of each model we have defined 'results' variable for storing model's accuracy and 'names' variable for storing algorithm name. Both these variables are of type list.

In next step inside the for loop we are iterating the models list. In this iteration we are using **KFold()** function of model_selection which provides train/test indices to split data in train/test sets. **It split dataset into k consecutive folds** (without shuffling by default).

For evaluating our metrics by cross-validation and also record fit/score times, we are using **cross_val_score()** function. . From the output it looks like that SVM or Support Vector Machine classifier has the highest estimated accuracy score (99%).

11. You can also create a plot of the model evaluation results and compare the spread and the mean accuracy of each model. There is a population of accuracy measures for each algorithm because each algorithm was evaluated 10 times (10-fold cross validation)-

```
fig = plt.figure()
fig.suptitle('Compare Algorithm Accuracy')
ax = fig.add_subplot(111)
plt.boxplot(results)
ax.set_xticklabels(names)
plt.show()
```

Fig 13.14

Once you run the above cell you will see below result-

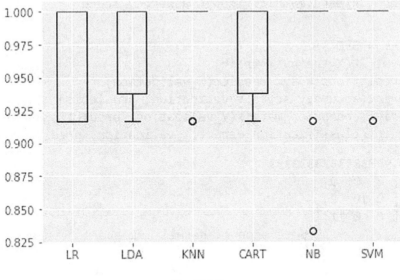

Fig 13.15

12. Now we can run the SVM model directly on the validation set and summarize the results as a final accuracy score, a confusion matrix and a classification report. **Always remember accuracy is not always an informative metric that's why evaluate the performance of your binary classifiers by computing the confusion matrix and generating a classification report**. For generating our accuracy score and report we will use sklearn's classification metrics module. Here **metrics.classification_report()** will build a text report showing the main classification metrics, **metrics.confusion_matrix()** will compute confusion matrix to evaluate the accuracy of a classification and **metrics.accuracy_score()** will tell us the accuracy classification score of our model-

```
#import required matrics
from sklearn.metrics import classification_report
from sklearn.metrics import confusion_matrix
from sklearn.metrics import accuracy_score
```

```
svm = SVC()
svm.fit(X_train, Y_train)
predictions = svm.predict(X_validation)
print(accuracy_score(Y_validation, predictions))
print(confusion_matrix(Y_validation, predictions))
print(classification_report(Y_validation, predictions))
```

```
0.9333333333333333
[[ 7  0  0]
 [ 0 10  2]
 [ 0  0 11]]
```

	precision	recall	f1-score	support
0	1.00	1.00	1.00	7
1	1.00	0.83	0.91	12
2	0.85	1.00	0.92	11
avg / total	0.94	0.93	0.93	30

Fig 13.16

To **train our model** we have used **.fit()** function which is a default function in many algorithms for training. , After training the model, to make predictions, we have used **.predict()** function call. Inside fit() method we pass two required arguments- features and target as numpy array. **The sklearn api requires data in numpy array format** only. Another point to remember is that there **should be no any missing values in data** otherwise you will face unexpected errors.

From the output, we can deduce that the accuracy is 0.933333 or 93%. The confusion matrix provides an indication of the three errors made. Finally, the classification report provides a breakdown of each class by precision, recall, f1-score and support showing excellent results (granted the validation dataset was small). The support gives the number of samples of the true response that lie in that class (no of species in our case on the test dataset).

Details of the report: Here, Classification report is a report of Precision/Recall/F1-score- for each element in your test data. In Multiclass problems, it is not a good idea to read Precision/Recall and F1-score over the whole data because any imbalance would make you feel you've reached better results. Confusion matrix, it is much detailed representation of what's going on with your labels. So, there are 7 [7+0+0] points in the first class (label 0). Out of these, your model was successful in identifying 7 of those correctly in label 0. Similarly look at second row. There were 12 [0+10+2] points in class 1, but 10 of them were marked correctly.

Coming to Recall/Precision. They are some of the mostly used measures in evaluating how good your system works. Now you had 7 points in first species (call it 0 species). Out of them your classifier was able to get 7 elements correctly. That's your recall. 7/7 = 1. Now look only at first column in the table. There is one cell with entry 7, rest all are zeros. This means your classifier marked 7 points in species 0, and all 7 of them were actually in species 0. This is precision. 7/7 = 1. Look at column marked 2. In this column, there are elements scattered in two rows. 11 of them [0+2+11=13] were marked correctly. Rest [2] are incorrect. So that reduces your precision.

13. Save your model in your disk so that next time you don't need to run all steps again in your notebook, instead you can predict any new iris species directly. For this purpose, you can use Python's **pickle** library. The pickle library serializes your machine learning algorithms and **saves** the serialized format to a file as shown in below-

```
# save the model to disk
import pickle
filename = 'finalized_model.sav'
pickle.dump(svm, open(filename, 'wb'))
# load the model from disk for next time you open this notebook
loaded_model = pickle.load(open(filename, 'rb'))
result = loaded_model.score(X_validation, Y_validation)
print(result)
```

0.9333333333333333

Fig 13.17

Running the example saves the model to *finalized_model.sav* in your local working directory. Load the saved model and evaluating it provides an estimate of accuracy of the model on unseen data. Later you can load this file to deserialize your model and use it to make new predictions.

Solving a Regression ML Problem

There are many different types of regression problems based on different data. The specific type of regressions we are going tolearn are called "generalized linear models". The important thing for you to know is that with this family of models, you need to pick a specific type of regression you're interested in. The -different type of data with respect to regression is as below

- **Linear**: When you are predicting a continuous value. (What temperature will it be today?)

- **Logistic**: When you are predicting which category, your observation is in. (Is this is a car or a bus?)

- **Poisson**: When you are predicting a count value. (How many cats will I see in the park?)

	Family	**Type of data**
Linear	Gaussian	Continuous
Logistic	Binomial	Categorical
Poisson	Poisson	Count

A quick guide to the three types of regression we've talked about.

Fig 13.18

About the problem: You are going to work on the Gapminder dataset. This dataset is already in clean state. GapMinder is a non-profit venture promoting sustainable global development and achievement of the United Nations Millennium Development Goals. It seeks to increase the use and understanding of statistics about social, economic and environmental development at local, national, and global levels.

Goal: Your goal will be to use this data to predict the life expectancy in a given country based on features such as the country's GDP, fertility rate, and population.

1. Load the dataset into Pandas data frame and inspect the columns and data types-

```
gapminder_df = pd.read_csv("E:/pg/bpb/BPB-Publications/Datasets/regression/gm_2008_region.csv")
```

```
gapminder_df.info()
<class 'pandas.core.frame.DataFrame'>
RangeIndex: 139 entries, 0 to 138
Data columns (total 10 columns):
population        139 non-null float64
fertility        139 non-null float64
HIV              139 non-null float64
CO2              139 non-null float64
BMI_male         139 non-null float64
GDP              139 non-null float64
BMI_female       139 non-null float64
life             139 non-null float64
child_mortality  139 non-null float64
Region           139 non-null object
```

Fig 13.19

Note	Always remember scikit-learn does not accept non-numerical features. In our case 'Region' is a categorical variable so you cannot include it in your training process until you handle it. You will learn how to handle this later.

2. In this dataset our target variable is 'life' and features variable is 'fertility'. Both these variables are of float data type but sklearn api accepts numpy array input. We need to convert our variables into arrays-

```
# Create arrays for features and target variable
y = gapminder_df['life'].values
X = gapminder_df['fertility'].values
```

Fig 13.20

3. If you check the dimension of the variables, you will notice that you are working on only one feature variable. With sklearn api you will need to reshape it-

```
# Print the dimensions of X and y before reshaping
print("Dimensions of target variable before reshaping: {}".format(y.shape))
print("Dimensions of feature variable before reshaping: {}".format(X.shape))
```

```
Dimensions of target variable before reshaping: (139,)
Dimensions of feature variable before reshaping: (139,)
```

Fig 13.21

After reshaping both variables dimension will be changed-

```
# Reshape X and y
y = y.reshape(-1,1)
X = X.reshape(-1,1)
# Print the dimensions of X and y after reshaping
print("Dimensions of target after reshaping: {}".format(y.shape))
print("Dimensions of feature variable after reshaping: {}".format(X.shape))
```

```
Dimensions of target after reshaping: (139, 1)
Dimensions of feature variable after reshaping: (139, 1)
```

Fig 13.22

4. Now to check co relation between different features of our dataframe, we can take help of heatmap function. For this instead of matplotlib library we will use seaborn library because it generates more beautiful plots so first import the seaborn library and then follow below code cell-

```
sns.heatmap(gapminder_df.corr(), square=True, cmap='RdYlGn')
plt.show()
```

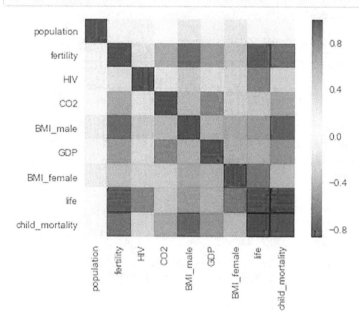

Fig 13.23

In above heat map, green cells show positive correlation, while cells that are in red show negative correlation. Here, we can say that life and fertility are poorly corelated. A linear regression should be able to capture this trend.

Next, we are going to solve our problem using **linear regression**. Before applying this, let's know some fundamentals of this algorithm. In this algorithm we try to fit a line to the data in such a way that it follows the equation: **y=ax+b or for higher dimensions y=a1x1+a2x2+b. Here y is the target, x is the single feature, a and b are the parameters of the model that you want to learn.** So here first question is **how to choose a and b?**

For this we define an **error function** (loss or cost function) for any given line and choose the line that minimizes the error function. In *sklearn* library when we train the data using *fit()* method it automatically apply this loss function behind the scene. This function is also called **Ordinary least squares** (OLS). The default accuracy metrics of this algo is R^2 (**R square**) instead of accuracy in classification problem.

5. Let's apply Linear Regression to our dataset without splitting it first-

```
# Import LinearRegression
from sklearn.linear_model import LinearRegression
# Create the regressor: reg
reg = LinearRegression()
# Create the prediction space
prediction_space = np.linspace(min(X), max(X)).reshape(-1,1)
# Fit the model to the data
reg.fit(X, y)
# Compute predictions over the prediction space: y_pred
y_pred = reg.predict(prediction_space)
# Print R^2
print(reg.score(X, y))
# Plot regression line
plt.plot(prediction_space, y_pred, color='black', linewidth=3)
plt.show()
```

0.6192442167740035

Fig 13.24

6. Now you will split the Gapminder dataset into training and testing sets, and then fit and predict a linear regression over all features just like we did for our classification problem. In addition to computing the R^2 score, you will also compute the Root Mean Squared Error (**RMSE**), which is another commonly used metric **to evaluate regression** models. Here R^2 score (R square) is a regression metric for evaluating predictions on regression machine learning problems-

```
# Import necessary modules
from sklearn.linear_model import LinearRegression
from sklearn.metrics import mean_squared_error
from sklearn.model_selection import train_test_split
# Create training and test sets
X_train, X_test, y_train, y_test = train_test_split(X, y, test_size = 0.3, random_state=42)
# Create the regressor: reg_all
reg_all = LinearRegression()
# Fit the regressor to the training data
reg_all.fit(X_train, y_train)
# Predict on the test data: y_pred
y_pred = reg_all.predict(X_test)
# Compute and print R^2 and RMSE
print("R^2: {}".format(reg_all.score(X_test, y_test)))
rmse = np.sqrt(mean_squared_error(y_test, y_pred))
print("Root Mean Squared Error: {}".format(rmse))
```

```
R^2: 0.7298987360907494
Root Mean Squared Error: 4.194027914110243
```

Fig 13.25

If you compare this output with the output of previous cell, you can easily say that all features has improved the model score because our model fit is increased from 0.619 to 0.729. Model performance is dependent on way the data is split. This makes sense, as the model has more information to learn from.

7. But as said earlier it is important to do cross validation because it maximizes the amount of data that is used to train the model. During the course of training, the model is not only trained, but also tested on all of the available data as explained below.

```
# Import the necessary modules
from sklearn.linear_model import LinearRegression
from sklearn.model_selection import cross_val_score
# Create a linear regression object: reg
reg = LinearRegression()
# Compute 5-fold cross-validation scores: cv_scores
cv_scores = cross_val_score(reg, X, y, cv=5)
# Print the 5-fold cross-validation scores
print(cv_scores)
# Print the average 5-fold cross-validation score
print("Average 5-Fold CV Score: {}".format(np.mean(cv_scores)))
```

```
[0.71001079 0.75007717 0.55271526 0.547501   0.52410561]
Average 5-Fold CV Score: 0.6168819644425119
```

Fig 13.26

In above example, we have applied 5-fold cross validation on the Gapminder data. By default, scikit-learn's *cross_val_score()* function uses R^2 (R square) as the metric of choice for regression. Since we are performing 5-fold cross-validation, the function will return 5 scores. Hence, we have computed these 5 scores and then taken their averages.

> **Note** Cross validation is essential but do not forget, the more folds you use, the more computationally expensive cross-validation becomes.
>
> Define the k as per your system capabilities.

Since linear regression minimizes a loss function by choosing a coefficient for each feature variables, large chosen coefficients can lead your model to overfit. To avoid this situation, we can alter the loss function and this technique is known as **regularization.** In this technique we try to find out most important feature and shrink the large coefficients to almost zero so that only important ones remain. Two regularization techniques are widely used in ML- **Lasso Regression** and **Ridge regression**. Let's understand each one by one-

- **Lasso Regression**:

Performs L1 regularization, i.e. adds penalty equivalent to absolute value of the magnitude of coefficients. Along with shrinking coefficients, lasso performs feature selection as well. Here some of the coefficients become exactly zero, which is equivalent to a particular feature being excluded from the model. It is majorly used to prevent overfitting as well as feature selection. The default value of regularization parameter in Lasso regression (given by alpha) is 1

- **Ridge Regression**:

Performs L2 regularization, i.e. adds penalty equivalent to square of the magnitude of coefficients. It includes all (or none) of the features in the model. Thus, the major advantage of ridge regression is coefficient shrinkage and reducing model complexity. It is majorly used to prevent overfitting. It generally works well even in presence of highly correlated features as it will include all of them in the model, but the coefficients will be distributed among them depending on the correlation.

Let's understand how you can apply Lasso with Python in breast cancer research dataset. This dataset is already there in sklearn api. First we will import the Lasso package from the *sklearn.linear_model* library followed by the breast cancer dataset from sklearn api and then we will apply the Lasso in our dataset as shown below.

```
from sklearn.linear_model import Lasso
from sklearn.datasets import load_breast_cancer
cancer = load_breast_cancer()
print(cancer.keys())
print(cancer.data.shape)
cancer_df = pd.DataFrame(cancer.data, columns=cancer.feature_names)
X = cancer.data
Y = cancer.target
X_train,X_test,y_train,y_test=train_test_split(X,Y, test_size=0.3, random_state=31)
lasso = Lasso()
lasso.fit(X_train,y_train)
train_score=lasso.score(X_train,y_train)
test_score=lasso.score(X_test,y_test)
coeff_used = np.sum(lasso.coef_!=0)
print("training score:", train_score )
print("test score: ", test_score)
print("number of features used: ", coeff_used)
plt.xlabel('Coefficient Index',fontsize=16)
plt.ylabel('Coefficient Magnitude',fontsize=16)
plt.legend(fontsize=13,loc=4)
plt.subplot(1,2,2)
plt.plot(lasso.coef_,alpha=0.7,linestyle='none',marker='*',markersize=5,color='red',label=r'Lasso; $\alpha = 1$',zorder=7)
plt.tight_layout()
plt.show()
```

Fig 13.27

Once you run the above cell you will see the following output-

```
dict_keys(['data', 'target', 'target_names', 'DESCR', 'feature_names'])
(569, 30)
training score: 0.5600974529893079
test score:   0.5832244618818156
number of features used:   4
```

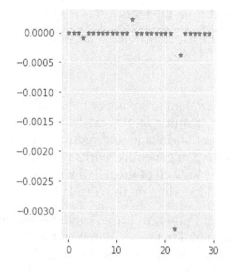

Fig 13.28

In our dataset there are total 30 features initially but on application of Lasso regression **only 4 features** are used; rest all are shrunk to zero (see the red stars on above plot). The training and test score are 56% and 58% respectively which are very low- it means our **model is underfitting.** Now you can reduce this under-fitting by increasing the number of iteration and by reducing the alpha. Try with alpha=0.0001 and number of feature =22 [lasso = Lasso(alpha=0.0001, max_iter=10e5)] and see how much accuracy do you get!

Next we will learn how to apply Ridge Regression in Python. Here we will use Boston house price dataset from sklearn api-

```
from sklearn.datasets import load_boston
from sklearn.linear_model import Ridge
boston=load_boston()
boston_df=pd.DataFrame(boston.data,columns=boston.feature_names)
boston_df['Price']=boston.target
newX=boston_df.drop('Price',axis=1)
newY=boston_df['Price']
```

Fig 13.29

Here axis=1 means we are applying logic to rows wise. We have separated the target column- Price from the dataframe and store it as target column.

```
X_train,X_test,y_train,y_test=train_test_split(newX,newY,test_size=0.3,random_state=3)
print(len(X_test), len(y_test))
lr = LinearRegression()
lr.fit(X_train, y_train)
rr = Ridge(alpha=0.01)
rr.fit(X_train, y_train)
train_score=lr.score(X_train, y_train)
test_score=lr.score(X_test, y_test)
Ridge_train_score = rr.score(X_train,y_train)
Ridge_test_score = rr.score(X_test, y_test)
print("linear regression train score:", train_score)
print("linear regression test score:", test_score)
print("ridge regression train score low alpha:", Ridge_train_score)
print("ridge regression test score low alpha:", Ridge_test_score)
plt.plot(rr.coef_,alpha=0.7,linestyle='none',marker='*',markersize=5,color='red',label=r'Ridge; $\alpha = 0.01$',zorder=7)
plt.plot(lr.coef_,alpha=0.4,linestyle='none',marker='o',markersize=7,color='green',label='Linear Regression')
plt.xlabel('Coefficient Index',fontsize=16)
plt.ylabel('Coefficient Magnitude',fontsize=16)
plt.legend(fontsize=13,loc=4)
plt.show()
```

Fig 13.30

Here, in X axis we plot the coefficient index which is features of our dataset. In our caseBoston data has 13 features.

Once you run the above code you will see following output-

```
152 152
linear regression train score: 0.7419034960343789
linear regression test score: 0.7146895989294312
ridge regression train score low alpha: 0.7419030253527293
ridge regression test score low alpha: 0.7145115044376255
```

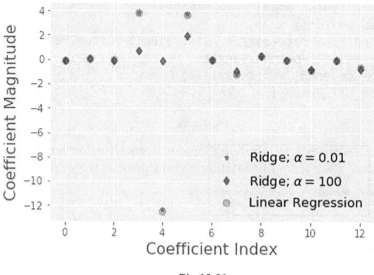

Fig 13.31

You will notice, in above plot that for low value of alpha (0.01) denoted as red star, when the coefficients are less restricted, the coefficient magnitudes are almost same as of linear regression. Try with alpha=100 and you will see that for this higher value of alpha (100), for coefficient indices 3,4,5 the magnitudes are considerably less compared to linear regression case. From above exercises you can say that Lasso is great for feature selection, but when building regression models, Ridge regression should be your first choice.

If you noticed, the steps, we have followed to solve classification and regression problems, have similarity. We can summarize the common steps in following simple words-

1. Perform the necessary imports

2. Instantiate your classifier or regressor

3. Split your dataset into training and test sets

4. Fit the model on your training data

5. Predict on your test set

How to Tune your ML Model?

Till now you have learnt required steps to build a ML model. But sometimes, implementing a model is not the ultimate solution. You may be required to fine tune your model for better accuracy. For the example explained above, you can tune your models-

1. by choosing the **right 'alpha'** parameter value in Lasso/Ridge regression

2. by choosing the **right 'n_neighbors'** parameter value in K-NN

Above parameters are chosen before training the model and called '**Hyperparameters'**. These parameters cannot be learnt by fitting the model. **So how you can choose the right one?** Till now only one possible solution is found- try with different hyperparameters values, fit all of them separately, do cross validation and then choose the right one after comparing the results.

Now you will learn how to do the same using **GridSearchCV** library which exhaustive searches over specified parameter values for an estimator. Here you only need to specify the hyperparameter as a dictionary in which keys are the hyperparameter's name like alpha or n_neighbors and the values in this dictionary is a list containing the values for which we choose the relevant hyperparameters.

Let's see how to use the **GridSearchCV with logistic regression**. Logistic Regression has a parameter- '**C'** which controls the inverse of the regularization strength, so a **large** 'C' can lead to an **overfit** model, while a **small** 'C' can lead to an **underfit** model. Now see how you can set up the hyperparameter grid (c_space) and perform grid-search cross-validation on a diabatic dataset.This dataset data set was prepared on diabetes patients for the use of participants for the 1994 AAAI Spring Symposium on Artificial Intelligence in Medicine-

```
from sklearn.linear_model import LogisticRegression
from sklearn.model_selection import GridSearchCV

df = pd.read_csv("E:/pg/bpb/BPB-Publications/Datasets/diabetes.csv")
print(df.columns)

y=df['diabetes']
X=df.drop('diabetes',axis=1)

#Setup the hyperparameter grid
c_space = np.logspace(-5, 8, 15)
param_grid = {'C': c_space}

logreg = LogisticRegression()
logreg_cv = GridSearchCV(logreg, param_grid, cv=5)
logreg_cv.fit(X, y)

print("Tuned Logistic Regression Parameters: {}".format(logreg_cv.best_params_))
print("Best score is {}".format(logreg_cv.best_score_))
```

Fig 13.32

Here in **param_grid** variable you can also use '**penalty**' argument along with 'C' to specify you want to use '**l1**' or '**l2**' **regularization**.

```
Index(['pregnancies', 'glucose', 'diastolic', 'triceps', 'insulin', 'bmi',
       'dpf', 'age', 'diabetes'],
      dtype='object')
Tuned Logistic Regression Parameters: {'C': 163789.3706954068}
Best score is 0.7721354166666666
```

Fig 13.33

In above output cell you can see the different properties of diabetes patients as columns. With proper hyperparameter grid setup we have achieved best score of our logistic regression model.

One drawback of GridSearchCV is- it can be **computationally expensive**, especially if you are searching over a large hyperparameter space and dealing with multiple hyperparameters. As an alternative you can also use **RandomizedSearchCV** in which a fixed number of hyperparameter settings is sampled from specified probability distributions. Let's understand how to use this in a decision tree classifier. As the name suggests the decision tree classifiers organized a series of test questions and conditions in a tree structure. Decision Tree Classifier poses a series of carefully crafted questions about the attributes of the test record. Each time it receive an answer, a follow-up question is asked until a conclusion about the class label of the record is reached-

```
# Import necessary modules
from scipy.stats import randint
from sklearn.tree import DecisionTreeClassifier
from sklearn.model_selection import RandomizedSearchCV

param_dist = {"max_depth": [3, None],
              "max_features": randint(1, 9),
              "min_samples_leaf": randint(1, 9),
              "criterion": ["gini", "entropy"]}

tree = DecisionTreeClassifier()
tree_cv = RandomizedSearchCV(tree, param_dist, cv=5)

tree_cv.fit(X, y)

print("Tuned Decision Tree Parameters: {}".format(tree_cv.best_params_))
print("Best score is {}".format(tree_cv.best_score_))

Tuned Decision Tree Parameters: {'criterion': 'entropy', 'max_depth': 3, 'max_features': 7, 'min_samples_leaf': 4}
Best score is 0.7447916666666666
```

Fig 13.34

In above code cell we have set the hyperparameter grid using RandomizedSearchCV to find the best parameters and as a result we found the best hyperparameters 'criterion', 'max_depth' and 'min_simple_leaf' as 'entropy', '3' and '4' respectively. You have now understood that hyperparameter tuning skill depend on your practice. The more you try with different parameters with different algorithms, the more you will be able to understand.

How to handle categorical variable in sklearn?

If you recollect, in one of the above example there is a categorical variable 'Region' in Gapmider dataset which is not accepted by sklearn api.You need to learn how to handle this case because sometimes it is not good to just leave such variables. One way to convert a non-numeric variable in desired format of sklearn is to binarize using Pandas **get_dummies()** function. Let's see how to do the same-

```
# handling categorical variable 'Region' by binarizing it(creating dummy variables)
# Create dummy variables: df_region
df_region = pd.get_dummies(df)

# Print the columns of df_region
print(df_region.columns)

# Drop 'Region_America' from df_region
df_region = pd.get_dummies(df, drop_first=True)

# Print the new columns of df_region
print(df_region.columns)
```

Fig 13.35

Here pd.get_dummies(df) is converting categorical variable of our dataframe into dummy/indicator variable. Once you run the above cell you will see that 'Region' column is suffixed by region names-

```
Index(['population', 'fertility', 'HIV', 'CO2', 'BMI_male', 'GDP',
       'BMI_female', 'life', 'child_mortality', 'Region_America',
       'Region_East Asia & Pacific', 'Region_Europe & Central Asia',
       'Region_Middle East & North Africa', 'Region_South Asia',
       'Region_Sub-Saharan Africa'],
     dtype='object')
```

Fig 13.36

Now you can perform regression technique on whole Gapmider dataset as below-

```
from sklearn.model_selection import cross_val_score
from sklearn.linear_model import Ridge

ridge = Ridge(alpha=0.5, normalize=True)
y=df_region['life'].values
X=df_region.drop('life', axis=1).values

# Perform 5-fold cross-validation: ridge_cv
ridge_cv = cross_val_score(ridge, X, y, cv=5)
print(ridge_cv)

[0.86808336 0.80623545 0.84004203 0.7754344  0.87503712]
```

Fig 13.37

Here axis=1 means we are applying logic to rows wise; for column wise operation change it to axis=0.

Advanced technique to handle missing data

You have already learn handling the missing data either by removing it or replacing it with mean, median or mode or forward /backward values in previous chapters. But what about if your dataset has many zero values? Here you will learn how to use Sklearn api to handle such values. **Sklearn.preprocessing** has **Imputer** package and Imputer has **transform()** function which we can use in following way to fill zero/ missing values in the Pima Indians Diabetes Dataset that involves predicting the onset of diabetes within 5 years in Pima Indians given medical details-

```
df = pd.read_csv('E:/pg/bpb/BPB-Publications/Datasets/pimaindians-diabetes.data.csv',header = None)
df.info()
```

```
<class 'pandas.core.frame.DataFrame'>
RangeIndex: 768 entries, 0 to 767
Data columns (total 9 columns):
0    768 non-null int64
1    768 non-null int64
2    768 non-null int64
3    768 non-null int64
4    768 non-null int64
5    768 non-null float64
6    768 non-null float64
7    768 non-null int64
8    768 non-null int64
dtypes: float64(2), int64(7)
```

Fig 13.38

Once you check the count of the dataset you will find that there are no any missing values here-

```
missing_values_count = df.isnull().sum()
print("count of missing values:\n", missing_values_count)
```

```
count of missing values:
 0    0
 1    0
 2    0
 3    0
 4    0
 5    0
 6    0
 7    0
 8    0
```

Fig 13.39

But you should not blindly believe above output, you must perform statistical analysis like below-

```
df.describe()
```

	0	1	2	3	4	5	6	7	8
count	768.000000	768.000000	768.000000	768.000000	768.000000	768.000000	768.000000	768.000000	768.000000
mean	3.845052	120.894531	69.105469	20.536458	79.799479	31.992578	0.471876	33.240885	0.348958
std	3.369578	31.972618	19.355807	15.952218	115.244002	7.884160	0.331329	11.760232	0.476951
min	0.000000	0.000000	0.000000	0.000000	0.000000	0.000000	0.078000	21.000000	0.000000
25%	1.000000	99.000000	62.000000	0.000000	0.000000	27.300000	0.243750	24.000000	0.000000
50%	3.000000	117.000000	72.000000	23.000000	30.500000	32.000000	0.372500	29.000000	0.000000
75%	6.000000	140.250000	80.000000	32.000000	127.250000	36.600000	0.626250	41.000000	1.000000
max	17.000000	199.000000	122.000000	99.000000	846.000000	67.100000	2.420000	81.000000	1.000000

Fig 13.40

Do compare the min value with the columns of the dataframe. Since this is a diabatic data, many attributes of this data cannot be zero for example blood pressure or Body mass index. Hence, you must replace such zero values with logical ones. This observation is very important, and you must review carefully, your data and the problem.

Let's first replace zeros of some columns with actual missing value- NaN and then we will handle NaN-

```
# mark some columns zero values as missing or NaN
import numpy as np
df[[1,2,3,4,5]] = df[[1,2,3,4,5]].replace(0, np.NaN)
print(df.isnull().sum())
```

```
0      0
1      5
2     35
3    227
4    374
5     11
6      0
7      0
8      0
```

Fig 13.41

As you already know that missing values in a dataset can cause errors with some machine learning algorithms like Linear Discriminant Analysis or LDA algorithm, let's impute these values and then we will apply LDA-

```
from sklearn.preprocessing import Imputer
# fill missing values with mean column values
values = df.values
imputer = Imputer()
transformed_values = imputer.fit_transform(values)
# count the number of NaN values in each column
print(np.isnan(transformed_values).sum())
```

```
0
```

Fig 13.42

Now you can easily apply LDA algorithm on imputed data-

```
# evaluate an LDA model on the dataset using k-fold cross validation
model = LinearDiscriminantAnalysis()
kfold = KFold(n_splits=3, random_state=7)
result = cross_val_score(model, transformed_values, y, cv=kfold, scoring='accuracy')
print(result.mean())
```

```
0.7669270833333334
```

Fig 13.43

That's it! It quite easy to impute zero values, right. Let's see another example of Impute with pipeline with another algorithm known as Support Vector Machine Classifier-

```
from sklearn.preprocessing import Imputer
from sklearn.svm import SVC
imp = Imputer(missing_values='NaN', strategy='most_frequent', axis=0)

# Instantiate the SVC classifier: clf
clf = SVC()

# Setup the pipeline with the required steps: steps
steps = [('imputation', imp),
         ('SVM', clf)]
```

Fig 13.44

Here **'steps' variable is a list of tuples where the first tuple consists of the imputation step and the second consists of the classifier**. This is **pipeline** concept for imputing. After setting it up you can use it for classification like below-

```
from sklearn.preprocessing import Imputer
from sklearn.pipeline import Pipeline
from sklearn.svm import SVC
from sklearn.model_selection import train_test_split
from sklearn.metrics import classification_report

# Setup the pipeline steps: steps
steps = [('imputation', Imputer(missing_values='NaN', strategy='most_frequent', axis=0)),
         ('SVM', SVC())]

# Create the pipeline: pipeline
pipeline = Pipeline(steps)

# Create training and test sets
X_train, X_test, y_train, y_test = train_test_split(X, y, test_size=0.3, random_state=42)

# Fit the pipeline to the train set
pipeline.fit(X_train, y_train)

# Predict the labels of the test set
y_pred = pipeline.predict(X_test)

# Compute metrics
print(classification_report(y_test, y_pred))
```

Fig 13.45

	precision	recall	f1-score	support
0.0	0.65	1.00	0.79	151
1.0	0.00	0.00	0.00	80
avg / total	0.43	0.65	0.52	231

Fig 13.46

See, how easy is to handle such data with pipeline!

Conclusion

You have now learnt fundamentals as well as some advanced technique of Supervised Machine Learning algorithms. You have also solved a real world supervised problem. But there is so much to explore and learn in this field. That can be only done if you try different approaches and algorithms by your own so try as much as you can till then go chase your dreams, have an awesome day, make every second count and see you later in next chapter of this book where you will learn about Unsupervised Machine Learning.

CHAPTER 14

Unsupervised Machine Learning

The main feature of unsupervised learning algorithms, when compared to classification and regression methods, is that input data are unlabelled (i.e. no labels or classes given) and the algorithm learns the structure of the data without any assistance. This is the world of unsupervised learning - you are not guiding, or supervising, the pattern discovery by some prediction task, but instead uncovering hidden structure from unlabelled data. Unsupervised learning encompasses a variety of techniques in machine learning, from clustering to dimension reduction to matrix factorization. In this chapter, you will learn the fundamentals of unsupervised learning and implement the essential algorithms using scikit-learn and scipy.

Structure

- Why Unsupervised Learning?
- Unsupervised Learning Techniques
- Kmeans Clustering
- Principal Component Analysis (PCA)
- Case Study
- Validation of Unsupervised Ml

Objective

After studying and practicing this chapter you will be familiar with Unsupervised learning and you will be able to cluster, transform, visualize, and extract insights from unlabeled datasets.

Why Unsupervised Learning?

In the unsupervised learning inputs (training data) are unlabelled and we have no output results to validate efficiency of the learning process. However, once the training process is complete, we are able to label our data. The described process is similar to how humans acquire knowledge through experience. Even though the machine works in the dark, it somehow manages to extract features and patterns from the probability distributions of data (e.g images, texts) which are fed to it.

However, why would we even need unsupervised learning if we have so many efficient and tested supervised ML methods around? There are several reasons for the growing popularity of unsupervised methods:

- Sometimes we don't know in advance to which class/type our data belongs. For example, in consumer segmentation problem, we don't know what similarities consumers really share and how they differ as groups.

- Structured data can be expensive and not always available. Supervised learning requires properly labelled, cleaned up, and regularized data. Even worse, many AI start-ups might not have access to structured data at all. To acquire data needed to train their AI systems, start-ups have to license it from commercial datasets specializing in data collection for supervised learning.

- Supervised methods are a good fit for classification and prediction, but not as suitable for content generation. Unsupervised learning is an excellent option when we want to generate content (e.g. images, videos) similar to the original training data.

- Now, thanks to the cheaper cloud-based computing power and new deep learning techniques, we may efficiently use unsupervised learning in combination with neural networks trained on powerful GPUs.

Unsupervised Learning Techniques

Some applications of unsupervised machine learning techniques include:

1. **Clustering** allows you to automatically split the dataset into groups according to similarity. Often, however, cluster analysis overestimates the similarity between groups and doesn't treat data points as individuals. For this reason, cluster analysis is a poor choice for applications like customer segmentation and targeting.

2. **Anomaly detection** can automatically discover unusual data points in your dataset. This is useful in pinpointing fraudulent transactions, discovering faulty pieces of hardware, or identifying an outlier caused by a human error during data entry.

3. **Association mining** identifies sets of items that frequently occur together in your dataset. Retailers often use it for **basket analysis**, because it allows analysts to discover goods often purchased at the same time and develop more effective marketing and merchandising strategies.

4. **Latent variable models** are commonly used for data pre-processing, such as reducing the number of features in a dataset (dimensionality reduction) or decomposing the dataset into multiple components.

The two unsupervised learning techniques we will explore are **clustering** the data into groups by similarity and **reducing dimensionality** to compress the data while maintaining its structure and usefulness-

Clustering

"**Clustering**" is the process of grouping similar entities together. The goal of this unsupervised machine learning technique is to find similarities in the data point and group similar data points together. Grouping similar entities together give us insight into underlying patterns of different groups. For example, you can identify different groups/segments of customers and market each group in a different way to maximize the revenue. Clustering is also used to reduces the dimensionality of the data when you are dealing with a copious number of variables. Most popular and widely used clustering algorithms are **K-mean Clustering, Hierarchical Clustering.**

K-mean Clustering

In **K-mean Clustering, K means the input which is how many clusters you want to find**. In this algorithm, you place K centroids in random locations in your space then using the Euclidean distance between data points and centroids, you assign each data point to the cluster which is close to it then recalculate the cluster centres as a mean of data points assigned to it and then again repeat above steps until no further changes occur. In mathematics, the **Euclidean distance** or **Euclidean metric** is the "ordinary" **straight-line distance between two points in Euclidean space**. With this distance, Euclidean space becomes a metric space and the **centroids** are like the heart of the cluster, **they capture the points closest to them and add them to the cluster**.

You might be thinking that **how do I decide the value of K in the first step?** One of the methods is called **"Elbow" method**- can be used to decide an optimal number of clusters. The idea is to run K-mean clustering on a range of K values and plot the "percentage of variance explained" on the Y-axis and "K" on X-axis. For example, in picture shown below you will notice that as we add more clusters after 3 it doesn't give much better modelling on the data. The first cluster adds much information, but at some point, the marginal gain will start dropping-

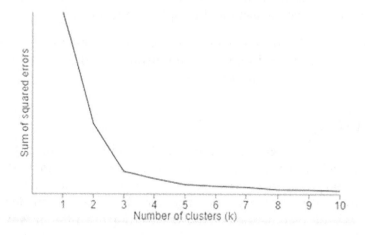

Fig 14.1

See the above plot- it almost looks like a human elbow structure. Let's see how to apply k-means on an actual dataset and evaluate a cluster. To understand and practice the code examples, kindly load the Unsupervised Learning notebook provided inside the code Bundle.

In this exercise you will get the poker training/testing dataset from a url and then perform k-means with Elbow method-

```
# read training and test data from the url link and save the file to your working directory
url = "http://archive.ics.uci.edu/ml/machine-learning-databases/poker/poker-hand-training-true.data"

urllib.request.urlretrieve(url, "E:/pg/bpb/BPB-Publications/Datasets/unsupervised/poker_train.csv")

url2 = "http://archive.ics.uci.edu/ml/machine-learning-databases/poker/poker-hand-testing.data"

urllib.request.urlretrieve(url2, "E:/pg/bpb/BPB-Publications/Datasets/unsupervised/poker_test.csv")

# read the data in and add column names
data_train = pd.read_csv("E:/pg/bpb/BPB-Publications/Datasets/unsupervised/poker_train.csv", header=None,
                names=['S1', 'C1', 'S2', 'C2', 'S3', 'C3','S4', 'C4', 'S5', 'C5', 'CLASS'])

data_test = pd.read_csv("E:/pg/bpb/BPB-Publications/Datasets/unsupervised/poker_test.csv", header=None,
                names=['S1', 'C1', 'S2', 'C2', 'S3', 'C3','S4', 'C4', 'S5', 'C5', 'CLASS'])
```

Fig 14.2

In above code cell, first we are reading the train and test data from a url using urllib.request.urlretrieve() function which takes url as one required argument. This function is the easiest way to store the content of a page in a variable so we are doing the same by storing the train and test data in url and url2 variables.

Here we have saved the training and test csv files in our local directory. From there we are reading and storing them in Pandas Dataframe for further processing. Next, we subset the train dataset-

```
# subset clustering variables
cluster=data_train[['S1', 'C1', 'S2', 'C2', 'S3', 'C3','S4', 'C4', 'S5', 'C5']]
```

Fig 14.3

Next, in order to cluster the data effectively, you'll need to **standardize** these features first. For equally contributing the variables, we will scale them using **preprocessing. scale()** function as below-

```
from sklearn import preprocessing
# standardize clustering variables to have mean=0 and sd=1 so that card suit and
# rank are on the same scale as to have the variables equally contribute to the analysis
clustervar = cluster.copy() # create a copy
clustervar['S1']=preprocessing.scale(clustervar['S1'].astype('float64'))
clustervar['C1']=preprocessing.scale(clustervar['C1'].astype('float64'))
clustervar['S2']=preprocessing.scale(clustervar['S2'].astype('float64'))
clustervar['C2']=preprocessing.scale(clustervar['C2'].astype('float64'))
clustervar['S3']=preprocessing.scale(clustervar['S3'].astype('float64'))
clustervar['C3']=preprocessing.scale(clustervar['C3'].astype('float64'))
clustervar['S4']=preprocessing.scale(clustervar['S4'].astype('float64'))
clustervar['C4']=preprocessing.scale(clustervar['C4'].astype('float64'))
clustervar['S5']=preprocessing.scale(clustervar['S5'].astype('float64'))
clustervar['C5']=preprocessing.scale(clustervar['C5'].astype('float64'))

# The data has been already split data into train and test sets
clus_train = clustervar
```

Fig 14.4

preprocessing.scale() function standardizes a dataset along any axis [Center to the mean and component wise scale to unit variance].

Next, for **computing** distance between each pair of the two collections of inputs you don't need to do any calculation. Using **scipy.spatial.distance's cdist** library we can do that. After calculating the distance, we will loop through each cluster and fit the model to the train set and then we will generate the predicted cluster assignment and append the mean distance by taking the sum divided by the shape as below-

```
from sklearn.cluster import KMeans

# k-means cluster analysis for 1-10 clusters due to the 10 possible class outcomes for poker hands
from scipy.spatial.distance import cdist
clusters=range(1,20)
meandist=[]

# loop through each cluster and fit the model to the train set
# generate the predicted cluster assingment and append the mean distance my taking the sum divided
for k in clusters:
    model=KMeans(n_clusters=k)
    model.fit(clus_train)
    clusassign=model.predict(clus_train)
    meandist.append(sum(np.min(cdist(clus_train, model.cluster_centers_, 'euclidean'), axis=1))
    / clus_train.shape[0])

"""
Plot average distance from observations from the cluster centroid
to use the Elbow Method to identify number of clusters to choose
"""
plt.plot(clusters, meandist)
plt.xlabel('Number of clusters')
plt.ylabel('Average distance')
plt.title('Selecting k with the Elbow Method') # pick the fewest number of clusters that reduces th
```

```
Text(0.5,1,'Selecting k with the Elbow Method')
```

Fig 14.5

Once you run the above cell you will see as shown in below output plot that 3 (see x-axis in the plot) will be right choice of k as after this you will not get better model. Basically, number of clusters = the x-axis value of the point that is the corner of the "elbow" (the plot looks often looks like an elbow)-

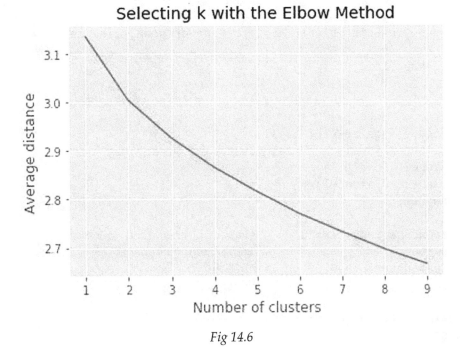

Fig 14.6

Hierarchical Clustering

Unlike K-mean clustering **Hierarchical clustering starts by assigning all data points as their own cluster**. As the name suggests it builds the hierarchy and in the next step, it combines the two nearest data point and merges it together to one cluster. Following are the steps to implement this technique-

1. Start with N clusters, assign each data point to its own cluster.

2. Find closest pair of clusters using Euclidean distance and merge them in to single cluster.

3. Calculate distance between two nearest clusters and combine until all items are clustered in to a single cluster.

In a nutshell, you can decide the optimal number of clusters by noticing which vertical lines can be cut by horizontal line without intersecting a cluster and covers the maximum distance. Let's see how you can use Hierarchical clustering on Iris dataset-

```
# calculate full dendrogram
from scipy.cluster.hierarchy import dendrogram, linkage
# generate the linkage matrix
Z = linkage(iris, 'ward')
# set cut-off to 50
max_d = 7.08                    # max_d as in max_distance

plt.figure(figsize=(25, 10))
plt.title('Iris Hierarchical Clustering Dendrogram')
plt.xlabel('Species')
plt.ylabel('distance')
dendrogram(
    Z,
    truncate_mode='lastp',   # show only the last p merged clusters
    p=150,                   # Try changing values of p
    leaf_rotation=90.,       # rotates the x axis labels
    leaf_font_size=8.,       # font size for the x axis labels
)
plt.axhline(y=max_d, c='k')
plt.show()
```

Fig 14.7

Here we are using **linkage() function** with **'ward'** argument **to obtain a hierarchical clustering of the iris samples,** and **dendrogram() to visualize the result**. Here 'ward' is a linkage method which minimizes the variant between the clusters. Once you run the above cell, it will display a plot like below-

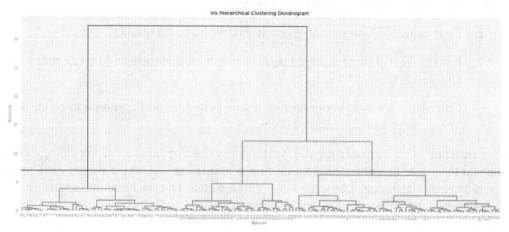

Fig 14.8

See, Dendrograms are a great way to illustrate the arrangement of the clusters produced by hierarchical clustering! In our example also you can see a black straight horizontal line between the clusters. This line is currently crossing the 3 clusters so number of clusters will be three in this case.

Remember, Hierarchical clustering can't handle big data well but K Means clustering can. In K Means clustering, as we start with an arbitrary choice of clusters, the results generated by running the algorithm multiple times might differ while results are reproducible in Hierarchical clustering.

t-SNE

Another clustering technique often used in visualization is **t-SNE** or **t-distributed stochastic neighbor embedding.** It basically maps higher dimension space to 2D or 3D space so that we can visualize a higher dimensional data. Basically, it's a dimensionality reduction technique.

In case of the Iris dataset which has four measurements, its samples are 4D. For this dataset t-SNE technique can map samples to 2D for easy visualization. In sklearn api you can use t-SNE from sklearn.ma library and then can use it's **fit_teransform()** method for fitting the model and transforming the data simultaneously. But it has one limit- you cannot extend it to include new samples, you have to start over each time. One important parameter of t-SNE is the **learning rate** which you choose according to the dataset but a value between 50-200 is often a fine choice. One strange behaviour of this technique is that every time you apply t-SNE, you will get different visualization result on the same dataset so don't be confused with this behaviour. **In fact, it is perfectly fine to run t-SNE a number of times (with the same data and parameters), and to select the visualization with the lowest value of the objective function as your final visualization.** One drawback of using this technique is it is memory consuming technique so be careful to apply on a simple computer otherwise you may get memory errors.

Let's see how you can use sklearn api to apply t-SNE in MNIST digit dataset. You can load this dataset from the sklearn.datasets api using fetch_mldata function as shown in below code cell

```
from sklearn.datasets import fetch_mldata
mnist = fetch_mldata("MNIST original")
X = mnist.data / 255.0
y = mnist.target
print(X.shape, y.shape)

(70000, 784) (70000,)
```

Fig 14.9

If you face any issue while loading the data from sklearn api, you can then download the dataset from any other resources like google or github or from the download link provided in the bookNext, import the basic libraries- numpy and pandas and then convert the above training data (X) into a pandas dataframe. From this newly created dataframe extract the target variable as shown in below code cell-

```
#convert the matrix and vector to a Pandas DataFrame
feat_cols = [ 'pixel'+str(i) for i in range(X.shape[1]) ]

df = pd.DataFrame(X,columns=feat_cols)
df['label'] = y
df['label'] = df['label'].apply(lambda i: str(i))

X, y = None, None

print('Size of the dataframe: {}'.format(df.shape))
```

```
Size of the dataframe: (70000, 785)
```

Fig 14.10

Next, we will take a random subset of the digits. The randomization is important as the dataset is sorted by its label (i.e., the first seven thousand or so are zeros, etc.). To ensure randomization we'll create a random permutation of the number 0 to 69,999 which allows us later to select the first five or ten thousand for our calculations and visualizations-

```
rndperm = np.random.permutation(df.shape[0])
```

Fig 14.11

We now have our dataframe and our randomization vector. Let's first check what these numbers actually look like. To do this we'll generate 30 plots of randomly selected images. Don't forget to import the matplotlib.pyplot as plt before running below code

```
plt.gray()
fig = plt.figure( figsize=(16,7) )
for i in range(0,30):
    ax = fig.add_subplot(3,10,i+1, title='Digit: ' + str(df.loc[rndperm[i],'label']) )
    ax.matshow(df.loc[rndperm[i],feat_cols].values.reshape((28,28)).astype(float))
plt.show()
```

Fig 14.12

The images are 28-by-28 pixel images and therefore have a total of 784 'dimensions', each holding the value of one specific pixel. What we can do is reduce the number of dimensions drastically whilst trying to retain as much of the 'variation' in the information as possible.

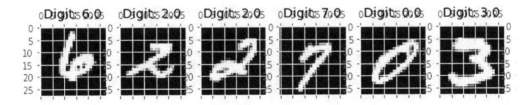

Fig 14.13

In case if you are not seeing actual image as output or seeing object as output; you need to put a semicolon after the plt.show() line i.e. plt.show();

To make sure we don't burden our machine in terms of memory and power/time we will only use the first 7,000 samples to run the algorithm on.

```
import time
from sklearn.manifold import TSNE

n_sne = 7000

time_start = time.time()
tsne = TSNE(n_components=2, verbose=1, perplexity=40, n_iter=300)
tsne_results = tsne.fit_transform(df.loc[rndperm[:n_sne],feat_cols].values)

print('t-SNE done! Time elapsed: {} seconds'.format(time.time()-time_start))
```

Fig 14.14

In above code cell we have taken the 7000 samples as a variable n_sne and then in the TSNE() function we are passing 'Dimension of the embedded space' as n_ components, 'Verbosity level' as verbose, 'Number of nearest neighbors' as perplexity and 'Maximum number of iterations for the optimization' as n_iter arguements. The fit_transform() method fits the data into an embedded space and returns that transformed output.

Based on my system configuration output looks like blow-

```
[t-SNE] Computing 121 nearest neighbors...
[t-SNE] Indexed 7000 samples in 0.329s...
[t-SNE] Computed neighbors for 7000 samples in 59.903s...
[t-SNE] Computed conditional probabilities for sample 1000 / 7000
[t-SNE] Computed conditional probabilities for sample 2000 / 7000
[t-SNE] Computed conditional probabilities for sample 3000 / 7000
[t-SNE] Computed conditional probabilities for sample 4000 / 7000
[t-SNE] Computed conditional probabilities for sample 5000 / 7000
[t-SNE] Computed conditional probabilities for sample 6000 / 7000
[t-SNE] Computed conditional probabilities for sample 7000 / 7000
[t-SNE] Mean sigma: 2.239101
[t-SNE] KL divergence after 250 iterations with early exaggeration: 83.187843
[t-SNE] Error after 300 iterations: 2.422179
t-SNE done! Time elapsed: 135.07717204093933 seconds
```

Fig 14.15

We can visualize the two dimensions by creating a scatter plot and coloring each sample by its respective label. This time we will use ggplot to visualize our data. To install this package with conda run one of the following in anaconda prompt:

1. conda install -c conda-forge ggplot

2. conda install -c conda-forge/label/gcc7 ggplot

3. conda install -c conda-forge/label/cf201901 ggplot

```
from ggplot import *
df_tsne = df.loc[rndperm[:n_sne],:].copy()
df_tsne['x-tsne'] = tsne_results[:,0]
df_tsne['y-tsne'] = tsne_results[:,1]

tsne_plot = ggplot( df_tsne, aes(x='x-tsne', y='y-tsne', color='label') ) \
        + geom_point(size=70,alpha=0.1) \
        + ggtitle("tSNE dimensions colored by digit")
tsne_plot
```

Fig 14.16

Once you run above code you will see below beautiful plot. In case if you are getting an object instead of plot, you need to run tsne_plot.show(); also after the last line of the above code.

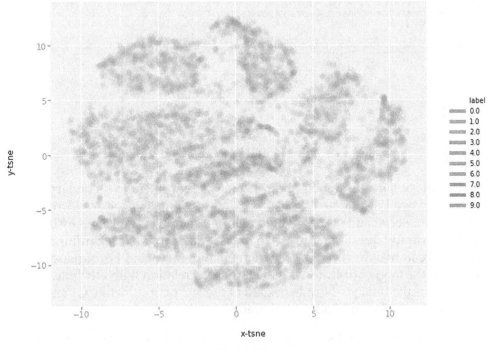

Fig 14.17

We can see that the digits are very clearly clustered in their own little group(See the label colors as each color is denoting a separate color). Same visualization you cannot do without t-SNE if you include higher dimensions.

Principal Component Analysis (PCA)

One of the most common tasks in unsupervised learning is dimensionality reduction. On one hand, dimensionality reduction may help with data visualization (e.g. t-SNA method) while, on the other hand, it may help deal with the multicollinearity of your data and prepare the data for a supervised learning method (e.g. decision trees). Multicollinearity of data is a type of disturbance in the data, and if present in the data the statistical inferences made about the data may not be reliable. Principal Component Analysis or PCA is one of the easiest, most intuitive, and most frequently used methods for dimensionality reduction.

PCA aligns the data with axes which means it rotates data samples to be aligned with axes in such a way that no information is lost. Here you can understand a principal component as direction of variance. Let's see how we can apply PCA on a student details dataset. Don't forget to rerun the required packages like pandas before running below line if you are starting your work

```
student_data_mat  = pd.read_csv("E:/pg/bpb/BPB-Publications/Datasets/unsupervised/PCA/student-mat.csv",delimiter=";")
student_data_por  = pd.read_csv("E:/pg/bpb/BPB-Publications/Datasets/unsupervised/PCA/student-por.csv",delimiter=";")
student_data = pd.merge(student_data_mat,student_data_por,how="outer")
student_data.head()
```

	school	sex	age	address	famsize	Pstatus	Medu	Fedu	Mjob	Fjob	...	famrel	freetime	goout	Dalc	Walc	health	absences	G1	G2	G3
0	GP	F	18	U	GT3	A	4	4	at_home	teacher	...	4	3	4	1	1	3	6	5	6	6
1	GP	F	17	U	GT3	T	1	1	at_home	other	...	5	3	3	1	1	3	4	5	5	6
2	GP	F	15	U	LE3	T	1	1	at_home	other	...	4	3	2	2	3	3	10	7	8	10
3	GP	F	15	U	GT3	T	4	2	health	services	...	3	2	2	1	1	5	2	15	14	15
4	GP	F	16	U	GT3	T	3	3	other	other	...	4	3	2	1	2	5	4	6	10	10

5 rows × 33 columns

Fig 14.18

This dataset contains the details about student achievement in secondary education of two Portuguese schools. The data attributes include student grades, demographic, social and school related features and it was collected by using school reports and questionnaires. Two datasets are provided regarding the performance in two distinct subjects: Mathematics (mat) and Portuguese language (por). Here the target attribute G3 has a strong correlation with attributes G2 and G1. G3 is the final year grade (issued at the 3rd period), while G1 and G2 correspond to the 1st and 2nd period grades.

Here some columns look like categorical variables so let's handle such columns-

```
student_data.isnull().values.any()
```

False

```
col_str = student_data.columns[student_data.dtypes == object]
```

```
from sklearn.preprocessing import LabelEncoder
lenc = LabelEncoder()
student_data[col_str] = student_data[col_str].apply(lenc.fit_transform)
```

Fig 14.19

Let's check the correlation between G1,G2 and G3 columns of the dataset using .corr() function-

```
print(student_data[["G1","G2","G3"]].corr())
```

```
       G1        G2        G3
G1  1.000000  0.858739  0.809142
G2  0.858739  1.000000  0.910743
G3  0.809142  0.910743  1.000000
```

Fig 14.20

From above output cell, you can easily say that G1,G2 and G3 are highly corelated, so we can drop G1 and G2 for further analysis-

```
# Since, G1,G2,G3 have very high correlation, we can drop G1,G2
student_data.drop(axis = 1,labels= ["G1","G2"])
```

Fig 14.21

Next step is to separate target and samples from the dataset and then can apply PCA easily using the **sklearn.decomposition** package. Here our target variable is G3 so we will separate it from the dataset. In below code cell we are putting the target in label variable and rest data in predictors variable. Later we import the PCA library form the sklearn.decomposition api and initialize it using PCA() function. Then we are using .fit() method to train our data, explained_variance_ration() method to get the percentage of variance explained by each of the selected components. Next, we are using numpy' cumsum() method which returns the cumulative sum of the elements along a given axis-

```
label = student_data["G3"].values
predictors = student_data[student_data.columns[:-1]].values
```

```
from sklearn.decomposition import PCA
pca = PCA(n_components=len(student_data.columns)-1)
pca.fit(predictors)
variance_ratio = pca.explained_variance_ratio_
variance_ratio_cum_sum=np.cumsum(np.round(pca.explained_variance_ratio_, decimals=4)*100)
print(variance_ratio_cum_sum)
plt.plot(variance_ratio_cum_sum)
plt.show()
```

Fig 14.22

Here, "**variance**" **means summative variance or multivariate variability or overall variability or total variability**. PCA **replaces** original variables with new variables, called **principal components**, which are orthogonal (i.e. they have zero covariations) and have variances (called **eigenvalues**) in decreasing order. Once you run the above cell, following plot will be displayed-

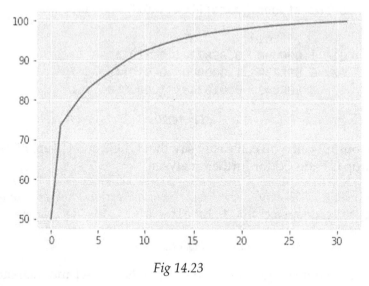

Fig 14.23

In above output, the red line is the regression line, or the set of the predicted values from the model. The variance explained can be understood as the ratio of the vertical spread of the regression line (i.e., from the lowest point on the line to the highest point on the line) to the vertical spread of the data (i.e., from the lowest data point to the highest data point).

Case Study

Until now you must have grasped basic knowledge of regression techniques. It's time to apply your knowledge on a real problem. Here you will work on MNIST computer vison dataset which consists 28 x 28 pixel images of digits. Let's import the train data first-

```
train = pd.read_csv("E:/pg/bpb/BPB-Publications/Datasets/regression/MNIST/train.csv")
print(train.shape)
train.head()
```

(42000, 785)

	label	pixel0	pixel1	pixel2	pixel3	pixel4	pixel5	pixel6	pixel7	pixel8	...	pixel774	pixel775	pixel776
0	1	0	0	0	0	0	0	0	0	0	...	0	0	0
1	0	0	0	0	0	0	0	0	0	0	...	0	0	0

Fig 14.24

The MNIST set consists of 42,000 rows and 785 columns. There 784 columns as well as one extra label column which is essentially a class label to state whether the row-wise contribution to each digit gives a 1 or a 9. Each row component contains a value between one and zero and this describes the intensity of each pixel.

Let's conduct some cleaning of the train data by saving the label feature and then removing it from the dataframe-

```
# save the labels to a Pandas series target
target = train['label']
# Drop the label feature
train = train.drop("label",axis=1)
```

Fig 14.25

Since our dataset consists of a relatively large number of features (columns), it is perfect time to apply Dimensionality Reduction method (PCA). For this it may be informative to observe how the variances look like for the digits in the MNIST dataset. Therefore, to achieve this, let us calculate the eigenvectors and eigenvalues of the covariance matrix as follows:

```
# Standardizing MNIST dataset features by removing the mean and scaling to unit variance
from sklearn.preprocessing import StandardScaler
train_X = train.values
train_X_std = StandardScaler().fit_transform(train_X)

# Calculating Eigenvectors and Eigenvalues of Covariance matrix
covariance_matrix = np.cov(train_X_std.T)
eigen_values, eigen_vectors = np.linalg.eig(covariance_matrix)

# Creating a list of (eigenvalue, eigenvector)
eigen_pairs = [ (np.abs(eigen_values[i]),eigen_vectors[:,i]) for i in range(len(eigen_values))]

# Sorting the eigenvalue, eigenvector pair from high to low
eigen_pairs.sort(key = lambda x: x[0], reverse= True)

# Calculating Individual and Cumulative explained variance
total_eigen_values = sum(eigen_values)
indivisual_exp_var = [(i/total_eigen_values)*100 for i in sorted(eigen_values, reverse=True)]
cumulative_exp_var = np.cumsum(indivisual_exp_var)
```

FIG 14.26

After calculating Individual Explained Variance and Cumulative Explained Variance values, let's use the Plotly visualization package to produce an interactive chart to showcase this. First import required Plotly libraries. If this ibrary is not installed in your notebook, install it using command '**conda install -c plotly plotly**'-

```
import plotly.offline as py
py.init_notebook_mode(connected=True)
from plotly.offline import init_notebook_mode, iplot
import plotly.graph_objs as go
import plotly.tools as tls
import seaborn as sns
```

Fig 14.27

Next, we will plot a simple scatter plot using Plotly. Since these plots are interactive, you can move up and down over it. In below code cell first we will set the scatter plot parameters like name, mode, color for cumulative and individual explained variances then we will append these two scatter plot variables into a subplot using make_subplots() function-

```
cumulative_plot = go.Scatter(
    x=list(range(784)),
    y= cumulative_exp_var,
    mode='lines+markers',
    name="'Cumulative Explained Variance'",
    line=dict(
        shape='spline',
        color = 'limegreen'
    )
)
individual_plot = go.Scatter(
    x=list(range(784)),
    y= indivisual_exp_var,
    mode='lines+markers',
    name="'Individual Explained Variance'",
    line=dict(
        shape='linear',
        color = 'black'
    )
)
fig = tls.make_subplots(insets=[{'cell': (1,1), 'l': 0.7, 'b': 0.5}],
                        print_grid=True)

fig.append_trace(cumulative_plot, 1, 1)
fig.append_trace(individual_plot,1,1)
fig.layout.title = 'Explained Variance plots - Full and Zoomed-in'
fig.layout.xaxis = dict(range=[0, 50], title = 'Feature columns')
fig.layout.yaxis = dict(range=[0, 40], title = 'Explained Variance')
iplot(fig)
```

Fig 14.28

Once you run the above cell, you will get following plot-

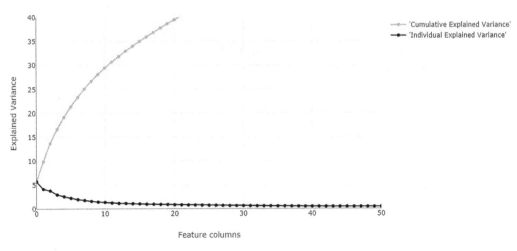

Fig 14.29

As we can see, out of our 784 features or columns approximately 90% of the Explained Variance can be described by using just over 200 over features. So, if you want to implement a PCA on this, extracting the top 200 features would be a very logical choice as they already account for the majority of the data.

Since the PCA method seeks to obtain the optimal directions (or eigenvectors) that captures the most variance (spreads out the data points the most). Therefore, it may be informative to visualize these directions and their associated eigenvalues. For speed, I will invoke PCA to only extract the top 30 eigenvalues (using Sklearn's **.components_ call**) from the digit dataset and visually compare the top 5 eigenvalues to some of the other smaller ones to see if we can glean any insights. Import the PCA package form sklearn.decomposition api if you are restarting your work and thenfollow as below:

```
# Invoke SKLearn's PCA method
n_components = 30
pca = PCA(n_components=n_components).fit(train.values)
eigenvalues = pca.components_.reshape(n_components, 28, 28)
# Extracting the PCA components ( eignevalues )
eigenvalues = pca.components_
```

Fig 14.30

```
n_row = 4
n_col = 7
# Plot the first 8 eignenvalues
plt.figure(figsize=(13,12))
for i in list(range(n_row * n_col)):
    offset =0
    plt.subplot(n_row, n_col, i + 1)
    plt.imshow(eigenvalues[i].reshape(28,28), cmap='jet')
    title_text = 'Eigenvalue ' + str(i + 1)
    plt.title(title_text, size=6.5)
    plt.xticks(())
    plt.yticks(())
plt.show()
```

Fig 14.31

Above cell will draw following looks like plots-

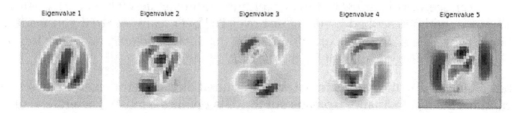

Fig 14.32

The subplots above portray the top 5 optimal directions or principal component axes that the PCA method has decided to generate for our digit dataset. If you compare the first component "Eigenvalue 1" to the 25th component "Eigenvalue 5", it is obvious that more complicated directions or components are being generated in the search to maximize variance in the new feature subspace.

Now using the Sklearn toolkit, we implement the Principal Component Analysis algorithm as follows:

```
# Delete our earlier created X object
del X
# Taking only the first N rows to speed things up
X= train[:6000].values
del train
# Standardising the values
X_std = StandardScaler().fit_transform(X)

# Call the PCA method with 5 components.
pca = PCA(n_components=5)
pca.fit(X_std)
X_5d = pca.transform(X_std)

# For cluster coloring in our Plotly plots, remember to also restrict the target values
Target = target[:6000]
```

Fig 14.33

In above code we are first normalising the data (actually no need to do so for this data set as they are all 1's and 0's) using Sklearn's convenient StandardScaler() call. Next, we invoke Sklearn's inbuilt PCA function by providing into its argument n_components, the number of components/dimensions we would like to project the data on. As a general practice for selecting the number of components or dimensions always look at the proportion of cumulative variance and the individual variance which you have already done earlier in this chapter.

Finally, we'll call both fit and transform methods which fits the PCA model with the standardised digit data set and then does a transformation by applying the dimensionality reduction on the data.

Imagine just for a moment, if we were not provided with the class labels to this digit set because PCA is an unsupervised method. How will we be able to separate out our data points in the new feature space? We can apply a clustering algorithm on our new PCA projection data and hopefully arrive at distinct clusters which would tell us something about the underlying class separation in the data.

To start off, we set up a KMeans clustering method with Sklearn's KMeans call and use the fit_predict method to compute cluster centers and predict cluster indices for the first and second PCA projections (to see if we can observe any appreciable clusters)-

```
from sklearn.cluster import KMeans
# Set a KMeans clustering with 9 components
kmeans = KMeans(n_clusters=9)
# Compute cluster centers and predict cluster indices
X_clustered = kmeans.fit_predict(X_5d)

trace_Kmeans = go.Scatter(x=X_5d[:, 0], y= X_5d[:, 1], mode="markers",
                    showlegend=False,
                    marker=dict(
                            size=8,
                            color = X_clustered,
                            colorscale = 'Portland',
                            showscale=False,
                            line = dict(
            width = 2,
            color = 'rgb(255, 255, 255)'
        )
                        ))
```

Fig 14.34

```
layout = go.Layout(
    title= 'KMeans Clustering',
    hovermode= 'closest',
    xaxis= dict(
          title= 'First Principal Component',
          ticklen= 5,
          zeroline= False,
          gridwidth= 2,
    ),
    yaxis=dict(
          title= 'Second Principal Component',
          ticklen= 5,
          gridwidth= 2,
    ),
    showlegend= True
)
data = [trace_Kmeans]
fig1 = dict(data=data, layout= layout)
# fig1.append_trace(contour_list)
py.iplot(fig1, filename="svm")
```

Fig 14.35

Output of above input looks like below-

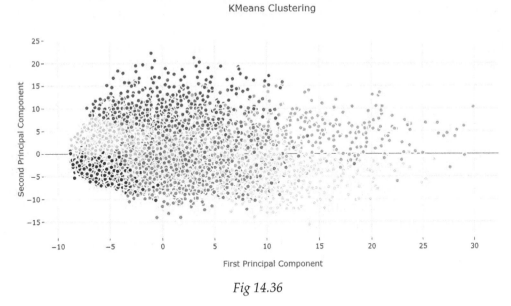

Fig 14.36

Visually, the clusters generated by the K-Means algorithm appear to provide a clearer demarcation amongst clusters as compared to naively adding in class labels into our PCA projections. This should come as no surprise as PCA is meant to be an unsupervised method and therefore not optimised for separating different class labels.

Validation of Unsupervised Ml

Validation of a unsupervised ML depends on which class of unsupervised algorithms you are referring to.

For example, dimensionality reduction techniques are generally evaluated by **computing the reconstruction error**. You can do this using similar techniques with respect to supervised algorithms, e.g. **by applying a k-fold cross validation** procedure.

Clustering algorithms are more difficult to evaluate. Internal metrics use only information on the computed clusters to evaluate if clusters are compact and well-separated. Also, you can have external metrics that perform a statistical testing on the structure of your data.

Density estimation is also rather difficult to evaluate, but there are a wide range of techniques which are mostly used for model tuning, e.g. **cross-validation procedures**.

In addition, unsupervised strategies are sometimes used in the context of a more complex workflow, in which an extrinsic performance function can be defined. For example, if clustering is used to create meaningful classes (e.g. clustering documents), it is possible to create an external dataset by hand-labelling and test the accuracy (the so-called gold standard). Similarly, if dimensionality reduction is used as a pre-processing step in a supervised learning procedure, the accuracy of the latter can be used as a proxy performance measure for the dimensionality reduction technique.

Conclusion

This chapter has taught you the basic concepts of Unsupervised learning along with practical use cases of dimensionality reduction techniques. It is strongly recommended you apply learnings from this chapter as well as other supervised dimensionality reduction technique- LDA and compare the results with each other. As always said practice more and more on different datasets and you will find new insights in every practice. In the next chapter you will learn how to handle time series data

CHAPTER 15

Handling Time-Series Data

In previous chapters you have learnt how to solve supervised and unsupervised machine learning problems. In this chapter you will gain knowledge to understand and work with time-series data. Whether it is analysing business trends, forecasting company revenue or exploring customer behaviour, every data scientist is likely to encounter time series data at some point during their work. Time series is a series of data points indexed (or listed or graphed) in time order. Therefore, the data is organized by relatively deterministic timestamps, and may, compared to random sample data, contain additional information that we can extract.

Structure

- Why Time-Series is important?
- How to handle Date and Time?
- Transforming a Time Series Data
- Manipulating a Time Series Data
- Comparing Time Series Growth Rates
- How to change Time Series Frequency?
- Conclusion

Objective

After studying this chapter, you will be able to manipulate and visualize the time-series data in order to extract meaningful statistics and other characteristics of the data.

Why Time-Series is important?

Since Time-Series is a collection of data points collected at constant time intervals; they are analysed to determine the long-term trend. Time series forecasting is the use of a model to predict future values based on previously observed values. That's in business scenarios like predicting stock price or predicting the weather conditions for tomorrow, time-series has significant role. In your day to day job you will cine across situations with time series-connected tasks. For example, think about the following frequent question a person may think daily—What will happen with our metrics in the next day/week/month? How many people will install the app? How much time will a user spend online? How many actions users will do? Analysing such kind of data can reveal things that at first where not clear, such as unexpected trends, correlations and forecast trends in the future bringing a competitive advantage to anyone who uses it. For these reasons Time-Series can be applied to a wide range of fields.

How to handle Date and Time?

Pandas has dedicated libraries for handling Time Series objects, particularly the **datetime64[ns]** class which stores time information and allows us to perform some operations really fast. Here 'ns' means nano-seconds. Besides Pandas, you will need **statsmodels** library that has tons of statistical modelling functions, including time series. You can install the statsmodels by running following command in anaconda prompt.

conda install -c anaconda statsmodels

When you load the data in a Pandas Dataframe, any column can contain date for time information, but it is most important as Dataframe index because it converts entire dataframe into a Time Series. The complete examples of this chapter is in Time Series Data.ipynb as a notebook. Let's understand first Pandas capability of handling Time Series data by importing basic libraries-

```
import pandas as pd
from datetime import datetime # for manually creating dates
```

Fig 15.1

Now we will create a pandas dataframe and will check its datatype as below-

```
# creating pandas timestamp
time_stamp = pd.Timestamp(datetime(2019,1,1))

# using a date string as datetime object
pd.Timestamp(datetime(2019,1,1)) == time_stamp
```

```
True
```

```
time_stamp
```

```
Timestamp('2019-01-01 00:00:00')
```

Fig 15.2

See the above cells, here the type of our time_stamp variable is 'Timestamp' and a default time with midnight value is added and date string also generates the same result which means you can use date as string also. Pandas Timestamp has various attributes like year, month, day, weekday_name etc to store time specific information which you can access as below-

```
time_stamp.year
```

```
2019
```

```
time_stamp.month
```

```
1
```

```
time_stamp.day
```

```
1
```

Fig 15.3

Pandas has also a data type for handling time periods. The **Period** object always has a frequency with month as default. It also has a method to convert between frequencies as well as you can convert period object to back in it's timestamp format. You can also convert a Timestamp object to period and vice versa. What to say more! You can even perform basic date arithmetic operations. Let' understand how you can practically implement this-

```
period = pd.Period('2019-01')
print("period:: ", period)

#convert period to daily from month
print(period.asfreq('D'))

#convert period to timestamp back
print(period.to_timestamp().to_period('M'))

#basic date arithmetic operation
print(period + 3)
```

```
period::  2019-01
2019-01-31
2019-01
2019-04
```

Fig 15.4

Next, you will create a Time Series with sequences of Dates using the Pandas **date_range()** function. This function returns a fixed frequency DatetimeIndex. You can also convert the index to period index just like Timestamp. See the below cells for each one and notice the data type in output cells-

```
index = pd.date_range(start='2018-1-1', periods=12, freq='M')
index
```

```
DatetimeIndex(['2018-01-31', '2018-02-28', '2018-03-31', '2018-04-30',
               '2018-05-31', '2018-06-30', '2018-07-31', '2018-08-31',
               '2018-09-30', '2018-10-31', '2018-11-30', '2018-12-31'],
              dtype='datetime64[ns]', freq='M')
```

```
index[0]
```

```
Timestamp('2018-01-31 00:00:00', freq='M')
```

```
index.to_period()
```

```
PeriodIndex(['2018-01', '2018-02', '2018-03', '2018-04', '2018-05', '2018-06',
             '2018-07', '2018-08', '2018-09', '2018-10', '2018-11', '2018-12'],
            dtype='period[M]', freq='M')
```

Fig 15.5

Now we can easily create a Time Series (Pandas DatetimeIndex). For example we will create a random 12 rows with 2 columns using **numpy.random.rand()** to match the date time index and then create our first time series as below-

```
pd.DataFrame({'date' : index}).info()
print("=========================================")
import numpy as np
my_data = np.random.rand(12, 2)
pd.DataFrame(data = my_data, index = index).info()
```

```
<class 'pandas.core.frame.DataFrame'>
RangeIndex: 12 entries, 0 to 11
Data columns (total 1 columns):
date     12 non-null datetime64[ns]
dtypes: datetime64[ns](1)
memory usage: 176.0 bytes
=========================================
<class 'pandas.core.frame.DataFrame'>
DatetimeIndex: 12 entries, 2018-01-31 to 2018-12-31
Freq: M
Data columns (total 2 columns):
0     12 non-null float64
1     12 non-null float64
dtypes: float64(2)
memory usage: 608.0 bytes
```

Fig 15.6

In above output cells you can see that each date in the resulting pd.DatetimeIndex is a pd.Timestamp and since this Timestamp has various attributes; you can easily access and obtain information about the date. In the following example we will create a week of data, iterate over the result, and obtain the dayofweek and weekday_name for each date-

```
# Create the range of dates here
seven_days = pd.date_range('2019-1-1', periods=7)

# Iterate over the dates and print the number and name of the weekday
for day in seven_days:
    print(day.dayofweek, day.weekday_name)
```

```
1 Tuesday
2 Wednesday
3 Thursday
4 Friday
5 Saturday
6 Sunday
0 Monday
```

Fig 15.7

Above mentioned examples will help you to handle and manipulate Time Series data with statsmodel library very easily. Next, you will learn how to transform a Time Series data.

Transforming a Time Series Data

While analysing the Time Series data it is common to transform your data into a better one. For example, your date column is in object form and you will need to parse this string object and then convert it to datetime64 data type or you may need to generate new data from existing Time Series data. That's why it is important to know all these transformations. Let's understand the importance of transformation by working on Google's stock price data which you can download from the download link provided at the start of the book-

```
google_df = pd.read_csv("E:/pg/bpb/BPB-Publications/Datasets/timeseries/stock_data/google.csv")
google_df.head()
```

	Date	Close
0	2014-01-02	556.00
1	2014-01-03	551.95
2	2014-01-04	NaN
3	2014-01-05	NaN
4	2014-01-06	558.10

Fig 15.8

The Date column looks fine at first look, but when you check it's data type, it's a string-

```
google_df.info()

<class 'pandas.core.frame.DataFrame'>
RangeIndex: 1094 entries, 0 to 1093
Data columns (total 2 columns):
Date     1094 non-null object
Close     756 non-null float64
dtypes: float64(1), object(1)
memory usage: 17.2+ KB
```

Fig 15.9

Since many machine learning algorithms don't accept string input, you must convert Data column data type to correct data type. You can convert a string data type to dateTime64[ns] using Pandas as shown below-

```
google_df.Date = pd.to_datetime(google_df.Date)
google_df.info()
```

```
<class 'pandas.core.frame.DataFrame'>
RangeIndex: 1094 entries, 0 to 1093
Data columns (total 2 columns):
Date     1094 non-null datetime64[ns]
Close    756 non-null float64
dtypes: datetime64[ns](1), float64(1)
```

Fig 15.10

Now our Date column is in correct data type and we can set it as index as below-

```
google_df.set_index('Date', inplace=True)
google_df.info()
```

```
<class 'pandas.core.frame.DataFrame'>
DatetimeIndex: 1094 entries, 2014-01-02 to 2016-12-30
Data columns (total 1 columns):
Close    756 non-null float64
dtypes: float64(1)
```

Fig 15.11

If you get error like keyerror: ['Date'], add 'drop=False' argument in the above code cell. So your new code will be **google_df.set_index('Date', inplace=True, drop=False)**

Here we are setting the Date column as index one and 'inplace=True' means don't create a new copy of DataFrame.

Now since you have corrected the date type, you can easily visualize the stock price data as shown below-

```
import matplotlib.pyplot as plt
%matplotlib inline
google_df.Close.plot(title='Google Stock closing Price')
plt.tight_layout()
plt.show()
```

Fig 15.12

You might have noticed here, there is no frequency in our date time index; The calendar day frequency can be set as shown below-

```
google_df.asfreq('D').info()
```

```
<class 'pandas.core.frame.DataFrame'>
DatetimeIndex: 1094 entries, 2014-01-02 to 2016-12-30
Freq: D
Data columns (total 1 columns):
Close     756 non-null float64
dtypes: float64(1)
```

Fig 15.13

After this transformation let's check the new data because there may be some null values added. So, it's good to check the head of the dataset as shown below-

```
google_df.asfreq('D').head()
```

	Close
Date	
2014-01-02	556.00
2014-01-03	551.95
2014-01-04	NaN
2014-01-05	NaN
2014-01-06	558.10

Fig 15.14

As you can see these new dates has missing values and this is called "**Upsampling**". It means higher frequency implies new dates and so missing values. We will handle this later in this chapter.

Manipulating a Time Series Data

Time Series data manipulation means shifting or lagging values back or forward in time, getting the difference in value for a given time period or computing the percent change over any number of periods. Pandas library has built in methods to achieve all such manipulations.

In the next example we will explore the power of Pandas. We will reload Google stock price data using Pandas DataFrame but with some additional parameters as below-

```
google_df = pd.read_csv("E:/pg/bpb/BPB-Publications/Datasets/timeseries/stock_data/google.csv",
                        parse_dates=['Date'],
                        index_col='Date')
google_df.head()
```

	Close
Date	
2014-01-02	556.00
2014-01-03	551.95
2014-01-04	NaN
2014-01-05	NaN
2014-01-06	558.10

Fig 15.15

In this case, while loading the dataset you will notice the date column is automatically transformed in correct format. Here Pandas does all parsing for you and provide us with properly formatted time series dataset!

Let's understand different methods of Pandas for manipulating our time series data. First we will see **shift()** method which by default shift by 1 period into future as below-

```
google_df['shifted'] = google_df.Close.shift()
google_df.head()
```

Date	Close	shifted
2014-01-02	556.00	NaN
2014-01-03	551.95	556.00
2014-01-04	NaN	551.95
2014-01-05	NaN	NaN
2014-01-06	558.10	NaN

Fig 15.16

Similarly, there is a **lagged()** method which by default shift by 1 period into past. You can try this in your notebook!

You can also calculate one period finance change or financial return using **div()** method and some arithmetic operation on it as below-

```
google_df['change'] = google_df.Close.div(google_df.shifted)
google_df.head()
```

Date	Close	shifted	change
2014-01-02	556.00	NaN	NaN
2014-01-03	551.95	556.00	0.992716
2014-01-04	NaN	551.95	NaN
2014-01-05	NaN	NaN	NaN
2014-01-06	558.10	NaN	NaN

Fig 15.17

```
google_df['return'] = google_df.change.sub(1).mul(100)
google_df.head()
```

Date	Close	shifted	change	return
2014-01-02	556.00	NaN	NaN	NaN
2014-01-03	551.95	556.00	0.992716	-0.728417
2014-01-04	NaN	551.95	NaN	NaN
2014-01-05	NaN	NaN	NaN	NaN
2014-01-06	558.10	NaN	NaN	NaN

Fig 15.18

You can also calculate the difference in value for two adjacent periods using **diff()** method. Try this in your notebook!

Since you are able to use above knowledge to visually compare a stock price series for Google, let us now shift 90 business days into both past and future like below-

```
# Set data frequency to business daily
google = google_df.asfreq('B')

# Create 'lagged' and 'shifted'
google['lagged'] = google.Close.shift(periods=-90)
google['shifted'] = google.Close.shift(periods=90)

# Plot the google price series
google.plot()
plt.show()
```

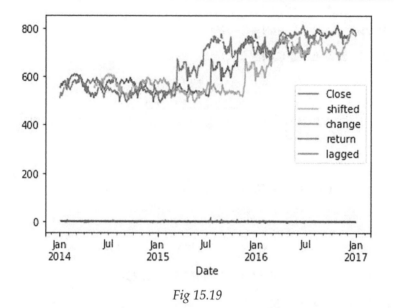

Fig 15.19

Thus, you can visually compare the time series to itself at different points in time.

Comparing Time Series Growth Rates

Comparing Time Series growth rate is a very common task and you will come across it in your time series analysis. Like comparing the stock performance. But this is not a piece of cake because stock price series are very hard to compare at different levels. There is a solution to tackle this problem- normalize price series to start at 100. To achieve this solution, you just need to divide all prices by first in series and multiply by 100. As a result, you will get first value as 1 and all prices relative to starting point. Let's apply this solution in our Google stock price data as below-

```
first_price = google.Close.iloc[0]
# normalize a single series
normalized = google.Close.div(first_price).mul(100)
normalized.plot(title='Google Normalized Price')
plt.show()
```

Fig 15.20

Notice the output plot here! It is starting at 100.

In the same way you can normalize multiple series also. We just need to ensure that row labels of our series align with the columns headers of the DataFrame. For this confirmation you don't need to worry because div() method will take care of this. example we are going to normalize different companies stock price as below-

```
price_df = pd.read_csv("E:/pg/bpb/BPB-Publications/Datasets/timeseries/stock_data/stock_data.csv",
                       parse_dates=['Date'],
                       index_col='Date')
price_df.head(3)
```

Date	AAPL	AMGN	AMZN	CPRT	EL	GS	ILMN	MA	PAA	RIO	TEF	UPS
2010-01-04	30.57	57.72	133.90	4.55	24.27	173.08	30.55	25.68	27.00	56.03	28.55	58.18
2010-01-05	30.63	57.22	134.69	4.55	24.18	176.14	30.35	25.61	27.30	56.90	28.53	58.28
2010-01-06	30.14	56.79	132.25	4.53	24.25	174.26	32.22	25.56	27.29	58.64	28.23	57.85

Fig 15.21

Now we will plot different stock prices of different companies using the plot() method . Here we will again use div() method to make ensure that row labels of our series align with the columns headers of the price_df as below-

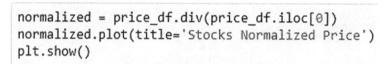

```
normalized = price_df.div(price_df.iloc[0])
normalized.plot(title='Stocks Normalized Price')
plt.show()
```

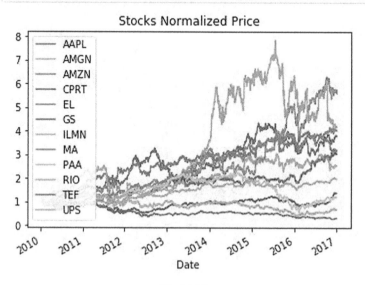

Fig 15.22

Once you normalize price of the stocks as shown above you can also compare the performance of various stocks against a benchmark. Let's learn this by comparing the three largest stocks from the NYSE to the Dow Jones Industrial Average datasets, which contains the 30 largest US companies as shown below.

```
# Import stock prices and index here
stocks = pd.read_csv('E:/pg/bpb/BPB-Publications/Datasets/timeseries/stock_data/nyse.csv',
                parse_dates=['date'], index_col='date')
dow_jones = pd.read_csv('E:/pg/bpb/BPB-Publications/Datasets/timeseries/stock_data/dow_jones.csv',
                parse_dates=['date'], index_col='date')

# Concatenate data and inspect result
data = pd.concat([stocks, dow_jones], axis=1)
print(data.info())

# Normalize and plot your data
data.div(data.iloc[0]).mul(100).plot()
plt.show()
```

Fig 15.23

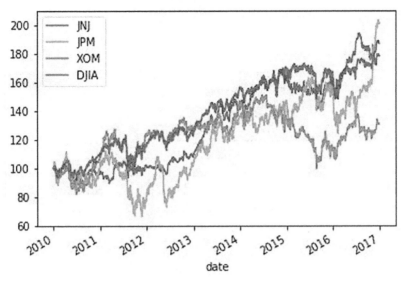

Fig 15.24

Next, we will learn how you can compare the performance of Microsoft (MSFT) and Apple (AAPL) to the S&P 500 dataset over the last 10 years as shown below.

```python
# Create tickers
tickers = ['MSFT', 'AAPL']

# Import stock data here
stocks = pd.read_csv('E:/pg/bpb/BPB-Publications/Datasets/timeseries/stock_data/msft_aapl.csv',
                     parse_dates=['date'], index_col='date')

# Import index here
sp500 = pd.read_csv('E:/pg/bpb/BPB-Publications/Datasets/timeseries/stock_data/sp500.csv',
                    parse_dates=['date'], index_col='date')

# Concatenate stocks and index here
data = pd.concat([stocks, sp500], axis=1).dropna()

# Normalize data
normalized = data.div(data.iloc[0]).mul(100)

# Subtract the normalized index from the normalized stock prices, and plot the result
normalized[tickers].sub(normalized['SP500'], axis=0).plot()
plt.show()
```

Fig 15.25

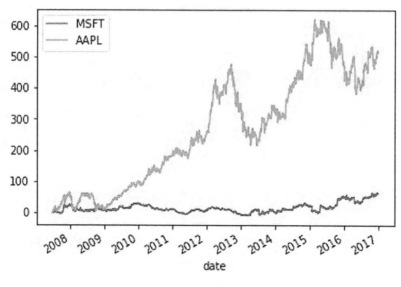

Fig 15.26

Now you can compare these stocks to the overall market, so that you can easily spot trends and outliers.

How to change Time Series Frequency?

Change in frequency also affects the data. If you are doing Upsampling then you should fill or handle the missing values and in case of Downsampling you should aggregate the existing data. First, we will find out the quarterly frequency of the time series data then from this quarterly frequency we will take out the monthly frequency so that in the last we can use this monthly frequency for upsampling and downsampling-

```
dates = pd.date_range(start='2018', periods=4, freq='Q')
my_data = range(1,5)
quaterly = pd.Series(data=my_data, index=dates)
quaterly
```

```
2018-03-31    1
2018-06-30    2
2018-09-30    3
2018-12-31    4
Freq: Q-DEC, dtype: int64
```

```
# upsampling quaterly to Month
monthly = quaterly.asfreq('M')
monthly
```

```
2018-03-31    1.0
2018-04-30    NaN
2018-05-31    NaN
2018-06-30    2.0
2018-07-31    NaN
2018-08-31    NaN
2018-09-30    3.0
2018-10-31    NaN
2018-11-30    NaN
2018-12-31    4.0
Freq: M, dtype: float64
```

Fig 15.27

Now let's see how we can achieve this in each case -

```
monthly = monthly.to_frame('baseline')
# handling missing values using forward fill
monthly['ffill'] = quaterly.asfreq('M', method='ffill')
# handling missing values using backward fill
monthly['bfill'] = quaterly.asfreq('M', method='bfill')
# handling missing values with 0
monthly['ffill'] = quaterly.asfreq('M', fill_value=0)
monthly
```

	baseline	ffill	bfill
2018-03-31	1.0	1	1
2018-04-30	NaN	0	2
2018-05-31	NaN	0	2
2018-06-30	2.0	2	2
2018-07-31	NaN	0	3

Fig 15.28

Now you will learn about interpolate() method. **Pandas dataframe.interpolate()** function is basically used to fill NA values in the dataframe or series. But, this is a very powerful function to fill the missing values. It uses various interpolation technique to fill the missing values rather than hard-coding the value. To understand the Pandas **interpolate()** method which Interpolate values according to different methods, let's take an example of a new dataset-

```
# Import & inspect data
data_df = pd.read_csv('E:/pg/bpb/BPB-Publications/Datasets/timeseries/stock_data/debt_unemployment.csv',
                      parse_dates=['date'],
                      index_col='date')
data_df.info()
```

```
<class 'pandas.core.frame.DataFrame'>
DatetimeIndex: 89 entries, 2010-01-01 to 2017-05-01
Data columns (total 2 columns):
Debt/GDP        29 non-null float64
Unemployment    89 non-null float64
dtypes: float64(2)
```

Fig 15.29

Now we will interpolate debt/GDP and compare to unemployment as below-

```
interpolated = data_df.interpolate()
interpolated.info()
```

```
<class 'pandas.core.frame.DataFrame'>
DatetimeIndex: 89 entries, 2010-01-01 to 2017-05-01
Data columns (total 2 columns):
Debt/GDP        89 non-null float64
Unemployment    89 non-null float64
dtypes: float64(2)
```

Fig 15.30

Later, we can visualize this as below-

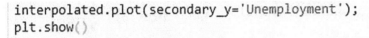

```
interpolated.plot(secondary_y='Unemployment');
plt.show()
```

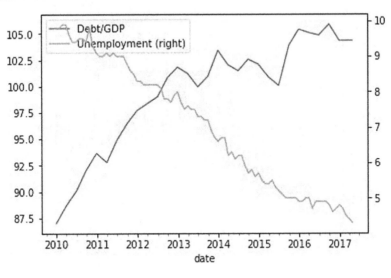

Fig 15.31

From above plot you can see Debt/GDP column of our dataframe as in blue line whereas Unemployment is in brown color. From the plot you can understand that,Debt/GDP rate is increasing with some variation in between 2015 and 2016 while Unemployment is decreasing steadily since 2010.

So far, we have done upsampling, fill logic and interpolation. Now we will learn how to do Downsampling. For downsampling you can choose option like mean, median or last value to fill missing values. For understanding this let's work on air quality dataset-

```
ozone_df = pd.read_csv('E:/pg/bpb/BPB-Publications/Datasets/timeseries/air_quality_data/ozone_nyla.csv',
                parse_dates=['date'], index_col='date')
ozone_df.info()
```

```
<class 'pandas.core.frame.DataFrame'>
DatetimeIndex: 6291 entries, 2000-01-01 to 2017-03-31
Data columns (total 2 columns):
Los Angeles    5488 non-null float64
New York       6167 non-null float64
dtypes: float64(2)
```

Fig 15.32

First, we calculate and plot the monthly average ozone trend as below-

```
ozone_df.resample('W').mean().plot();
plt.show()
```

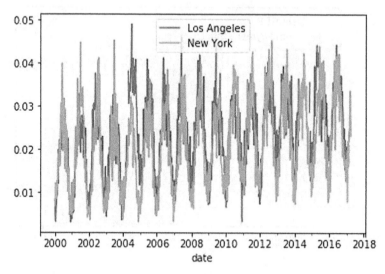

Fig 15.33

Next, we calculate and plot the annual average ozone trend as below-

```
ozone_df.resample('A').mean().plot();
plt.show();
```

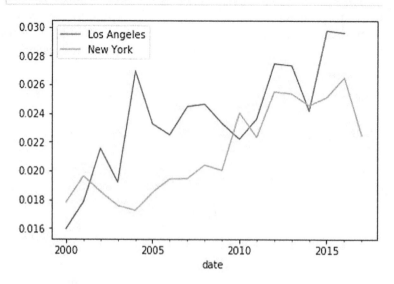

Fig 15.34

You can easily see that how does changing the resampling period change the plot of the time series.

Now you can compare higher-frequency stock price series to lower-frequency economic time series easily. As a first example, let's compare the quarterly GDP growth rate to the quarterly rate of return on the (resampled) Dow Jones Industrial index of 30 large US stocks. GDP growth is reported at the beginning of each quarter for the previous quarter. To calculate matching stock returns, you'll resample the stock index to quarter start frequency using the alias 'QS', and aggregating using the *.first()* observations as below-

```
# Import and inspect gdp_growth
gdp_growth = pd.read_csv('E:/pg/bpb/BPB-Publications/Datasets/timeseries/stock_data/gdp_growth.csv',
                         parse_dates=['date'], index_col='date')
gdp_growth.info()

# Import and inspect djia
djia = pd.read_csv('E:/pg/bpb/BPB-Publications/Datasets/timeseries/stock_data/djia.csv',
                   parse_dates=['date'], index_col='date')
djia.info()
```

```
<class 'pandas.core.frame.DataFrame'>
DatetimeIndex: 41 entries, 2007-01-01 to 2017-01-01
Data columns (total 1 columns):
gdp_growth    41 non-null float64
dtypes: float64(1)
memory usage: 656.0 bytes
<class 'pandas.core.frame.DataFrame'>
DatetimeIndex: 2610 entries, 2007-06-29 to 2017-06-29
Data columns (total 1 columns):
djia     2519 non-null float64
dtypes: float64(1)
memory usage: 40.8 KB
```

Fig 15.35

Since we have stored the data as a dataframe, let's calculate quarterly return and plot it with respect to GDP growth as below-

```
# Calculate djia quarterly returns
djia_quarterly = djia.resample('QS').first()
djia_quarterly_return = djia_quarterly.pct_change().mul(100)

# Concatenate, rename and plot djia_quarterly_return and gdp_growth
data = pd.concat([gdp_growth, djia_quarterly_return], axis=1)
data.columns = ['gdp', 'djia']

data.plot()
plt.show();
```

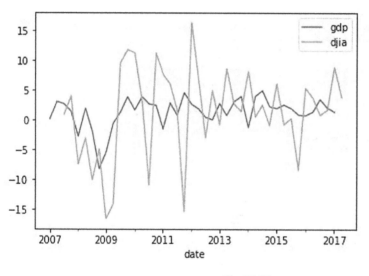

Fig 15.36

Let's explore how the monthly mean, median and standard deviation of daily S&P500 returns have trended over the last 10 years. In this example we will aggregate the mean, median and standard deviation with *resample()* method-

```
# Import data
sp500 = pd.read_csv('E:/pg/bpb/BPB-Publications/Datasets/timeseries/stock_data/sp500.csv',
                    parse_dates=['date'], index_col='date')

# Calculate daily returns here
daily_returns = sp500.squeeze().pct_change()

# Resample and calculate statistics
stats = daily_returns.resample('M').agg(['mean', 'median', 'std'])

stats.plot()
plt.show()
```

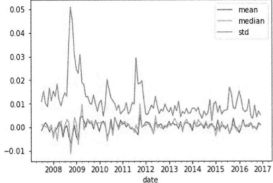

Fig 15.37

From the above plot you can easily see the statistical average methods like mean as a blue line, green as standard deviation and orange as median of daily S&P500 returns in last 10 years.

Conclusion

In this chapter you have learnt how to manipulate and visualize Time Series data. If you practice above exercise in your notebook, Time Series data is no more difficult for you to understand. But to know more you need to practice more with new data. The learning from this chapter will definitely help you when you will work with stock price prediction or weather prediction or sales data. In the next chapter you will learn different time Series forecasting machine learning methods.

## CHAPTER 16

Time-Series Methods

In the previous chapter you have learnt techniques of manipulating and visualizing varying types of Time Series data analysis. In this chapter you will learn various Time Series forecasting methods using the statsmodels library. These statistical techniques are important to know before applying any machine learning model on a Time Series data. You will learn different APIs of this library to forecast Time Series by working on different examples. Having a working code example as a starting point will greatly accelerate your progress when you will apply these methods with machine learning models. All the examples mentioned in this chapter, you can also find in a notebook named as Time Series Methods.ipynb.

Structure

- What is Time-Series is forecasting?
- Basic Steps in Forecasting
- Time Series Forecasting Techniques
- Forecast future traffic to a Web page
- Conclusion

Objective

After studying this chapter, you will be familiar with various time series forecasting methods and apply the techniques to forecast any time series problem.

What is Time-Series forecasting?

Time series forecasting is an important area of machine learning because there are so many prediction problems present in this world that involves time component. Since Time series adds an explicit order dependence between observations-a time dimension; this additional dimension is both a constraint and a structure that provides a source of additional information. Making predictions about the future is called extrapolation in the classical statistical handling of time series data. More modern fields focus on the topic and refer to it as time series forecasting.

Forecasting involves taking models fit on historical data and using them to predict future observations. An important distinction in forecasting is that the future is completely unpredictable and must only be estimated from what has already happened. Some examples of Time Series forecasting are- forecasting the closing price of a stock each day, forecasting product sales in units sold each day for a store, forecasting the number of passengers through a train station each day, forecasting unemployment for a state each quarter, forecasting the average price of petrol in a city each day etc.

Basic Steps in Forecasting

Famous Statisticians and Econometricians- Dr. Hyndman and Dr. Athanasopoulos has summarized 5 basic forecasting steps as below-

1. **Defining Business Problem** - The careful consideration of who requires the forecast and how the forecast will be used.

2. **Information Gathering** - The collection of historical data to analyse and model data. This also includes getting access to domain experts and gathering information that can help to best interpret the historical information, and ultimately the forecasts that will be made.

3. **Preliminary Exploratory Analysis**- The use of simple tools, like graphing and summary statistics, to better understand the data. Review plots and summarize and note obvious temporal structures, like trends seasonality, anomalies like missing data, corruption, and outliers, and any other structures that may impact forecasting.

4. **Choosing and Fitting Models**- Evaluate two, three, or a suite of models of varying types on the problem. Models are configured and fit to the historical data.

5. **Using and Evaluating a Forecasting Model**- The model is used to make forecasts and the performance of those forecasts is evaluated and skill of the models estimated.

Above mentioned basic steps are very useful and effective so always remember and apply same whenever you deal with Time Series data.

Time Series Forecasting Techniques

Statsmodels library has many methods for Time Series forecasting. You must know some of these Time Series methods/techniques because you will not get a better accuracy only applying a machine learning algorithm to a time series data. Following are some common techniques which we will cover in this chapter-

1. Autoregression (AR)

2. Moving Average (MA)

3. Autoregressive Moving Average (ARMA)

4. Autoregressive Integrated Moving Average (ARIMA)

5. Seasonal Autoregressive Integrated Moving-Average (SARIMA)

6. Seasonal Autoregressive Integrated Moving-Average with Exogenous Regressors (SARIMAX)

7. Vector Autoregression Moving-Average (VARMA)

8. Holt Winter's Exponential Smoothing (HWES)

Autoregression (AR)

Autoregression is a time series model that uses observations from previous time steps as input to a regression equation to predict the value at the next time step. An autoregression model makes an assumption that the observations at previous time steps are useful to predict the value at the next time step. This relationship between variables is called **correlation**. If both variables change in the same direction (e.g. go up together or down together), this is called a positive correlation. If the variables move in opposite directions as values change (e.g. one goes up and one goes down), then this is called negative correlation. The method is suitable for univariate time series without trend and seasonal components. Following is an example of using Autoregression model using statsmodels' api-

```
# Autoregression(AR) example
from statsmodels.tsa.ar_model import AR
from random import random
# create a sample dataset
data = [a + random() for a in range(1, 100)]
# fit model
model = AR(data)
model_fit = model.fit()
# make prediction
prediction = model_fit.predict(len(data), len(data))
prediction
```

```
array([100.6504561])
```

Fig 16.1

In above code cell we fit the unconditional maximum likelihood of an AR(p) process using statsmodels.tsa.ar_model.AR.fit() and later we return the in-sample and out-of-sample prediction using the predict() method. The predict() method takes first argument as the starting number of forecasting and second argument takes a number where you want to end the forecasting. In our case the autoregression model has predicted values as 100.65 for a sample dataset.

Moving Average (MA)

This algorithm helps us to forecast new observations based on a time series. This algorithm uses smoothing methods. The moving average algorithm is used only on time series that DOESN'T have a trend. This method is suitable for univariate time series without trend and seasonal components. It consists of making the arithmetic mean of the last n observations contained by the time series to forecast the next observation.

We can use the ARMA class to create an MA model and setting a zeroth-order AR model. We must specify the order of the MA model in the order argument shown as below-

```
# Moving Average(MA) example
from statsmodels.tsa.arima_model import ARMA
from random import random
# create a sample dataset
data = [a + random() for a in range(1, 100)]
# fit model
model = ARMA(data, order=(0, 1))
model_fit = model.fit(disp=False)
# make prediction
ma_predict = model_fit.predict(len(data), len(data))
ma_predict
```

array([75.32920306])

Fig 16.2

In above code cell we have fit MA model by exact maximum likelihood via Kalman filter using *statsmodels.tsa.arima_model.fit()* method with *disp* as false parameter and later we return the in-sample and out-of-sample prediction using the predict() method. In our sample dataset example we are getting moving average prediction as 75.33.

Autoregressive Moving Average (ARMA)

In ARMA forecasting model both autoregression analysis and moving average methods are applied to a well-behaved time series data. ARMA assumes that the time series is stationary-fluctuates more or less uniformly around a time-invariant mean. Non-stationary series need to be differenced one or more times to achieve stationarity. ARMA models are considered inappropriate for impact analysis or for data that incorporates random 'shocks.'

```
# ARMA example
from statsmodels.tsa.arima_model import ARMA
from random import random
# create a sample dataset
data = [random() for x in range(1, 100)]
# fit model
model = ARMA(data, order=(2, 1))
model_fit = model.fit(disp=False)
# make prediction
arma_pred = model_fit.predict(len(data), len(data))
arma_pred
```

array([0.58318755])

Fig 16.3

In above code cell we have fit ARIMA(p,d,q) model by exact maximum likelihood via Kalman filter using statsmodels.tsa.arima_model.fit() method and later we return the in-sample and out-of-sample prediction using the predict() method. Here disp argument controls the frequency of the output during the iterations. The predict() method forecasted 0.58 as the prediction of our sample dataset.

Autoregressive Integrated Moving Average (ARIMA)

ARIMA method combines both Autoregression (AR) and Moving Average (MA) methods as well as a differencing pre-processing step of the sequence to make the sequence stationary, called integration (I). ARIMA models can represent a wide range of time series data, and are used generally in computing the probability of a future value lying between any two limits. Although this method can handle data with a trend, it does not support time series with a seasonal component. ARIMA models are denoted with the notation ARIMA(p, d, q). These three parameters account for seasonality, trend, and noise in data.

```python
# ARIMA example
from statsmodels.tsa.arima_model import ARIMA
from random import random
# create a sample dataset
data = [x + random() for x in range(1, 100)]
# fit model
model = ARIMA(data, order=(1, 1, 1))
model_fit = model.fit(disp=False)
# make prediction
arima_pred = model_fit.predict(len(data), len(data), typ='levels')
arima_pred
```

```
array([100.57016203])
```

Fig 16.4

In above code cell we fit the ARIMA(p,d,q) model by exact maximum likelihood via Kalman filter and then predicted it's ARIMA model in-sample and out-of-sample using .predict() method.

Seasonal Autoregressive Integrated Moving-Average (SARIMA)

An extension to ARIMA that supports the direct modelling of the seasonal component of the series is called SARIMA. SARIMA model combines the ARIMA model with the ability to perform the same autoregression, differencing, and moving average modelling at the seasonal level. This method is suitable for univariate time series with trend and/or seasonal components. The big difference between an ARIMA model and a SARIMA model is the addition of seasonal error components to the model-

```python
# SARIMA example
from statsmodels.tsa.statespace.sarimax import SARIMAX
from random import random
# create a sample dataset
data = [x + random() for x in range(1, 100)]
# fit model
model = SARIMAX(data, order=(1, 1, 1), seasonal_order=(1, 1, 1, 1))
model_fit = model.fit(disp=False)
# make prediction
sarima_pred = model_fit.predict(len(data), len(data))
sarima_pred
```

array([100.5407515])

Fig 16.5

In code cell we have Fit the model by maximum likelihood via Kalman filter and then we have returned the fitted values using predict() method. Here the SARIMAX method have one extra argument- seasonal_order() which has 4 parameters. The (p,d,q,s) order of the seasonal component of the model for the AR parameters, differences, MA parameters, and periodicity.

must be an integer indicating the integration order of the process, while p and q may either be an integer indicating the AR and MA orders (so that all lags up to those orders are included) or else iterables giving specific AR and / or MA lags to include. s is an integer giving the periodicity (number of periods in season), often it is 4 for quarterly data or 12 for monthly data. Default is no seasonal effect. The same SARIMA model with an X factor you will see next.

Seasonal Autoregressive Integrated Moving-Average with Exogenous Regressors (SARIMAX)

The SARIMAX model is an extension of the SARIMA model that also includes the modelling of exogenous variables. Here exogenous variables are also called covariates and can be thought of as parallel input sequences that have observations at the same time steps as the original series. The method is suitable for univariate time series with trend and/or seasonal components and exogenous variables.

```
# SARIMAX example
from statsmodels.tsa.statespace.sarimax import SARIMAX
from random import random
# create datasets
data1 = [x + random() for x in range(1, 100)]
data2 = [x + random() for x in range(101, 200)]
# fit model
model = SARIMAX(data1, exog=data2, order=(1, 1, 1), seasonal_order=(0, 0, 0, 0))
model_fit = model.fit(disp=False)
# make prediction
exog2 = [200 + random()]
sarimax_pred = model_fit.predict(len(data1), len(data1), exog=[exog2])
sarimax_pred
```

```
array([100.09306379])
```

Fig 16.6

Consider an example of food supply chain research. During retail stage of food supply chain (FSC), food waste and stock-outs occur mainly due to inaccurate sales forecasting which leads to inappropriate ordering of products. The daily demand for a fresh food product is affected by external factors, such as seasonality, price reductions and holidays. In order to overcome this complexity and inaccuracy, while doing sales forecasting try to consider all the possible demand influencing factors. SARIMAX model which tries to account all the effects due to the demand influencing factors, to forecast the daily sales of perishable foods in a retail store; it is found that the SARIMAX model improves the traditional Seasonal Autoregressive Integrated Moving Average (SARIMA) model.

Vector Autoregression Moving-Average (VARMA)

The VARMA method models the next step in each time series using an ARMA model. It is the generalization of ARMA to multiple parallel time series, e.g. multivariate time series. The method is suitable for multivariate time series without trend and seasonal components.

```python
# VARMA example
from statsmodels.tsa.statespace.varmax import VARMAX
from random import random
# create dataset with dependency
data = list()
for i in range(100):
    v1 = random()
    v2 = v1 + random()
    row = [v1, v2]
    data.append(row)
# fit model
model = VARMAX(data, order=(1, 1))
model_fit = model.fit(disp=False)
# make prediction
varma_pred = model_fit.forecast()
varma_pred
```

```
array([[0.58299814, 1.10249435]])
```

Fig 16.7

From above code example you can see that the VARMAX class in Statsmodels allows estimation of VAR, VMA, and VARMA models (through the order argument), optionally with a constant term (via the trend argument). Exogenous regressors may also be included (as usual in Statsmodels, by the exog argument), and in this way a time trend may be added. Finally, the class allows measurement error (via the measurement_error argument) and allows specifying either a diagonal or unstructured innovation covariance matrix (via the error_cov_type argument).

Holt Winter's Exponential Smoothing (HWES)

The Holt Winter's Exponential Smoothing (HWES) also called the Triple Exponential Smoothing method and it models the next time step as an exponentially weighted linear function of observations at prior time steps, taking trends and seasonality into account. The method is suitable for univariate time series with trend and/or seasonal components.

```python
# HWES example
from statsmodels.tsa.holtwinters import ExponentialSmoothing
from random import random
# create dataset
data = [x + random() for x in range(1, 100)]
# fit model
model = ExponentialSmoothing(data)
model_fit = model.fit()
# make prediction
hwes_pred = model_fit.predict(len(data), len(data))
hwes_pred
```

```
array([99.90409631])
```

Fig 16.8

Exponential smoothing promise you the possibility of peeking into the future by building models and you can solve these kind of problems- How many iPhone XR will be sold in first 7 months? What's the demand trend for Tesla after Elon musk smokes weed on a live show? Will this winter be warm?

Forecast future traffic to a Web page

Now it's time to apply the learnings from this and previous chapter to an actual time series problem. In the following exercise your goal is to forecast future traffic to Wikipedia pages. The dataset required form this exercise you can download from our repository. Let's start our analysis by loading the dataset-

```
train = pd.read_csv('E:/pg/bpb/BPB-Publications/Datasets/timeseries/wiki/train_1.csv').fillna(0)
train.head()
```

	Page	2015-07-01	2015-07-02	2015-07-03	2015-07-04	2015-07-05	2015-07-06	2015-07-07	2015-07-08	2015-07-09	...	2016-12-22	2016-12-23
0	2NE1_zh.wikipedia.org_all-access_spider	18.0	11.0	5.0	13.0	14.0	9.0	9.0	22.0	26.0	...	32.0	63.0
1	2PM_zh.wikipedia.org_all-access_spider	11.0	14.0	15.0	18.0	11.0	13.0	22.0	11.0	10.0	...	17.0	42.0
2	3C_zh.wikipedia.org_all-access_spider	1.0	0.0	1.0	1.0	0.0	4.0	0.0	3.0	4.0	...	3.0	1.0
3	4minute_zh.wikipedia.org_all-access_spider	35.0	13.0	10.0	94.0	4.0	26.0	14.0	9.0	11.0	...	32.0	10.0
4	52_Hz_I_Love_You_zh.wikipedia.org_all-access_s...	0.0	0.0	0.0	0.0	0.0	0.0	0.0	0.0	0.0	...	48.0	9.0

5 rows × 551 columns

Fig 16.9

The training dataset has 5 rows and 551 columns. Let's find first how language affects the web traffic. For this we will use a simple regular expression to search for the language code in the Wikipedia URL. First import the **re** library and then follow below code

```
def get_language(page):
    res = re.search('[a-z][a-z].wikipedia.org',page)
    if res:
        return res[0][0:2]
    return 'na'

train['lang'] = train.Page.map(get_language)
from collections import Counter
Counter(train.lang)
```

```
Counter({'de': 18547,
         'en': 24108,
         'es': 14069,
         'fr': 17802,
         'ja': 20431,
         'na': 17855,
         'ru': 15022,
         'zh': 17229})
```

Fig 16.10

For each language Wikipedia has different pages. To make easy our analysis we will create dataframes to hold each language as below-

```
lang_sets = {}
lang_sets['de'] = train[train.lang=='de'].iloc[:,0:-1]
lang_sets['en'] = train[train.lang=='en'].iloc[:,0:-1]
lang_sets['es'] = train[train.lang=='es'].iloc[:,0:-1]
lang_sets['fr'] = train[train.lang=='fr'].iloc[:,0:-1]
lang_sets['ja'] = train[train.lang=='ja'].iloc[:,0:-1]
lang_sets['na'] = train[train.lang=='na'].iloc[:,0:-1]
lang_sets['ru'] = train[train.lang=='ru'].iloc[:,0:-1]
lang_sets['zh'] = train[train.lang=='zh'].iloc[:,0:-1]

sums = {}
for key in lang_sets:
    sums[key] = lang_sets[key].iloc[:,1:].sum(axis=0) / lang_sets[key].shape[0]
```

Fig 16.11

Let's plot all the different sets on the same plot to know how the total number of views changes over time-

```
days = [r for r in range(sums['en'].shape[0])]
fig = plt.figure(1,figsize=[10,10])
plt.ylabel('Views per Wiki Page')
plt.xlabel('Day')
plt.title('Wiki Pages in Different Languages')
labels={'en':'English','ja':'Japanese','de':'German',
        'na':'Media','fr':'French','zh':'Chinese',
        'ru':'Russian','es':'Spanish'
       }

for key in sums:
    plt.plot(days,sums[key],label = labels[key] )

plt.legend()
plt.show()
```

Fig 16.12

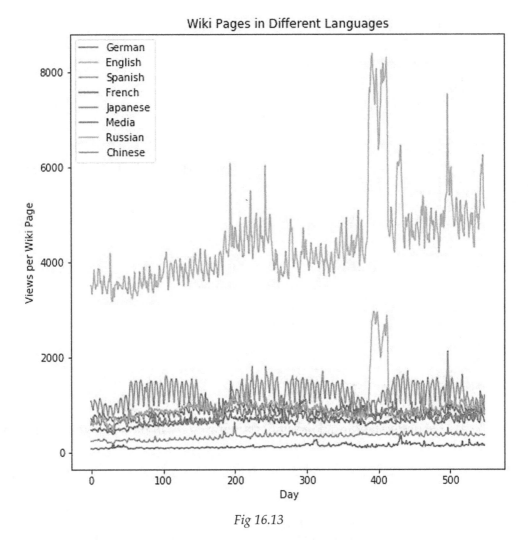

Fig 16.13

From above plot you can deduce the following- English shows much higher number of views per page. This is expected since Wikipedia is a US-based site. The English and Russian plots show very large spikes around day 400. There's also a strange pattern in the English data around day 200. The Spanish data (see the green line) is very interesting too. There is a clear periodic structure there, with a ~1 week fast period and what looks like a significant dip around every 6 months or so.

Since it looks like there is some periodic structure here, we will plot each of these separately so that the scale is more visible. Along with the individual plots, we will also look at the magnitude of the Fast Fourier Transform (FFT) because Peaks in the FFT show us the strongest frequencies in the periodic signal. You can import the fft from the scipy.fftpack api, calculate the magnitude of fft using numpy as below-

```
from scipy.fftpack import fft
def plot_with_fft(key):

    fig = plt.figure(1,figsize=[15,5])
    plt.ylabel('Views per Page')
    plt.xlabel('Day')
    plt.title(labels[key])
    plt.plot(days,sums[key],label = labels[key] )

    fig = plt.figure(2,figsize=[15,5])
    fft_complex = fft(sums[key])
    fft_mag = [np.sqrt(np.real(x)*np.real(x)+np.imag(x)*np.imag(x)) for x in fft_complex]
    fft_xvals = [day / days[-1] for day in days]
    npts = len(fft_xvals) // 2 + 1
    fft_mag = fft_mag[:npts]
    fft_xvals = fft_xvals[:npts]

    plt.ylabel('FFT Magnitude')
    plt.xlabel(r"Frequency [days]$^{-1}$")
    plt.title('Fourier Transform')
    plt.plot(fft_xvals[1:],fft_mag[1:],label = labels[key] )
    plt.axvline(x=1./7,color='red',alpha=0.3)
    plt.axvline(x=2./7,color='red',alpha=0.3)
    plt.axvline(x=3./7,color='red',alpha=0.3)

    plt.show()
for key in sums:
    plot_with_fft(key)
```

Fig 16.14

For the ease of understanding, I am only showing German plot, rest you can see in your notebook-

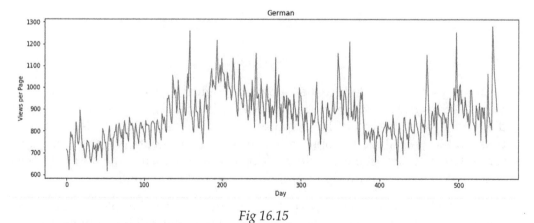

Fig 16.15

Once you see all the plots in your notebook, you will find following insights- while the Spanish data has the strongest periodic features compared to most of the other languages. For some reason the Russian and media data do not seem to reveal any pattern . I plotted red lines where a period of 1, 1/2, and 1/3 weeks patterns would appear. We see that the periodic features are mainly at 1 and 1/2 week. This is not surprising since browsing habits may differ on weekdays compared to weekends, leading to peaks in the FFTs at frequencies of n/(1 week) for integer n.

We've learned now that not all page views are smooth. There is some regular variation from day to day, but there are also large effects that can happen quite suddenly. A model likely will not be able to predict the sudden spikes unless it can be fed more information about what is going on in the world that day.

Now we will look at the most popular pages, which are generally going to be the main pages for the languages in this dataset. We will loop over the language sets using for loop and then look over the pages using the key 'Pages' for each language. After calculating the total we will sort the results and descending order. Following function will do this for us-

```python
# For each language get highest few pages
npages = 5
top_pages = {}
for key in lang_sets:
    print(key)
    sum_set = pd.DataFrame(lang_sets[key][['Page']])
    sum_set['total'] = lang_sets[key].sum(axis=1)
    sum_set = sum_set.sort_values('total',ascending=False)
    print(sum_set.head(10))
    top_pages[key] = sum_set.index[0]
    print('\n\n')
```

Fig 16.16

Above cell will generate popular pages list for all languages, here is an example of German language-

```
de
```

	Page	total
139119	Wikipedia:Hauptseite_de.wikipedia.org_all-acce...	1.603934e+09
116196	Wikipedia:Hauptseite_de.wikipedia.org_mobile-w...	1.112689e+09
67049	Wikipedia:Hauptseite_de.wikipedia.org_desktop_...	4.269924e+08
140151	Spezial:Suche_de.wikipedia.org_all-access_all-...	2.234259e+08
66736	Spezial:Suche_de.wikipedia.org_desktop_all-agents	2.196368e+08
140147	Spezial:Anmelden_de.wikipedia.org_all-access_a...	4.029181e+07
138800	Special:Search_de.wikipedia.org_all-access_all...	3.988154e+07
68104	Spezial:Anmelden_de.wikipedia.org_desktop_all-...	3.535523e+07
68511	Special:MyPage/toolserverhelferleinconfig.js_d...	3.258496e+07

Fig 16.17

Let's analyse more! We have seen earlier, the statsmodels package includes quite a few tools for doing time series analysis. Here, I'll show the autocorrelation and partial autocorrelation for the most-viewed page for each language. Both methods show correlations of the signal with a delayed version of itself. At each lag, the partial autocorrelation tries to show the correlation at that lag after removing correlations at shorter lags-

```python
from statsmodels.tsa.stattools import pacf
from statsmodels.tsa.stattools import acf
for key in top_pages:
    fig = plt.figure(1,figsize=[10,5])
    ax1 = fig.add_subplot(121)
    ax2 = fig.add_subplot(122)
    cols = train.columns[1:-1]
    data = np.array(train.loc[top_pages[key],cols])
    data_diff = [data[i] - data[i-1] for i in range(1,len(data))]
    autocorr = acf(data_diff)
    pac = pacf(data_diff)

    x = [x for x in range(len(pac))]
    ax1.plot(x[1:],autocorr[1:])

    ax2.plot(x[1:],pac[1:])
    ax1.set_xlabel('Lag')
    ax1.set_ylabel('Autocorrelation')
    ax1.set_title(train.loc[top_pages[key],'Page'])

    ax2.set_xlabel('Lag')
    ax2.set_ylabel('Partial Autocorrelation')
    plt.show()
```

Fig 16.18

You will see in most cases strong correlations and anticorrelations every 7 days due to weekly effects. For the partial autocorrelation, the first week seems to be the strongest and then things start settling down-

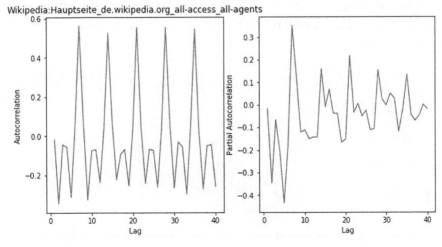

Wikipedia:Hauptseite_de.wikipedia.org_all-access_all-agents

Fig 16.19

Let's apply one of the classical statistical forecasting method -ARIMA model for a small set of pages and then we will see the insights we get from these plots -

```
cols = train.columns[1:-1]
for key in top_pages:
    data = np.array(train.loc[top_pages[key],cols],'f')
    result = None
    with warnings.catch_warnings():
        warnings.filterwarnings('ignore')
        try:
            arima = ARIMA(data,[2,1,4])
            result = arima.fit(disp=False)
        except:
            try:
                arima = ARIMA(data,[2,1,2])
                result = arima.fit(disp=False)
            except:
                print(train.loc[top_pages[key],'Page'])
                print('\tARIMA failed')
    pred = result.predict(2,599,typ='levels')
    x = [i for i in range(600)]
    i=0

    plt.plot(x[2:len(data)],data[2:] ,label='Data')
    plt.plot(x[2:],pred,label='ARIMA Model')
    plt.title(train.loc[top_pages[key],'Page'])
    plt.xlabel('Days')
    plt.ylabel('Views')
    plt.legend()
    plt.show()
```

Fig 16.20

Above code will plot the data as blue line and ARIMA model will be denoted as orange line for each language. Some of the plots will look like below. Rest plots you can see in your notebook-

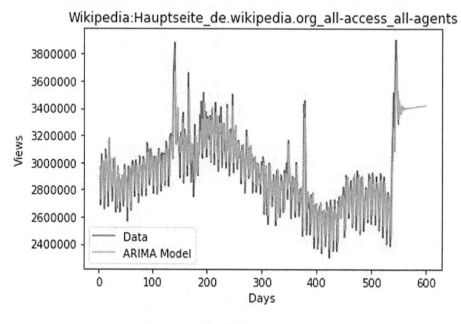

Fig 16.21

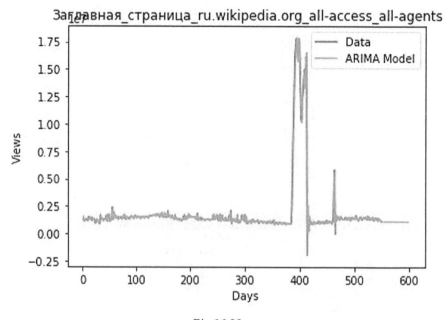

Fig 16.22

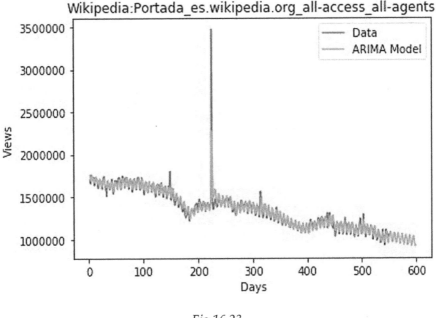

Fig 16.23

Take a good look at all plots and you will understand that ARIMA model in some cases is able to predict the weekly substructure of the signal effectively. In other cases, it seems to just give a linear fit. This is potentially very useful in weekly, substructure of the signal.

What will happen when you just blindly apply the ARIMA model to the whole dataset? Try this and you will see that the results are not nearly as good as just using a basic median model.

Conclusion

The time series method of forecasting is the most reliable when the data represents a broad time period. Information about conditions can be extracted by measuring data at various time intervals -- e.g., hourly, daily, monthly, quarterly, annually or at any other time interval. Forecasts are the soundest when based on large numbers of observations for longer time periods to measure patterns in conditions. To get more confidence start working on any new stock or weather dataset and apply this chapter learnings in forcasting. In the next chapter you will be gone through various case study examples.

CHAPTER 17

Case Study-1

In previous chapters you have learnt basics and some advanced concepts with the help of real-world data science problems. To begin the journey of a data scientist, as I mentioned earlier, the more you practice your learning, the more you will gain confidence. Let us work on some case studies covering application of Supervised and Unsupervised machine learning techniques. These case studies will walk you through different business domains and get you grips as a data scientist.

Case Study 1: Predict whether or not an applicant will be able to repay a loan

Your Goal:- In our first study you are working for an insurance client and help them with implementing a machine learning model to predict the probability of whether or not an applicant will be able to repay a loan.

Your Client: - Your client is an international consumer finance provider with operations in 10 countries.

About Dataset :- Client has given his datasets having static data for all applications. One row represents one loan in their data which you can download from our repository.

Our Baseline ML Models:- In this example I am going to apply logistic regression and random forest algorithms.

Since the objective of this competition is to use historical loan application data to predict whether or not an applicant will be able to repay a loan; this is a standard supervised classification task. Let's import all required basic libraries and read the datasets-

```
# numpy and pandas for data manipulation
import numpy as np
import pandas as pd

# sklearn preprocessing for dealing with categorical variables
from sklearn.preprocessing import LabelEncoder

# Suppress warnings
import warnings
warnings.filterwarnings('ignore')

# matplotlib and seaborn for plotting
import matplotlib.pyplot as plt
%matplotlib inline
import seaborn as sns
```

```
# load and explore training data
train_df = pd.read_csv('E:/pg/bpb/BPB-Publications/Datasets/Case Studies/case_study_1/application_train.csv')
print('Training data shape: ', train_df.shape)
train_df.head()
```

Fig 17.1

Training data shape: (307511, 122)

	SK_ID_CURR	TARGET	NAME_CONTRACT_TYPE	CODE_GENDER	FLAG_OWN_CAR	FLAG_OWN_REALTY
0	100002	1	Cash loans	M	N	Y
1	100003	0	Cash loans	F	N	N
2	100004	0	Revolving loans	M	Y	Y
3	100006	0	Cash loans	F	N	Y
4	100007	0	Cash loans	M	N	Y

5 rows × 122 columns

Fig 17.2

The training data has 307511 observations (each one a separate loan) and 122 features (variables) including the TARGET (the label we want to predict). Details related to every loan is present in a row and is identified by the feature SK_ID_CURR. The training application data comes with the TARGET indicating 0: the loan was repaid or 1: the loan was not repaid. Similarly, we will check the testing dataset also provided in a separate file named *application_test.csv*-

```
# load and explore testing data
test_df = pd.read_csv('E:/pg/bpb/BPB-Publications/Datasets/Case Studies/case_study_1/application_test.csv')
print('Testing data shape: ', test_df.shape)
test_df.head()
```

Testing data shape: (48744, 121)

	SK_ID_CURR	NAME_CONTRACT_TYPE	CODE_GENDER	FLAG_OWN_CAR	FLAG_OWN_REALTY	CNT_CHILDREN	AMT_INCOME_TOTAL
0	100001	Cash loans	F	N	Y	0	135000.0
1	100005	Cash loans	M	N	Y	0	99000.0
2	100013	Cash loans	M	Y	Y	0	202500.0
3	100028	Cash loans	F	N	Y	2	315000.0
4	100038	Cash loans	M	Y	N	1	180000.0

5 rows × 121 columns

Fig 17.3

In next step we will do Exploratory Data Analysis (EDA); this is an open-ended process where we calculate statistics and make figures to find trends, anomalies, patterns, or relationships within the data. The target is what we are asked to predict: either a 0 for the loan was repaid on time, or a 1 indicating the client had payment difficulties. We will first examine the number of loans falling into each category. From below plot you can say that this is an imbalanced class problem. It indicates more loans were repaid on time compared to the loans that were defaulted.

```
train_df['TARGET'].value_counts()
```

```
0    282686
1     24825
Name: TARGET, dtype: int64
```

```
"""
0 means the loan was repaid on time
1 indicating the client had payment difficulties
"""
```

```
train_df['TARGET'].astype(int).plot.hist()
```

```
<matplotlib.axes._subplots.AxesSubplot at 0x14ee2ebfc50>
```

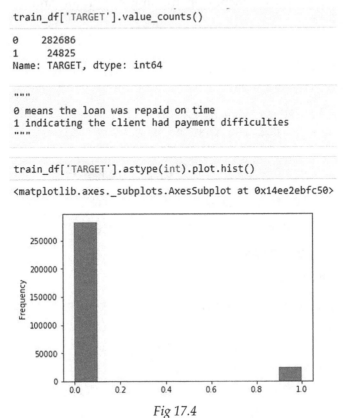

Fig 17.4

Let's examine missing values. Here we will look at the number and percentage of missing values in each column by writing a function. Remember it is a coding standard to write some common functionalities in a function-

```
# check number and percentage of missing values in each column
def missing_values_table(df):
    mis_val = df.isnull().sum() # Total missing values
    mis_val_percent = 100 * df.isnull().sum() / len(df) # Percentage of missing values
    mis_val_table = pd.concat([mis_val, mis_val_percent], axis=1) # Make a table with the results
    mis_val_table_ren_columns = mis_val_table.rename(
    columns = {0 : 'Missing Values', 1 : '% of Total Values'}) # Rename the columns

    # Sort the table by percentage of missing descending
    mis_val_table_ren_columns = mis_val_table_ren_columns[
        mis_val_table_ren_columns.iloc[:,1] != 0].sort_values(
    '% of Total Values', ascending=False).round(1)

    # Print some summary information
    print ("Your selected dataframe has " + str(df.shape[1]) + " columns.\n"
        "There are " + str(mis_val_table_ren_columns.shape[0]) +
        " columns that have missing values.")

    # Return the dataframe with missing information
    return mis_val_table_ren_columns
```

Fig 17.5

Now we will apply above function in training dataframe and we will fill these missing values later-

```
# Missing values statistics
missing_values = missing_values_table(train_df)
missing_values.head()
```

```
Your selected dataframe has 122 columns.
There are 67 columns that have missing values.
```

	Missing Values	% of Total Values
COMMONAREA_MEDI	214865	69.9
COMMONAREA_AVG	214865	69.9
COMMONAREA_MODE	214865	69.9
NONLIVINGAPARTMENTS_MEDI	213514	69.4
NONLIVINGAPARTMENTS_MODE	213514	69.4

Fig 17.6

Let's now look at the number of unique entries in each of the object (categorical) columns-

```
# data types of each type of column
train_df.dtypes.value_counts()
```

```
float64     65
int64       41
object      16
dtype: int64
```

```
# Number of unique classes in each object column
train_df.select_dtypes('object').apply(pd.Series.nunique, axis = 0)
```

```
NAME_CONTRACT_TYPE            2
CODE_GENDER                   3
FLAG_OWN_CAR                  2
FLAG_OWN_REALTY               2
NAME_TYPE_SUITE               7
NAME_INCOME_TYPE              8
NAME_EDUCATION_TYPE           5
NAME_FAMILY_STATUS            6
NAME_HOUSING_TYPE             6
OCCUPATION_TYPE              18
WEEKDAY_APPR_PROCESS_START    7
ORGANIZATION_TYPE            58
FONDKAPREMONT_MODE            4
HOUSETYPE_MODE                3
WALLSMATERIAL_MODE            7
EMERGENCYSTATE_MODE           2
```

Fig 17.7

Let's encode these Categorical Variables or above object data types columns. We will follow following thumb rule - If we only have two unique values for a categorical variable (such as Male/Female), then label encoding method is fine, but for more than 2 unique categories, one-hot encoding method is the safe option to handle categorical features-

```
le = LabelEncoder()
le_count = 0

for col in train_df:
    if train_df[col].dtype == 'object':
        # If 2 or fewer unique categories
        if len(list(train_df[col].unique())) <= 2:
            # Train on the training data
            le.fit(train_df[col])
            # Transform both training and testing data
            train_df[col] = le.transform(train_df[col])
            test_df[col] = le.transform(test_df[col])
            # Keep track of how many columns were label encoded
            le_count += 1

print('%d columns were label encoded.' % le_count)
```

```
3 columns were label encoded.
```

Fig 17.8

```
# one-hot encoding of categorical variables
train_df = pd.get_dummies(train_df)
test_df = pd.get_dummies(test_df)
print('Training Features shape: ', train_df.shape)
print('Testing Features shape: ', test_df.shape)
```

```
Training Features shape:  (307511, 243)
Testing Features shape:  (48744, 239)
```

Fig 17.9

One-hot encoding has created more columns in the training data because there were some categorical variables with categories not represented in the testing data. To remove the columns in the training data that are not in the testing data, we need to align the dataframes.

First, we extract the target column from the training data (because this is not in the testing data, but we need to keep this information). When we do the align, we must make sure to set axis = 1 to align the dataframes based on the columns and not on the rows-

```
# seperate target variable
train_labels = train_df['TARGET']
# combine the training and testing data, keep only columns present in both dataframes
train_df, test_df = train_df.align(test_df, join = 'inner', axis = 1)
# add the target back in
train_df['TARGET'] = train_labels

print('Training Features shape: ', train_df.shape)
print('Testing Features shape: ', test_df.shape)
```

```
Training Features shape:  (307511, 240)
Testing Features shape:  (48744, 239)
```

Fig 17.10

Now the training and testing datasets have the same features which is required for machine learning. One problem we always want to lookout before doing EDA is find anomalies within the data. These may be due to mis-typed numbers, errors in measuring equipment, or they could be valid but extreme measurements. One way to support anomalies quantitatively is by looking at the statistics of a column using the describe method. Try using the .describe() on DAYS_EMPLOYED column and see what you find-

```
anomalous_clients = train_df[train_df['DAYS_EMPLOYED'] == 365243]
non_anomalous_clients = train_df[train_df['DAYS_EMPLOYED'] != 365243]
print('The non-anomalies default on %0.2f%% of loans' % (100 * non_anomalous_clients['TARGET'].mean()))
print('The anomalies default on %0.2f%% of loans' % (100 * anomalous_clients['TARGET'].mean()))
print('There are %d anomalous days of employment' % len(anomalous_clients))
```

```
The non-anomalies default on 8.66% of loans
The anomalies default on 5.40% of loans
There are 55374 anomalous days of employment
```

Fig 17.11

It turns out that the anomalies have a lower rate of default. Handling the anomalies depends on the exact situation, with no set rules. One of the safest approaches is just to set the anomalies to a missing value and then have them filled in (using Imputation) before machine learning.

In our case we will fill in the anomalous values with not a number (np.nan) and then create a new boolean column indicating whether or not the value was anomalous-

```
# Create an anomalous flag column
train_df['DAYS_EMPLOYED_ANOM'] = train_df["DAYS_EMPLOYED"] == 365243

# Replace the anomalous values with nan
train_df['DAYS_EMPLOYED'].replace({365243: np.nan}, inplace = True)

train_df['DAYS_EMPLOYED'].plot.hist(title = 'Days Employment Histogram')
plt.xlabel('Days Employment')
plt.show()
```

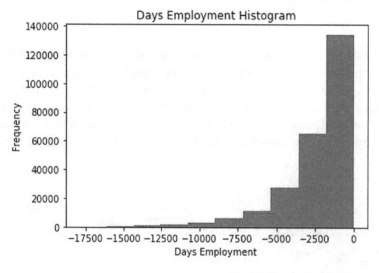

Fig 17.12

As an extremely important note, anything we do to the training data we also have to do to the testing data. So repeat the above step in testing dataset by your own. Now that we have dealt with the categorical variables and the outliers, we'll look for correlations between the features and the target. We can calculate the Pearson correlation coefficient between every variable and the target using the .corr dataframe method-

```
# Find correlations with the target and sort
correlations = train_df.corr()['TARGET'].sort_values()
# Display correlations
print('Most Positive Correlations:\n', correlations.tail())
print('\nMost Negative Correlations:\n', correlations.head())
```

```
Most Positive Correlations:
 REGION_RATING_CLIENT            0.058899
REGION_RATING_CLIENT_W_CITY     0.060893
DAYS_EMPLOYED                   0.074958
DAYS_BIRTH                      0.078239
TARGET                          1.000000
Name: TARGET, dtype: float64

Most Negative Correlations:
 EXT_SOURCE_3                          -0.178919
EXT_SOURCE_2                          -0.160472
EXT_SOURCE_1                          -0.155317
NAME_EDUCATION_TYPE_Higher education  -0.056593
CODE_GENDER_F                         -0.054704
Name: TARGET, dtype: float64
```

Fig 17.13

Let's take a look at some of more significant correlations: the DAYS_BIRTH is the most positive correlation. (except for TARGET because the correlation of a variable with itself is always 1!). DAYS_BIRTH is the age in days of the client at the time of the loan in negative days (for whatever reason!). The correlation is positive, but the value of this feature is actually negative, meaning that as the client gets older, they are less likely to default on their loan (ie the target == 0). That's a little confusing, so we will take the absolute value of the feature and then the correlation will be negative-

```
# Find the correlation of the positive days since birth and target
train_df['DAYS_BIRTH'] = abs(train_df['DAYS_BIRTH'])
train_df['DAYS_BIRTH'].corr(train_df['TARGET'])
```

```
-0.07823930830982712
```

Fig 17.14

As the client gets older, there is a negative linear relationship with the target meaning that as clients get older, they tend to repay their loans on time more often. Let's start looking at this variable. First, we can make a histogram of the age. We will put the x axis in years to make the plot a little more understandable-

```
plt.hist(train_df['DAYS_BIRTH'] / 365, edgecolor = 'k', bins = 25)
plt.title('Age of Client'); plt.xlabel('Age (years)'); plt.ylabel('Count')
plt.show()
```

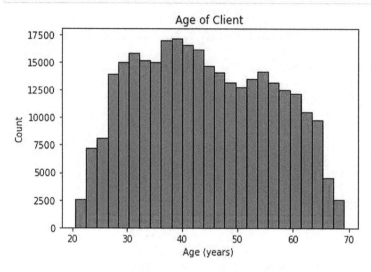

Fig 17.15

By itself, the distribution of age does not tell us much more than that! There are no outliers (no any age more than 70 years) as all the ages are reasonable. Next, we will try two simple feature construction methods for feature engineering: Polynomial features and Domain knowledge features. Polynomial models are a great tool for determining which input factors drive responses and in what direction . In Polynomial method, we make features that are powers of existing features as well as interaction terms between existing features and in Domain knowledge we use our logic specific to a domain-

```
# Make a new dataframe for polynomial features
poly_features = train_df[['EXT_SOURCE_1', 'EXT_SOURCE_2', 'EXT_SOURCE_3', 'DAYS_BIRTH', 'TARGET']]
poly_features_test = test_df[['EXT_SOURCE_1', 'EXT_SOURCE_2', 'EXT_SOURCE_3', 'DAYS_BIRTH']]

# imputer for handling missing values
from sklearn.preprocessing import Imputer
imputer = Imputer(strategy = 'median')

poly_target = poly_features['TARGET']

poly_features = poly_features.drop(columns = ['TARGET'])

# Need to impute missing values
poly_features = imputer.fit_transform(poly_features)
poly_features_test = imputer.transform(poly_features_test)

from sklearn.preprocessing import PolynomialFeatures
poly_transformer = PolynomialFeatures(degree = 3)
```

Fig 17.16

```
# Train the polynomial features
poly_transformer.fit(poly_features)
# Transform the features
poly_features = poly_transformer.transform(poly_features)
poly_features_test = poly_transformer.transform(poly_features_test)
print('Polynomial Features shape: ', poly_features.shape)
```

```
Polynomial Features shape:   (307511, 35)
```

Fig 17.17

Above code will create a considerable number of new features. To get the names you have to use the polynomial features **get_feature_names()** method. In this method pass the input features names and it will show outputas below-

```
# get the names
poly_transformer.get_feature_names(input_features = ['EXT_SOURCE_1', 'EXT_SOURCE_2', 'EXT_SOURCE_3', 'DAYS_BIRTH'])[:15]
```

```
['1',
 'EXT_SOURCE_1',
 'EXT_SOURCE_2',
 'EXT_SOURCE_3',
 'DAYS_BIRTH',
 'EXT_SOURCE_1^2',
 'EXT_SOURCE_1 EXT_SOURCE_2',
 'EXT_SOURCE_1 EXT_SOURCE_3',
 'EXT_SOURCE_1 DAYS_BIRTH',
 'EXT_SOURCE_2^2',
 'EXT_SOURCE_2 EXT_SOURCE_3',
 'EXT_SOURCE_2 DAYS_BIRTH',
 'EXT_SOURCE_3^2',
 'EXT_SOURCE_3 DAYS_BIRTH',
 'DAYS_BIRTH^2']
```

Fig 17.18

There are 35 features with individual features raised to powers up to degree 3 and interaction terms. Now, we can see whether any of these new features are correlated with the target-

```
# Create a dataframe of the features
poly_features = pd.DataFrame(poly_features,
                    columns = poly_transformer.get_feature_names(['EXT_SOURCE_1', 'EXT_SOURCE_2',
                                                                  'EXT_SOURCE_3', 'DAYS_BIRTH']))

# Add in the target
poly_features['TARGET'] = poly_target

# Find the correlations with the target
poly_corrs = poly_features.corr()['TARGET'].sort_values()

# Display most negative and most positive
print(poly_corrs.head())
print(poly_corrs.tail())
```

```
EXT_SOURCE_2 EXT_SOURCE_3                    -0.193939
EXT_SOURCE_1 EXT_SOURCE_2 EXT_SOURCE_3       -0.189605
EXT_SOURCE_2 EXT_SOURCE_3 DAYS_BIRTH         -0.181283
EXT_SOURCE_2^2 EXT_SOURCE_3                  -0.176428
EXT_SOURCE_2 EXT_SOURCE_3^2                  -0.172282
Name: TARGET, dtype: float64
DAYS_BIRTH        -0.078239
DAYS_BIRTH^2      -0.076672
DAYS_BIRTH^3      -0.074273
TARGET             1.000000
1                       NaN
Name: TARGET, dtype: float64
```

Fig 17.19

It is evident that most of the new variables have a greater (in terms of absolute magnitude) correlation with the target than the original features. When we build machine learning models, we can try with and without these features to determine if they actually help the model learn. We will add these features to a copy of the training and testing data and then evaluate models with and without the features because many times in machine learning, the only way to know if an approach will work is to try it out-

```
# Put test features into dataframe
poly_features_test = pd.DataFrame(poly_features_test,
                     columns = poly_transformer.get_feature_names(['EXT_SOURCE_1', 'EXT_SOURCE_2',
                                                                    'EXT_SOURCE_3', 'DAYS_BIRTH']))

# Merge polynomial features into training dataframe
poly_features['SK_ID_CURR'] = train_df['SK_ID_CURR']
app_train_poly = train_df.merge(poly_features, on = 'SK_ID_CURR', how = 'left')

# Merge polnomial features into testing dataframe
poly_features_test['SK_ID_CURR'] = test_df['SK_ID_CURR']
app_test_poly = test_df.merge(poly_features_test, on = 'SK_ID_CURR', how = 'left')

# Align the dataframes
app_train_poly, app_test_poly = app_train_poly.align(app_test_poly, join = 'inner', axis = 1)

# Print out the new shapes
print('Training data with polynomial features shape: ', app_train_poly.shape)
print('Testing data with polynomial features shape:  ', app_test_poly.shape)

Training data with polynomial features shape:  (307511, 275)
Testing data with polynomial features shape:   (48744, 275)
```

Fig 17.20

Let's do feature engineering by domain knowledge. We can make a couple features that attempt to capture what we think may be important for telling whether a client will default on a loan. For this you need to read about client for example here you can read about the client from their website or google. and their business by your own and then create new features-

```
# Domain Knowledge Features
app_train_domain = train_df.copy()
app_test_domain = test_df.copy()

app_train_domain['CREDIT_INCOME_PERCENT'] = app_train_domain['AMT_CREDIT'] / app_train_domain['AMT_INCOME_TOTAL']
app_train_domain['ANNUITY_INCOME_PERCENT'] = app_train_domain['AMT_ANNUITY'] / app_train_domain['AMT_INCOME_TOTAL']
app_train_domain['CREDIT_TERM'] = app_train_domain['AMT_ANNUITY'] / app_train_domain['AMT_CREDIT']
app_train_domain['DAYS_EMPLOYED_PERCENT'] = app_train_domain['DAYS_EMPLOYED'] / app_train_domain['DAYS_BIRTH']

#repeat for test
app_test_domain['CREDIT_INCOME_PERCENT'] = app_test_domain['AMT_CREDIT'] / app_test_domain['AMT_INCOME_TOTAL']
app_test_domain['ANNUITY_INCOME_PERCENT'] = app_test_domain['AMT_ANNUITY'] / app_test_domain['AMT_INCOME_TOTAL']
app_test_domain['CREDIT_TERM'] = app_test_domain['AMT_ANNUITY'] / app_test_domain['AMT_CREDIT']
app_test_domain['DAYS_EMPLOYED_PERCENT'] = app_test_domain['DAYS_EMPLOYED'] / app_test_domain['DAYS_BIRTH']
```

Fig 17.21

Now we will make a baseline model. In this example I am going to use Logistic Regression and Random Forest Model but you must apply some new models also. To get a baseline, we will use all features after encoding the categorical variables. We will pre-process the data by filling in the missing values (imputation) and normalizing the range of the features (feature scaling). The following code performs these pre-processing steps-

```
# get a baseline
from sklearn.preprocessing import MinMaxScaler, Imputer
# Drop the target from the training data
if 'TARGET' in train_df:
    train = train_df.drop(columns = ['TARGET'])
else:
    train = train_df.copy()
# Feature names
features = list(train.columns)
# Copy of the testing data
test = test_df.copy()
# Median imputation of missing values
imputer = Imputer(strategy = 'median')
# Scale each feature to 0-1
scaler = MinMaxScaler(feature_range = (0, 1))
# Fit on the training data
imputer.fit(train)
# Transform both training and testing data
train = imputer.transform(train)
test = imputer.transform(test_df)
# Repeat with the scaler
scaler.fit(train)
train = scaler.transform(train)
test = scaler.transform(test)
print('Training data shape: ', train.shape)
print('Testing data shape: ', test.shape)
```

```
Training data shape:  (307511, 240)
Testing data shape:  (48744, 240)
```

Fig 17.22

Now we create the model train the model using *.fit() method as shown below.*

```
from sklearn.linear_model import LogisticRegression
# Make the model with the specified regularization parameter
log_reg = LogisticRegression(C = 0.0001)
# Train on the training data
log_reg.fit(train, train_labels)
```

```
LogisticRegression(C=0.0001, class_weight=None, dual=False,
        fit_intercept=True, intercept_scaling=1, max_iter=100,
        multi_class='ovr', n_jobs=1, penalty='12', random_state=None,
        solver='liblinear', tol=0.0001, verbose=0, warm_start=False)
```

Fig 17.23

Now that the model has been trained, we can use it to make predictions as shown below. We want to predict the probabilities of not paying a loan, so we use the model *predict.proba()* method. This will return a m x 2 array where m is the number of observations. The first column is the probability of the target being 0 and the second column is the probability of the target being 1 (so for a single row, the two columns must sum to 1). We want the probability the loan is not repaid, so we will select the second column-

```
# Make predictions
# Make sure to select the second column only
log_reg_pred = log_reg.predict_proba(test)[:, 1]
```

Fig 17.24

Now we will prepare our submission format in a csv format so that you can share it to the client. There will be only two columns: SK_ID_CURR and TARGET in csv.

We will create a dataframe named *submit* in this format from the test set and the predictions as shown below.

```
# Submission dataframe
submit = test_df[['SK_ID_CURR']]
submit['TARGET'] = log_reg_pred
submit.head()
```

	SK_ID_CURR	TARGET
0	100001	0.087750
1	100005	0.163957
2	100013	0.110238
3	100028	0.076575
4	100038	0.154924

Fig 17.25

Later we save this in a csv file with the .to_csv() method of dataframes as shown below.

```
# Save the submission to a csv file
submit.to_csv('E:/pg/bpb/BPB-Publications/Datasets/Case Studies/case_study_1/log_reg_baseline.csv', index = False)
```

Fig 17.26

Now try a second model- Random forest on the same training data to see how that affects performance.

```
from sklearn.ensemble import RandomForestClassifier
# Make the random forest classifier
random_forest = RandomForestClassifier(n_estimators = 100, random_state = 50, verbose = 1, n_jobs = -1)
```

Fig 17.27

Here like any other model we have initialized the Random Forest Classifier model with some parameters like no of estimators, random state, verbose and no of jobs. These parameters you can modify and try with different values.

```
# Train on the training data
random_forest.fit(train, train_labels)
# Extract feature importances
feature_importance_values = random_forest.feature_importances_
feature_importances = pd.DataFrame({'feature': features, 'importance': feature_importance_values})
# Make predictions on the test data
predictions = random_forest.predict_proba(test)[:, 1]

[Parallel(n_jobs=-1)]: Done  42 tasks      | elapsed:   32.6s
[Parallel(n_jobs=-1)]: Done 100 out of 100 | elapsed:  1.2min finished
[Parallel(n_jobs=4)]: Done  42 tasks      | elapsed:    0.3s
[Parallel(n_jobs=4)]: Done 100 out of 100 | elapsed:    0.7s finished
```

```
# Make a submission dataframe
submit = test_df[['SK_ID_CURR']]
submit['TARGET'] = predictions
# Save the submission dataframe
submit.to_csv('E:/pg/bpb/BPB-Publications/Datasets/Case Studies/case_study_1/random_forest_baseline.csv', index = False)
```

Fig 17.28

Now we will make Predictions using Engineered Features as shown above. The only way to see if the above created Polynomial Features and Domain knowledge improved the model is to train a test a model on these features. We can then compare the submission performance to the one without these features to gauge the effect of our feature engineering as shown below.

```python
poly_features_names = list(app_train_poly.columns)
# Impute the polynomial features
imputer = Imputer(strategy = 'median')

poly_features = imputer.fit_transform(app_train_poly)
poly_features_test = imputer.transform(app_test_poly)

# Scale the polynomial features
scaler = MinMaxScaler(feature_range = (0, 1))

poly_features = scaler.fit_transform(poly_features)
poly_features_test = scaler.transform(poly_features_test)

random_forest_poly = RandomForestClassifier(n_estimators = 100, random_state = 50, verbose = 1, n_jobs = -1)
```

Fig 17.29

```python
# Train on the training data
random_forest_poly.fit(poly_features, train_labels)

# Make predictions on the test data
predictions = random_forest_poly.predict_proba(poly_features_test)[:, 1]

[Parallel(n_jobs=-1)]: Done  42 tasks      | elapsed:   47.0s
[Parallel(n_jobs=-1)]: Done 100 out of 100 | elapsed:  1.8min finished
[Parallel(n_jobs=4)]: Done  42 tasks      | elapsed:   0.1s
[Parallel(n_jobs=4)]: Done 100 out of 100 | elapsed:   0.4s finished

# Make a submission dataframe
submit = test_df[['SK_ID_CURR']]
submit['TARGET'] = predictions

# Save the submission dataframe
submit.to_csv('E:/pg/bpb/BPB-Publications/Datasets/Case Studies/case_study_1/random_forest_baseline_engineered.csv',
```

Fig 17.30

In the same way we should also check domain features like we did using logistic model earlier-

```python
app_train_domain = app_train_domain.drop(columns = 'TARGET')
domain_features_names = list(app_train_domain.columns)
# Impute the domainnomial features
imputer = Imputer(strategy = 'median')
domain_features = imputer.fit_transform(app_train_domain)
domain_features_test = imputer.transform(app_test_domain)
# Scale the domainnomial features
scaler = MinMaxScaler(feature_range = (0, 1))
domain_features = scaler.fit_transform(domain_features)
domain_features_test = scaler.transform(domain_features_test)
random_forest_domain = RandomForestClassifier(n_estimators = 100, random_state = 50, verbose = 1, n_jobs = -1)
# Train on the training data
random_forest_domain.fit(domain_features, train_labels)
# Extract feature importances
feature_importance_values_domain = random_forest_domain.feature_importances_
feature_importances_domain = pd.DataFrame({'feature': domain_features_names, 'importance': feature_importance_values_domain})
# Make predictions on the test data
predictions = random_forest_domain.predict_proba(domain_features_test)[:, 1]

[Parallel(n_jobs=-1)]: Done  42 tasks      | elapsed:   31.8s
[Parallel(n_jobs=-1)]: Done 100 out of 100 | elapsed:  1.2min finished
[Parallel(n_jobs=4)]: Done  42 tasks      | elapsed:   0.3s
[Parallel(n_jobs=4)]: Done 100 out of 100 | elapsed:   0.7s finished
```

Fig 17.31

```
# Make a submission dataframe
submit = test_df[['SK_ID_CURR']]
submit['TARGET'] = predictions
# Save the submission dataframe
submit.to_csv('E:/pg/bpb/BPB-Publications/Datasets/Case Studies/case_study_1/random_forest_baseline_domain.csv', index = False)
```

Fig 17.32

You can measure each model prediction by ROC AUC metric. Calculate this for each above-mentioned models and see if there is any improvement in accuracy.

Now to see which variables are the most relevant, we can look at the feature importances of the random forest. We may use these feature importance as a method of dimensionality reduction in future work. So it is important to do this step also-

```
def plot_feature_importances(df):
    # Sort features according to importance
    df = df.sort_values('importance', ascending = False).reset_index()

    # Normalize the feature importances to add up to one
    df['importance_normalized'] = df['importance'] / df['importance'].sum()

    # Make a horizontal bar chart of feature importances
    plt.figure(figsize = (8, 4))
    ax = plt.subplot()

    # Need to reverse the index to plot most important on top
    ax.barh(list(reversed(list(df.index[:15]))),
            df['importance_normalized'].head(15),
            align = 'center', edgecolor = 'k')

    # Set the yticks and labels
    ax.set_yticks(list(reversed(list(df.index[:15]))))
    ax.set_yticklabels(df['feature'].head(15))

    # Plot labeling
    plt.xlabel('Normalized Importance'); plt.title('Feature Importances')
    plt.show()
    return df
```

Fig 17.33

```
# Show the feature importances for the default features
feature_importances_sorted = plot_feature_importances(feature_importances)
```

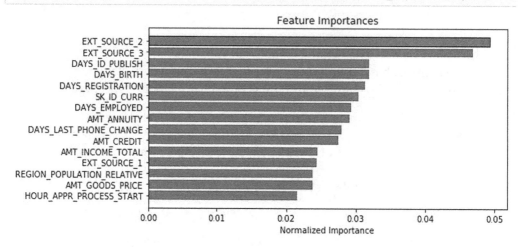

Fig 17.34

As expected, the most important features are those dealing with EXT_SOURCE and DAYS_BIRTH. We can see that there are only a handful of features with significant importance to the model, which suggests we may be able to drop many of the features without a decrease in performance (and we may even see an increase in performance.)

Conclusion

In this exercise you have made a baseline model to solve an actual supervised machine learning problem. We have tried with LR and Random Forest classifiers but there are other model waiting for you to extend this base model and see how to improve the accuracy of the model. Try to apply different models and don't forget to check the performance of your model using ROC AUC metric!

## CHAPTER 18

Case Study-2

Your Goal:- Build a prediction model that will accurately classify which text messages are spam.

About Dataset:- The SMS Spam Collection is a set of SMS tagged messages that have been collected for SMS Spam research. It contains one set of SMS messages in English of 5,574 messages, tagged according being ham (legitimate) or spam. The files contain one message per line. Each line is composed by two columns: v1 contains the label (ham or spam) and v2 contains the raw text in spam.csv file.

Our ML Models:- Multinomial Naive Bayes and Support Vector Machines.

Let's import required basic libraries and load the dataset in a Pandas dataframe-

```
import numpy as np
import pandas as pd
import matplotlib.pyplot as plt
from collections import Counter
from sklearn import feature_extraction, model_selection, naive_bayes, metrics, svm
from IPython.display import Image
import warnings
warnings.filterwarnings("ignore")
%matplotlib inline
```

Fig 18.1

In this case study we will use naïve bayes and support vector machine algorithms. In the above block of code, we have imported these two libraries along with some basic ones.

```
text_df = pd.read_csv('E:/pg/bpb/BPB-Publications/Datasets/Case Studies/case_study_2/spam.csv', encoding='latin-1')
text_df.head()
```

	v1	v2	Unnamed: 2	Unnamed: 3	Unnamed: 4
0	ham	Go until jurong point, crazy.. Available only ...	NaN	NaN	NaN
1	ham	Ok lar... Joking wif u oni...	NaN	NaN	NaN
2	spam	Free entry in 2 a wkly comp to win FA Cup fina...	NaN	NaN	NaN
3	ham	U dun say so early hor... U c already then say...	NaN	NaN	NaN
4	ham	Nah I don't think he goes to usf, he lives aro...	NaN	NaN	NaN

Fig 18.2

Although this dataset is in clean state but before proceeding further it is always best practice to check the data type of the columns or missing values which you can check using .info() and .isnull() methods. Let's check the distribution of spam vs non-spam messages by plotting them. Since we have two categories, it is always good to plot a bar or pie chart to see the distribution. So first we will draw the bar chart and then we will plot a pie chart-

```
# Distribution of spam/non-spam
count_class = pd.value_counts(text_df["v1"], sort= True)
count_class.plot(kind= 'bar', color= ["green", "red"])
plt.title('Distribution of spam vs non-spam')
plt.show()
```

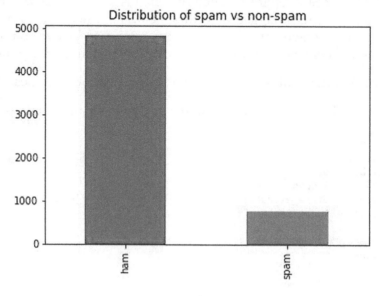

Fig 18.3

Above same result but in another visualization way you can plot as pie chart like below which demonstrate result in percentage-

```
count_class.plot(kind= 'pie', autopct='%1.0f%%')
plt.title('% distribution')
plt.ylabel('')
plt.show()
```

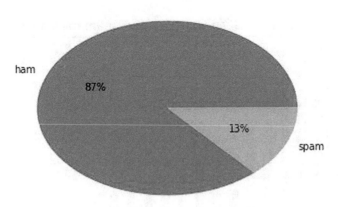

Fig 18.4

From the above chart you can easily see that 13% messages are defined as spam while rest are not spam. Next, we will see the frequencies of each word in spam and non-spam texts. For this calculation I am going to use **collections.Counter()** because it stores elements as dictionary keys, and their counts are stored as dictionary values-

```
# find frequencies of words in the spam and non-spam messages
ham_count = Counter(" ".join(text_df[text_df['v1']=='ham']["v2"]).split()).most_common(20)
ham_df = pd.DataFrame.from_dict(ham_count)
ham_df = ham_df.rename(columns={0: "words in non-spam", 1 : "count"})

spam_count = Counter(" ".join(text_df[text_df['v1']=='spam']["v2"]).split()).most_common(20)
spam_df = pd.DataFrame.from_dict(spam_count)
spam_df = spam_df.rename(columns={0: "words in spam", 1 : "count"})
```

Fig 18.5

In above code cell we are counting the frequencies of spam and ham messages using the Counter() function and then storing each count in separate dataframes- ham_df and spam_df. Later we are plotting the frequencies. First we plot most frequently appearing words in non-spam mesages as shown below-

```
# plot frequency of words in ham
ham_df.plot.bar(legend = False, color = 'green')
y_pos = np.arange(len(ham_df["words in non-spam"]))
plt.xticks(y_pos, ham_df["words in non-spam"])
plt.title('More frequent words in non-spam messages')
plt.xlabel('words')
plt.ylabel('number')
plt.show()
```

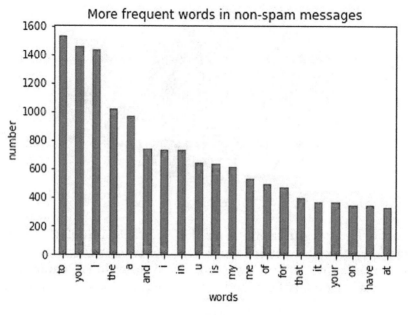

Fig 18.6

Later we plot, most frequently appearing words in spam messages.

```
# plot frequency of words in spam
spam_df.plot.bar(legend = False, color = 'red')
y_pos = np.arange(len(spam_df["words in spam"]))
plt.xticks(y_pos, spam_df["words in spam"])
plt.title('More frequent words in spam messages')
plt.xlabel('words')
plt.ylabel('number')
plt.show()
```

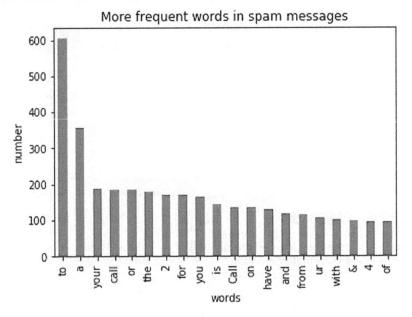

Fig 18.7

From above plots you can see that the majority of frequent words in both classes are **stop words** such as 'to', 'a', 'or' and so on. With stop words we refer to the most common words in a language which have very rare or no meaning in machine learning. It will be good to remove such words. Besides this creating new features is also a good choice to improve model accuracy.

We'll learn how to do this in two simple steps. The **sklearn.feature_extraction** module can be used to extract features in a format supported by machine learning algorithms from datasets consisting of formats such as text . We will use sklearn's **CountVectorizer** api to to convert a collection of text documents to a matrix of token counts and remove stop words as shown below-

```
# remove the stop words and create new features
f = feature_extraction.text.CountVectorizer(stop_words = 'english')
X = f.fit_transform(text_df["v2"])
np.shape(X)
```

(5572, 8404)

Fig 18.8

With this we have created more than 8400 new features.

Now we will start the predictive analysis. We will first map spam messages as '1' and no- spam messages as '0'. Later, we will split our data set in training set and test set-

```
text_df["v1"] = text_df["v1"].map({'spam':1,'ham':0})
X_train, X_test, y_train, y_test = model_selection.train_test_split(X, text_df['v1'], test_size=0.33, random_state=42)
print([np.shape(X_train), np.shape(X_test)])
```

[(3733, 8404), (1839, 8404)]

Fig 18.9

We will train different Bayes models by changing the regularization parameter and evaluate the accuracy, recall and precision of the model with the test set-

```
list_alpha = np.arange(1/100000, 20, 0.11)
score_train = np.zeros(len(list_alpha))
score_test = np.zeros(len(list_alpha))
recall_test = np.zeros(len(list_alpha))
precision_test= np.zeros(len(list_alpha))
count = 0
for alpha in list_alpha:
    bayes = naive_bayes.MultinomialNB(alpha=alpha)
    bayes.fit(X_train, y_train)
    score_train[count] = bayes.score(X_train, y_train)
    score_test[count]= bayes.score(X_test, y_test)
    recall_test[count] = metrics.recall_score(y_test, bayes.predict(X_test))
    precision_test[count] = metrics.precision_score(y_test, bayes.predict(X_test))
    count = count + 1
```

Fig 18.10

In above code cell we are first defining parameters used in Naïve Bayes in our case we are using Multi Nomial Naïve Bayes algorithm. Process of training is same as other sklearn api- fit the model and then make prediction. For computing the recall we are using **metrics.recall_score()** function.

The recall is the ratio tp / (tp + fn) where tp is the number of true positives and fn the number of false negatives. Recall is intuitively the ability of the classifier to find all the positive samples so the best value is 1 and the worst value is 0.

After computing the recall we are also computing the precision which is the ratio of tp / (tp + fp) where tp is the number of true positives and fp the number of false positives. Precision is intuitively the ability of the classifier not to label as positive a sample that is negative.

Next in below code cell we are calculating our model performance using different matrices-

```
# Let's see some learning models and their metrics
matrix = np.matrix(np.c_[list_alpha, score_train, score_test, recall_test, precision_test])
models = pd.DataFrame(data = matrix, columns =
                ['alpha', 'Train Accuracy', 'Test Accuracy', 'Test Recall', 'Test Precision'])
models.head()
```

	alpha	Train Accuracy	Test Accuracy	Test Recall	Test Precision
0	0.00001	0.998661	0.974443	0.920635	0.895753
1	0.11001	0.997857	0.976074	0.936508	0.893939
2	0.22001	0.997857	0.977162	0.936508	0.900763
3	0.33001	0.997589	0.977162	0.936508	0.900763
4	0.44001	0.997053	0.977162	0.936508	0.900763

Fig 18.11

As you can see different learning models with their precisions I above output cell, now we will select the model with the best test precision as shown in below code cell-

```
best_index = models['Test Precision'].idxmax()
models.iloc[best_index, :]
```

```
alpha             15.730010
Train Accuracy     0.979641
Test Accuracy      0.969549
Test Recall        0.777778
Test Precision     1.000000
Name: 143, dtype: float64
```

Fig 18.12

From above output cell we can see that train and test accuracy score is almost same which means there is no overfitting in our model. Let's check also if there is more than one model with 100% precision –

```
models[models['Test Precision']==1].head()
```

	alpha	Train Accuracy	Test Accuracy	Test Recall	Test Precision
143	15.73001	0.979641	0.969549	0.777778	1.0
144	15.84001	0.979641	0.969549	0.777778	1.0
145	15.95001	0.979641	0.969549	0.777778	1.0
146	16.06001	0.979373	0.969549	0.777778	1.0
147	16.17001	0.979373	0.969549	0.777778	1.0

Fig 18.13

As you can see there are more than one models having 100% precision but there is some point differences in alpha and train accuracy score. Let's select model which has more test accuracy-

```
best_index = models[models['Test Precision']==1]['Test Accuracy'].idxmax()
bayes = naive_bayes.MultinomialNB(alpha=list_alpha[best_index])
bayes.fit(X_train, y_train)
models.iloc[best_index, :]
```

```
alpha               15.730010
Train Accuracy       0.979641
Test Accuracy        0.969549
Test Recall          0.777778
Test Precision       1.000000
Name: 143, dtype: float64
```

Fig 18.14

From above output you can easily say that model which have alpha score as 15.730010. train accuracy is as 0.979641 and test accuracy is 0.969549 is our best model and that is at the index number 143. Let's also generate confusion Matrix for our Naïve Bayes Classifier-

```
# Confusion matrix with naive bayes classifier
m_confusion_test = metrics.confusion_matrix(y_test, bayes.predict(X_test))
pd.DataFrame(data = m_confusion_test, columns = ['Predicted 0', 'Predicted 1'],
        index = ['Actual 0', 'Actual 1'])
```

	Predicted 0	Predicted 1
Actual 0	1587	0
Actual 1	56	196

Fig 18.15

See the above confusion matrix result and you can say that we misclassify 56 spam messages as non-spam emails whereas we don't misclassify any non-spam message and our model has 96.95% test accuracy which you have find out just earliar. Now we will repeat above steps with our second model- Support Vector Machine.

```
# repeat same steps with Support Vector Machine
list_C = np.arange(500, 2000, 100)
score_train = np.zeros(len(list_C))
score_test = np.zeros(len(list_C))
recall_test = np.zeros(len(list_C))
precision_test= np.zeros(len(list_C))
count = 0
for C in list_C:
    svc = svm.SVC(C=C)
    svc.fit(X_train, y_train)
    score_train[count] = svc.score(X_train, y_train)
    score_test[count]= svc.score(X_test, y_test)
    recall_test[count] = metrics.recall_score(y_test, svc.predict(X_test))
    precision_test[count] = metrics.precision_score(y_test, svc.predict(X_test))
    count = count + 1
```

Fig 18.16

```
matrix = np.matrix(np.c_[list_C, score_train, score_test, recall_test, precision_test])
models = pd.DataFrame(data = matrix, columns =
            ['C', 'Train Accuracy', 'Test Accuracy', 'Test Recall', 'Test Precision'])
models.head()
```

	C	Train Accuracy	Test Accuracy	Test Recall	Test Precision
0	500.0	0.994910	0.982599	0.873016	1.0
1	600.0	0.995982	0.982599	0.873016	1.0
2	700.0	0.996785	0.982599	0.873016	1.0
3	800.0	0.997053	0.983143	0.876984	1.0
4	900.0	0.997589	0.983143	0.876984	1.0

```
best_index = models['Test Precision'].idxmax()
models.iloc[best_index, :]
```

```
C                   500.000000
Train Accuracy        0.994910
Test Accuracy         0.982599
Test Recall           0.873016
Test Precision        1.000000
Name: 0, dtype: float64
```

Fig 18.17

```
models[models['Test Precision']==1].head()
```

	C	Train Accuracy	Test Accuracy	Test Recall	Test Precision
0	500.0	0.994910	0.982599	0.873016	1.0
1	600.0	0.995982	0.982599	0.873016	1.0
2	700.0	0.996785	0.982599	0.873016	1.0
3	800.0	0.997053	0.983143	0.876984	1.0
4	900.0	0.997589	0.983143	0.876984	1.0

```
best_index = models[models['Test Precision']==1]['Test Accuracy'].idxmax()
svc = svm.SVC(C=list_C[best_index])
svc.fit(X_train, y_train)
models.iloc[best_index, :]
```

```
C                 800.000000
Train Accuracy      0.997053
Test Accuracy       0.983143
Test Recall         0.876984
Test Precision      1.000000
Name: 3, dtype: float64
```

Fig 18.18

```
m_confusion_test = metrics.confusion_matrix(y_test, svc.predict(X_test))
pd.DataFrame(data = m_confusion_test, columns = ['Predicted 0', 'Predicted 1'],
            index = ['Actual 0', 'Actual 1'])
```

	Predicted 0	Predicted 1
Actual 0	1587	0
Actual 1	31	221

Fig 18.19

In this case, we misclassify 31 spam as non-spam messages whereas we don't misclassify any non-spam message indicating the SVC model has 98.3% test accuracy which is better than our Naïve Bayes model. That completes our goal!

Now you can classify any new text to spam or non-spam with the help of your SVM model as shown below-

```
# predicting a new text using our svm model
Y = ["A loan for £950 is approved for you if you receive this SMS. 1 min verification & cash in 1 hr at www.example.co.uk
f = feature_extraction.text.CountVectorizer(stop_words = 'english')
f.fit(text_df["v2"])
X = f.transform(Y)
res=svc.predict(X)
if res==1:
    print('This text is spam')
else:
    print('This text is not a spam')
```

This text is spam

Fig 18.20

As you can see in above output cell I have added a new sentence for testing our model. Here first we store it in a variable as we used 'Y' for this then we have initialized the CountVectorizer() function with English stop words. Next, we have trained the model and after transformation of our newly sentence we are predicting the outcome and our model has recognised this sentence as spam which is correct prediction.

Conclusion

If you follow this case-study, you will find that classifying any mail or message is not a tough task. Gmail, Yahoo Mail and other email platforms are already using similar types of algorithms for such task. Naïve Bayes and Support Vector Machines are the two most used algorithms in spam vs non-spam classification problems. What next you can do this with this model is, try different parameters and see what variation in accuracy you can achieve with your changes.

CHAPTER 19

Case Study-3

Your Goal:- Build a film recommendation engine .

About Dataset:- TMDB dataset contains around 5000 movies and TV series with data on the plot, cast, crew, budget, and revenues. The credit csv (tmdb_5000_credits. csv) contains the movie id, title, cast, crew details while movie csv file (tmdb_5000_movies.csv) contains the movie budget, genre, revenue, popularity etc.

Main ML Libraries:- TfidfVectorizer and CountVectorizer

About Recommendation Engine:- A recommendation engine filters the data using different algorithms and recommends the most relevant items to users. It first captures the past behaviour of a customer and based on that, recommends products which the users might be likely to buy. Here we will build a movie recommendation engine based on popularity and content-based engines.

Let's load the datasets and explore them first to have a better understanding of the data-

```
credits = pd.read_csv('E:/pg/bpb/BPB-Publications/Datasets/Case Studies/case_study_3/tmdb_5000_credits.csv')
credits.info()
```

```
<class 'pandas.core.frame.DataFrame'>
RangeIndex: 4803 entries, 0 to 4802
Data columns (total 4 columns):
movie_id    4803 non-null int64
title       4803 non-null object
cast        4803 non-null object
crew        4803 non-null object
dtypes: int64(1), object(3)
memory usage: 150.2+ KB
```

Fig 19.1

```
movies = pd.read_csv('E:/pg/bpb/BPB-Publications/Datasets/Case Studies/case_study_3/tmdb_5000_movies.csv')
movies.info()
```

```
<class 'pandas.core.frame.DataFrame'>
RangeIndex: 4803 entries, 0 to 4802
Data columns (total 20 columns):
budget                 4803 non-null int64
genres                 4803 non-null object
homepage               1712 non-null object
id                     4803 non-null int64
keywords               4803 non-null object
original_language      4803 non-null object
original_title         4803 non-null object
overview               4800 non-null object
popularity             4803 non-null float64
production_companies   4803 non-null object
production_countries   4803 non-null object
release_date           4802 non-null object
revenue                4803 non-null int64
runtime                4801 non-null float64
spoken_languages       4803 non-null object
status                 4803 non-null object
tagline                3959 non-null object
title                  4803 non-null object
vote_average           4803 non-null float64
vote_count             4803 non-null int64
dtypes: float64(3), int64(4), object(13)
```

Fig 19.2

Now before starting our analysis first we will think about a metric which can rate or score a movie because since a movie with 7.9 average rating and only 2 votes cannot be considered better than the movie with 7.8 as as average rating but 45 votes. In the movie's dataset vote_count, vote_average is already present. We just have to find out mean vote across the whole data which can be calculates as shown below.

```
# calculate mean vote
C = movies['vote_average'].mean()
C
```

6.092171559442011

Fig 19.3

It shows a mean rating for all the movies is approximately 6 on a scale of 10.

The next step is to determine an appropriate value for the minimum votes required to be listed in the chart. We will use 90th percentile as our cutoff. In other words, for a movie to feature in the charts, it must have more votes than at least 90% of the movies in the list-

```
# calculate minimum votes required to be listed in the chart
m = movies['vote_count'].quantile(0.9)
m
```

1838.4000000000015

Fig 19.4

Now, we can filter out the movies that qualify for the chart-

```
# filter out the movies that qualify for the chart
q_movies = movies.copy().loc[movies['vote_count'] >= m]
q_movies.shape
```

(481, 23)

Fig 19.5

We see that there are 481 movies which qualify to be in this list. Now, we need to calculate our metric for each qualified movie.

To do this, we will define a function, *weighted_rating()*. This function will calculate our metric for each qualified movie. Next, we will also define a new feature called *score*, the value of this feature is calculated by applying this *weighted_rating()* function to our DataFrame of qualified movies. This is our first step towards making our first very basic recommender. For writing weighted_rating() function you can take help from the IMDB site itself by following below link-

https://help.imdb.com/article/imdb/track-movies-tv/faq-for-imdb-ratings/ G67Y87TFYYP6TWAV#

Same formula I have represented as below function for your easiness-

```
# calculate our metric for each qualified movie
def weighted_rating(x, m=m, C=C):
    v = x['vote_count']
    R = x['vote_average']
    # Calculation based on the IMDB formula
    return (v/(v+m) * R) + (m/(m+v) * C)
```

```
# Define a new feature 'score' and calculate its value with `weighted_rating()`
q_movies['score'] = q_movies.apply(weighted_rating, axis=1)
#Sort movies based on score calculated above
q_movies = q_movies.sort_values('score', ascending=False)
#Print the top 5 movies
q_movies[['title', 'vote_count', 'vote_average', 'score']].head()
```

	title	vote_count	vote_average	score
1881	The Shawshank Redemption	8205	8.5	8.059258
662	Fight Club	9413	8.3	7.939256
65	The Dark Knight	12002	8.2	7.920020
3232	Pulp Fiction	8428	8.3	7.904645
96	Inception	13752	8.1	7.863239

Fig 19.6

Now, let's understand how to visualize popular five movies got from the above code cell-

```
# plot 5 popular movies
popular_movies = movies.sort_values('popularity', ascending=False)
plt.figure(figsize=(12,4))
plt.barh(popular_movies['title'].head(),popular_movies['popularity'].head(), align='center',
    color='yellow')
plt.gca().invert_yaxis()
plt.xlabel("Popularity")
plt.title("Popular Movies")
```

```
Text(0.5,1,'Popular Movies')
```

Fig 19.7

See! It was quite easy to create a first basic popularity-based recommendation engine. But there is something to keep in mind is that these **popularity-based recommender** provide a general chart of recommended movies to all the users. They are not sensitive to the interests and tastes of a particular user. Now we will tackle this problem also and we will create a more refined system- **content based recommendation** engine by including other columns like overview, cast, crew, keyword, tagline etc. in our analysis. For this we need to handle these texts so that a machine learning model can understand them. We will use **scikit-learn**'s built-in **TfIdfVectorizer** class that produces the TF-IDF matrix in a couple of lines. In this matrix each column represents a word in the overview vocabulary (all the words that appear in at least one document) and each column represents a movie, as before. **TfIdfVectorizer** has two parts- **TF or Term Frequency** and **Inverse Document Frequency (idf)**.

TF simply tells us - How many times a particular word appears in a single doc and IDF solves the frequent and rare words in a given doc. After importing this library, we will initialize it with stop word parameter as English. – This stop_words parameter is used to remove less-meaningful English words.

Then we are handling missing values in overview column as shown below-

```python
from sklearn.feature_extraction.text import TfidfVectorizer
tfidf = TfidfVectorizer(stop_words='english')
# handle missing values
movies['overview'] = movies['overview'].fillna('')
tfidf_matrix = tfidf.fit_transform(movies['overview'])
tfidf_matrix.shape
```

```
(4803, 20978)
```

Fig 19.8

With this matrix in hand, we can now compute a similarity score. We will be using the cosine similarity to calculate a numeric quantity that denotes the similarity between two movies. We use the cosine similarity score since it is independent of magnitude (or size) and is relatively easy and fast to calculate. Cosine similarity is a metric used to measure how similar the documents are irrespective of their size.

Since we have used the TF-IDF vectorizer, calculating the dot product will directly give us the cosine similarity score. Therefore, we will use **sklearn's linear_kernel()** instead of cosine_similarities() since it is faster in executing inputs-

```python
from sklearn.metrics.pairwise import linear_kernel
# compute the cosine similarity matrix
cosine_sim = linear_kernel(tfidf_matrix, tfidf_matrix)
```

Fig 19.9

Now we are going to define a function that takes in a movie title as an input and outputs a list of the 10 most similar movies. Firstly, for this, we need a reverse mapping of movie titles and DataFrame indices. In other words, we need a mechanism to identify the index of a movie in our metadata DataFrame, given its title-

```
# construct a reverse map of indices and movie titles
indices = pd.Series(movies.index, index=movies['title']).drop_duplicates()
```

Fig 19.10

Next we will define our recommendation function that will do the following steps-

- Set the index of the movie given its title

- Get the list of cosine similarity scores for that particular movie with all movies

- Convert it into a list of tuples where the first element is its position and the second is the similarity score

- Sort the aforementioned list of tuples based on the similarity scores; that is, the second element

- Get the top 10 elements of this list.

- Ignore the first element as it refers to self (the movie most similar to a particular movie is the movie itself)

- In the last return the titles corresponding to the indices of the top elements

```
# define our recommendation function
def get_recommendations(title, cosine_sim=cosine_sim):
    idx = indices[title]
    sim_scores = list(enumerate(cosine_sim[idx]))
    sim_scores = sorted(sim_scores, key=lambda x: x[1], reverse=True)
    sim_scores = sim_scores[1:11]
    movie_indices = [i[0] for i in sim_scores]

    return movies['title'].iloc[movie_indices]
```

Fig 19.11

```
# test our function
get_recommendations('Spectre')
```

```
1343              Never Say Never Again
4071              From Russia with Love
3162                        Thunderball
1717                         Safe Haven
11                  Quantum of Solace
4339                             Dr. No
29                              Skyfall
1880                        Dance Flick
3336            Diamonds Are Forever
1743                          Octopussy
Name: title, dtype: object
```

Fig 19.12

That's great! Our recommendation engine has been improved.

Let's make it more mature by including following metadata: the 3 top actors, the director, related genres and the movie plot keywords. From the cast, crew and keywords features, we need to extract the three most important actors, the director and the keywords associated with that movie. Right now, our data is present in the form of "stringified" lists, we need to convert it into a safe and usable structure-

```
# parse the stringified features into their corresponding python objects
from ast import literal_eval
features = ['cast', 'crew', 'keywords', 'genres']
for feature in features:
    movies[feature] = movies[feature].apply(literal_eval)
```

Fig 19.13

Next, we'll write functions that will help us to extract the required information from each feature-

```
# Get the director's name from the crew feature
def get_director(x):
    for i in x:
        if i['job'] == 'Director':
            return i['name']
    return np.nan
```

```
# Returns the list top 3 elements or entire list
def get_list(x):
    if isinstance(x, list):
        names = [i['name'] for i in x]
        if len(names) > 3:
            names = names[:3]
        return names
    return []
```

```
# Define new director, cast, genres and keywords features that are in a suitable form
movies['director'] = movies['crew'].apply(get_director)
features = ['cast', 'keywords', 'genres']
for feature in features:
    movies[feature] = movies[feature].apply(get_list)
```

Fig 19.14

```
# Print the new features
movies[['title', 'cast', 'director', 'keywords', 'genres']].head()
```

	title	cast	director	keywords	genres
0	Avatar	[Sam Worthington, Zoe Saldana, Sigourney Weaver]	James Cameron	[culture clash, future, space war]	[Action, Adventure, Fantasy]
1	Pirates of the Caribbean: At World's End	[Johnny Depp, Orlando Bloom, Keira Knightley]	Gore Verbinski	[ocean, drug abuse, exotic island]	[Adventure, Fantasy, Action]
2	Spectre	[Daniel Craig, Christoph Waltz, Léa Seydoux]	Sam Mendes	[spy, based on novel, secret agent]	[Action, Adventure, Crime]
3	The Dark Knight Rises	[Christian Bale, Michael Caine, Gary Oldman]	Christopher Nolan	[dc comics, crime fighter, terrorist]	[Action, Crime, Drama]
4	John Carter	[Taylor Kitsch, Lynn Collins, Samantha Morton]	Andrew Stanton	[based on novel, mars, medallion]	[Action, Adventure, Science Fiction]

Fig 19.15

The next step would be to convert the names and keyword instances into lowercase and strip all the spaces between them. This is done so that our vectorizer doesn't count the John of "John Cena" and "John Cleese" as the same-

```
# Function to convert all strings to lower case and strip names of spaces
def clean_data(x):
    if isinstance(x, list):
        return [str.lower(i.replace(" ", "")) for i in x]
    else:
        if isinstance(x, str):
            return str.lower(x.replace(" ", ""))
        else:
            return ''
```

```
# Apply clean_data function to our features.
features = ['cast', 'keywords', 'director', 'genres']
for feature in features:
    movies[feature] = movies[feature].apply(clean_data)
```

Fig 19.16

We are now in a position to create our "metadata soup", which is a string that contains all the metadata that we want to feed to our vectorizer (namely actors, director and keywords)-

```
def create_soup(x):
    return ' '.join(x['keywords']) + ' ' + ' '.join(x['cast']) + ' ' + x['director'] + ' ' + ' '.join(x['genres'])
movies['soup'] = movies.apply(create_soup, axis=1)
```

Fig 19.17

Now we will use **sklearn's CountVectorizer()** instead of TF-IDF to remove stop words and transform our newly created soup column-

```
from sklearn.feature_extraction.text import CountVectorizer
count = CountVectorizer(stop_words='english')
count_matrix = count.fit_transform(movies['soup'])
```

```
# compute the Cosine Similarity matrix based on the count_matrix
from sklearn.metrics.pairwise import cosine_similarity
cosine_sim2 = cosine_similarity(count_matrix, count_matrix)
```

Fig 19.18

```
# test our get_recommendations() function with our new arguement
get_recommendations('Spectre', cosine_sim2)
```

```
29                      Skyfall
11            Quantum of Solace
1084            The Glimmer Man
1234             The Art of War
2156                 Nancy Drew
4638    Amidst the Devil's Wings
62          The Legend of Tarzan
3373    The Other Side of Heaven
4                   John Carter
72                 Suicide Squad
Name: title, dtype: object
```

Fig 19.19

Wow! You see that our recommendation engine has been successful in capturing more information due to more metadata and has given us (arguably) better recommendations. Still there are lots of work pending for you to improve your engine like the language of the film was not checked: in fact, this could be important to get sure that the films recommended are in the same language than the one choosen by the user.

Add this feature in your model and see if you get any better results. This is one example of recommendation engine which you can use as a base model. You can extend this model for different problems like product recommendation or a product category recommendation.

## CHAPTER 20

Case Study-4

Your Goal:- Online property companies offer valuations of houses using machine learning techniques. The aim of this case study is to predict the house sales in King County, Washington State, USA using regression.

About Dataset:- This dataset contains house sale prices for King County, which includes Seattle. It includes homes sold between May 2014 and May 2015 as described in kc_house_data.csv.

Our ML Model:- Linear Regression and Polynomial Regression.

Let's first read the housing data for which I have defined an empty dataframe named as *evaluation*. This dataframe includes Mean Squared Error (MSE), R-squared and Adjusted R-squared which are the important metrics to compare different models. Having a R-squared value closer to one and smaller MSE means a better fit. In the following example, I will calculate these values and store it in this dataframe with my results For this purpose first we will import all basic libraries along with sklearn library

```python
import numpy as np
import pandas as pd
from sklearn.model_selection import train_test_split
from sklearn import linear_model
from sklearn.neighbors import KNeighborsRegressor
from sklearn.preprocessing import PolynomialFeatures
from sklearn import metrics
import matplotlib.pyplot as plt
import seaborn as sns
from mpl_toolkits.mplot3d import Axes3D
%matplotlib inline
```

```python
# create evaluation metrics
evaluation = pd.DataFrame({'Model': [],
                           'Details':[],
                           'Mean Squared Error (MSE)':[],
                           'R-squared (training)':[],
                           'Adjusted R-squared (training)':[],
                           'R-squared (test)':[],
                           'Adjusted R-squared (test)':[]})
```

Fig 20.1

After creating our evaluation dataframe, we will load the King County dataset in a dataframe and will look into the head of this-

```python
# read and explore data
df = pd.read_csv('E:/pg/bpb/BPB-Publications/Datasets/Case Studies/case_study_4/kc_house_data.csv')
df.head()
```

	id	date	price	bedrooms	bathrooms	sqft_living	sqft_lot	floors	waterfront	view	...	grade	sqft_above	sqft_basement	yr_built
0	7129300520	20141013T000000	221900.0	3	1.00	1180	5650	1.0	0	0	...	7	1180	0	1955
1	6414100192	20141209T000000	538000.0	3	2.25	2570	7242	2.0	0	0	...	7	2170	400	1951
2	5631500400	20150225T000000	180000.0	2	1.00	770	10000	1.0	0	0	...	6	770	0	1933
3	2487200875	20141209T000000	604000.0	4	3.00	1960	5000	1.0	0	0	...	7	1050	910	1965
4	1954400510	20150218T000000	510000.0	3	2.00	1680	8080	1.0	0	0	...	8	1680	0	1987

5 rows × 21 columns

Fig 20.2

Please note here when we model a linear relationship between a response and just one explanatory variable, this is called simple linear regression. Here I want to predict house prices so our response variable is price. However, for a simple model we also need to select a feature. When I look at the columns of the dataset, living area (sqft) seemed the most important feature.

When we examine the correlation matrix, we may observe that price has the highest correlation coefficient with living area (sqft) and this also supports my opinion. Thus, I decided to use living area (sqft) as feature but if you want to examine the relationship between price and another feature, you may prefer that feature This logic we will apply in our dataframe but we will first split our dataset into 80:20 ratio so that we will train on 80% data and then validate our model on 20 % data. Then we will separate the target variable- price from the training dataset and then we wil fit the Linear regression model on this training and target input using fit() method. Same we will aplly for the testing dataset. Then we will predict the result on test data using predict() method. At last we will calculate the loss of our model using Mean Squared Error metric as below-

```python
%%capture
train_data,test_data = train_test_split(df,train_size = 0.8,random_state=3)

lr = linear_model.LinearRegression()
X_train = np.array(train_data['sqft_living'], dtype=pd.Series).reshape(-1,1)
y_train = np.array(train_data['price'], dtype=pd.Series)
lr.fit(X_train,y_train)

X_test = np.array(test_data['sqft_living'], dtype=pd.Series).reshape(-1,1)
y_test = np.array(test_data['price'], dtype=pd.Series)

pred = lr.predict(X_test)
msesm = format(np.sqrt(metrics.mean_squared_error(y_test,pred)),'.3f')
rtrsm = format(lr.score(X_train, y_train),'.3f')
rtesm = format(lr.score(X_test, y_test),'.3f')

print ("Average Price for Test Data: {:.3f}".format(y_test.mean()))
print('Intercept: {}'.format(lr.intercept_))
print('Coefficient: {}'.format(lr.coef_))

r = evaluation.shape[0]
evaluation.loc[r] = ['Simple Model','-',msesm,rtrsm,'-',rtesm,'-']
evaluation
```

Fig 20.3

In the last three lines of the above code cell, we are using our evaluation dataframe to calculate the metric by passing the metric scores- msesm, rtrsm and rtesm.

You will notice in the below output, we are getting mean squared error or regression loss as 254289.149 for our simple model -

```
Average Price for Test Data: 539744.130
Intercept: -47235.81130290043
Coefficient: [282.2468152]

C:\Users\prateek1.gupta\AppData\Local\Continuum\anaconda3\lib\site-packages\sklearn\model_selection\_split.py:2026: FutureWarni
ng: From version 0.21, test_size will always complement train_size unless both are specified.
  FutureWarning)
```

	Adjusted R-squared (test)	Adjusted R-squared (training)	Details	Mean Squared Error (MSE)	Model	R-squared (test)	R-squared (training)
0	Simple Model		-	254289.149		0.492	-	0.496	-
1	Simple Model		-	254289.149		0.492	-	0.496	-
2	Simple Model		-	254289.149		0.492	-	0.496	-

Fig 20.4

Because we have just two dimensions at the simple regression, it is easy to draw it. The below chart determines the result of the simple regression. It does not look like a perfect fit but when we work with real world datasets, having a perfect fit is not easy-

```
plt.figure(figsize=(6.5,5))
plt.scatter(X_test,y_test,color='darkgreen',label="Data", alpha=.1)
plt.plot(X_test,lr.predict(X_test),color="red",label="Predicted Regression Line")
plt.xlabel("Living Space (sqft)", fontsize=15)
plt.ylabel("Price ($)", fontsize=15)
plt.xticks(fontsize=13)
plt.yticks(fontsize=13)
plt.legend()

plt.gca().spines['right'].set_visible(False)
plt.gca().spines['top'].set_visible(False)
```

Fig 20.5

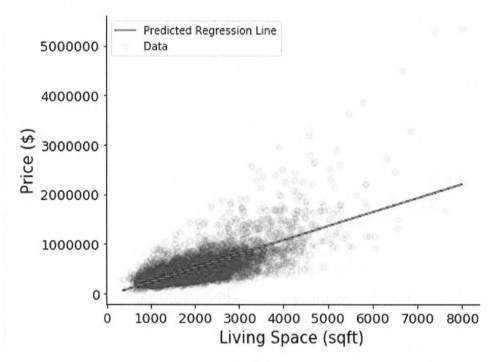

Fig 20.6

In the above case, we have used a simple linear regression and found a poor fit because data looks scattered around the line.

In order to improve this model, I am planning to add more features. However, in this case we should be careful about the overfit which can be detected by the high difference between the training and test evaluation metrics. When we have more than one feature in a linear regression, it is defined as multiple regression. Then, it is time to check the correlation matrix before fitting a multiple regression.

Having too many features in a model is not always a good thing because it might cause overfit and worse results when we want to predict values for a new dataset. Thus, if a feature does not improve your model a lot, not adding it may be a better choice.

Another important thing is correlation, if there is very high correlation between two features, keeping both of them is not a good idea (most of the times). For instance, sqt_above and sqt_living columns in the datasets are highly correlated. This can be estimated when you look at the definitions of the dataset.

Just to be sure, you can double-check this by looking at the correlation matrix which we are going to draw next. However, this does not mean that you must remove one of the highly correlated features. For instance: bathrooms and sqrt_living. They are highly correlated, but I do not think that the relation among them is the same as the relation between sqt_living and sqt_above. Let's draw a correlation matrix with all these features

```
features = ['price','bedrooms','bathrooms','sqft_living','sqft_lot','floors',
            'waterfront','view','condition','grade','sqft_above','sqft_basement',
            'yr_built','yr_renovated','zipcode','sqft_living15','sqft_lot15']

mask = np.zeros_like(df[features].corr(), dtype=np.bool)
mask[np.triu_indices_from(mask)] = True

f, ax = plt.subplots(figsize=(16, 12))
plt.title('Pearson Correlation Matrix',fontsize=25)

sns.heatmap(df[features].corr(),linewidths=0.25,vmax=1.0,square=True,cmap="BuGn_r",
            linecolor='w',annot=True,mask=mask,cbar_kws={"shrink": .75});
```

Fig 20.7

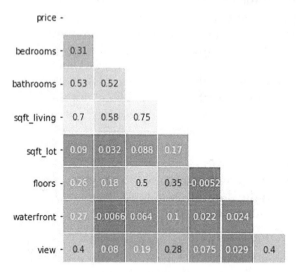

Pearson Correlation Matrix

Fig 20.8

After looking into the correlation matrix, we can examine the features and reach some useful analytical conclusions. Furthermore, plotting charts and examining the data before applying a model is a very good practice because we may detect some possible outliers or decide to do some normalizations. This is not a must, but getting to know the data using visualization is always good.

Now to determine bedrooms, floors or bathrooms/bedrooms vs price comparison, I preferred boxplot because we have numerical data but they are not continuous as 1,2,... bedrooms, 2.5, 3,... floors (probably 0.5 stands for the penthouse)-

```
f, axes = plt.subplots(1, 2,figsize=(15,5))
sns.boxplot(x=train_data['bedrooms'],y=train_data['price'], ax=axes[0])
sns.boxplot(x=train_data['floors'],y=train_data['price'], ax=axes[1])
axes[0].set(xlabel='Bedrooms', ylabel='Price')
axes[1].yaxis.set_label_position("right")
axes[1].yaxis.tick_right()
axes[1].set(xlabel='Floors', ylabel='Price')

f, axe = plt.subplots(1, 1,figsize=(12.18,5))
sns.boxplot(x=train_data['bathrooms'],y=train_data['price'], ax=axe)
axe.set(xlabel='Bathrooms / Bedrooms', ylabel='Price');
```

Fig 20.9

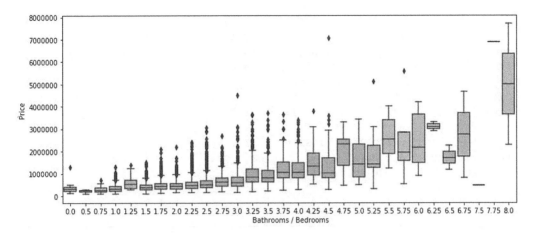

Fig 20.10

Let's create a complex model manually-to find out if we get a better regression loss or not. For this purpose, we will include six features of the dataset for predicting the outcome and then we will repeat the same steps as we have done earlier-

```
features1 = ['bedrooms','bathrooms','sqft_living','sqft_lot','floors','zipcode']
complex_model_1 = linear_model.LinearRegression()
complex_model_1.fit(train_data[features1],train_data['price'])

print('Intercept: {}'.format(complex_model_1.intercept_))
print('Coefficients: {}'.format(complex_model_1.coef_))

pred1 = complex_model_1.predict(test_data[features1])
msecm1 = format(np.sqrt(metrics.mean_squared_error(y_test,pred1)),'.3f')
rtrcm1 = format(complex_model_1.score(train_data[features1],train_data['price']),'.3f')
artrcm1 = format(adjustedR2(complex_model_1.score(train_data[features1],train_data['price']),train_data.shape[0],len(features1)),
rtecm1 = format(complex_model_1.score(test_data[features1],test_data['price']),'.3f')
artecm1 = format(adjustedR2(complex_model_1.score(test_data[features1],test_data['price']),test_data.shape[0],len(features1)),'.3

r = evaluation.shape[0]
evaluation.loc[r] = ['Complex Model-1','-',msecm1,rtrcm1,artrcm1,rtecm1,artecm1]
evaluation.sort_values(by = 'R-squared (test)', ascending=False)
```

Fig 20.11

```
Intercept: -57221293.13485877
Coefficients: [-5.68950279e+04  1.13310062e+04  3.18389287e+02 -2.90807628e-01
 -5.79609821e+03  5.84022824e+02]
```

	Adjusted R-squared (test)	Adjusted R-squared (training)	Details	Mean Squared Error (MSE)	Model	R-squared (test)	R-squared (training)
3	Complex Model-1		-	248514.011	0.514 0.514	0.519	0.518
0	Simple Model		-	254289.149	0.492 -	0.496	-
1	Simple Model		-	254289.149	0.492 -	0.496	-
2	Simple Model		-	254289.149	0.492 -	0.496	-

Fig 20.12

From above output you can say that uur first complex model decreased the Mean Squared Error to 248514.011. Which means we can add additional features to our model and again plot boxplots for further examination as shown in the next example.

```
f, axes = plt.subplots(1, 2,figsize=(15,5))
sns.boxplot(x=train_data['waterfront'],y=train_data['price'], ax=axes[0])
sns.boxplot(x=train_data['view'],y=train_data['price'], ax=axes[1])
axes[0].set(xlabel='Waterfront', ylabel='Price')
axes[1].yaxis.set_label_position("right")
axes[1].yaxis.tick_right()
axes[1].set(xlabel='View', ylabel='Price')

f, axe = plt.subplots(1, 1,figsize=(12.18,5))
sns.boxplot(x=train_data['grade'],y=train_data['price'], ax=axe)
axe.set(xlabel='Grade', ylabel='Price');
```

Fig 20.13

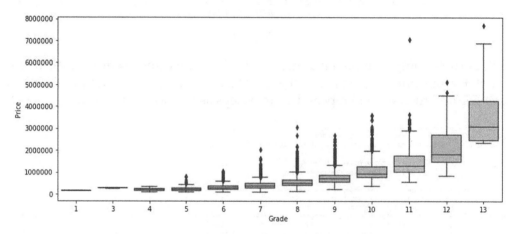

Fig 20.14

Let's add some more features and repeat the same steps-

```
features2 = ['bedrooms','bathrooms','sqft_living','sqft_lot','floors','waterfront','view',
             'grade','yr_built','zipcode']
complex_model_2 = linear_model.LinearRegression()
complex_model_2.fit(train_data[features2],train_data['price'])

print('Intercept: {}'.format(complex_model_2.intercept_))
print('Coefficients: {}'.format(complex_model_2.coef_))

pred2 = complex_model_2.predict(test_data[features2])
msecm2 = format(np.sqrt(metrics.mean_squared_error(y_test,pred2)),'.3f')
rtrcm2 = format(complex_model_2.score(train_data[features2],train_data['price']),'.3f')
artrcm2 = format(adjustedR2(complex_model_2.score(train_data[features2],train_data['price']),train_data.shape[0],len(features2)),
rtecm2 = format(complex_model_2.score(test_data[features2],test_data['price']),'.3f')
artecm2 = format(adjustedR2(complex_model_2.score(test_data[features2],test_data['price']),test_data.shape[0],len(features2)),'.3

r = evaluation.shape[0]
evaluation.loc[r] = ['Complex Model-2','-',msecm2,rtrcm2,artrcm2,rtecm2,artecm2]
evaluation.sort_values(by = 'R-squared (test)', ascending=False)
```

Fig 20.15

```
Intercept: 13559209.611222725
Coefficients: [-3.80981692e+04  5.03031727e+04  1.71370475e+02 -2.68019419e-01
  2.21944912e+04  5.53865017e+05  4.70338164e+04  1.23642184e+05
 -3.88306990e+03 -6.82180496e+01]
```

	Adjusted R-squared (test)	Adjusted R-squared (training)	Details	Mean Squared Error (MSE)	Model	R-squared (test)	R-squared (training)
4		Complex Model-2	-	210486.689	0.651	0.650	0.655	0.654
3		Complex Model-1	-	248514.011	0.514	0.514	0.519	0.518
0		Simple Model	-	254289.149	0.492	-	0.496	-
1		Simple Model	-	254289.149	0.492	-	0.496	-
2		Simple Model	-	254289.149	0.492	-	0.496	-

Fig 20.16

From above result you can see that adding more features in our complex model 2 is decreasing the regression log i.e. in our case it is now 210486.689. Always remember for the linear models the main idea is to fit a straight line to our data. However, if the data has a quadratic distribution, this time choosing a quadratic function and applying a polynomial transformation may give us better results. Let's see how can we choose a quadratic function and apply the polynomial transformation below -

```
polyfeat = PolynomialFeatures(degree=2)
X_trainpoly = polyfeat.fit_transform(train_data[features2])
X_testpoly = polyfeat.fit_transform(test_data[features2])
poly = linear_model.LinearRegression().fit(X_trainpoly, train_data['price'])

predp = poly.predict(X_testpoly)
msepoly1 = format(np.sqrt(metrics.mean_squared_error(test_data['price'],pred)),'.3f')
rtrpoly1 = format(poly.score(X_trainpoly,train_data['price']),'.3f')
rtepoly1 = format(poly.score(X_testpoly,test_data['price']),'.3f')

polyfeat = PolynomialFeatures(degree=3)
X_trainpoly = polyfeat.fit_transform(train_data[features2])
X_testpoly = polyfeat.fit_transform(test_data[features2])
poly = linear_model.LinearRegression().fit(X_trainpoly, train_data['price'])

predp = poly.predict(X_testpoly)
msepoly2 = format(np.sqrt(metrics.mean_squared_error(test_data['price'],pred)),'.3f')
rtrpoly2 = format(poly.score(X_trainpoly,train_data['price']),'.3f')
rtepoly2 = format(poly.score(X_testpoly,test_data['price']),'.3f')

r = evaluation.shape[0]
evaluation.loc[r] = ['Polynomial Regression','degree=2',msepoly1,rtrpoly1,'-',rtepoly1,'-']
evaluation.loc[r+1] = ['Polynomial Regression','degree=3',msepoly2,rtrpoly2,'-',rtepoly2,'-']
evaluation.sort_values(by = 'R-squared (test)', ascending=False)
```

Fig 20.17

In above code cell, we have first initialized the Polynomial Features with degree 2 for generating polynomial and interaction features. Then we have fit and transform these features using fit_transform() method and then we have train our linear regression model using fit() method as we did earlier.

Next, we repeat the same step but for degree 3. After this you can calculate each degree' regression log and score and then apply our evaluation dataframe to it just like we did earlier.

You will get following result after executing the above steps.

	Adjusted R-squared (test)	Adjusted R-squared (training)	Details	Mean Squared Error (MSE)	Model	R-squared (test)	R-squared (training)
6	Polynomial Regression	degree=3	254289.149	0.749	-	0.723	-
5	Polynomial Regression	degree=2	254289.149	0.730	-	0.716	-
4	Complex Model-2	-	210486.689	0.651	0.650	0.655	0.654
3	Complex Model-1	-	248514.011	0.514	0.514	0.519	0.518
0	Simple Model	-	254289.149	0.492	-	0.496	-
1	Simple Model	-	254289.149	0.492	-	0.496	-
2	Simple Model	-	254289.149	0.492	-	0.496	-

Fig 20.18

When we look at the above evaluation table, MSE values is confusing to select which is best model because many models have same MSE value. For removing this confusion, we must see the R-squared (test) values also. R-squared value closer to 100% denotes a good correlation so in our case it seems our 3rd degree Polynomial Regression model is the best model for our problem having a 74.9% R-squared value. That complete our goal!

Always start with a simple model and then increase it's complexity by adding it's features and check different evaluation metric scores. Although it is time consuming process, it is one of the best way to get a stable and highly accurate model.

Try to add some new features, check evaluation metric and see if you are getting a more valid score or not.

Index

CPSIA information can be obtained
at www.ICGtesting.com
Printed in the USA
LVHW101521170520
655861LV00007B/872